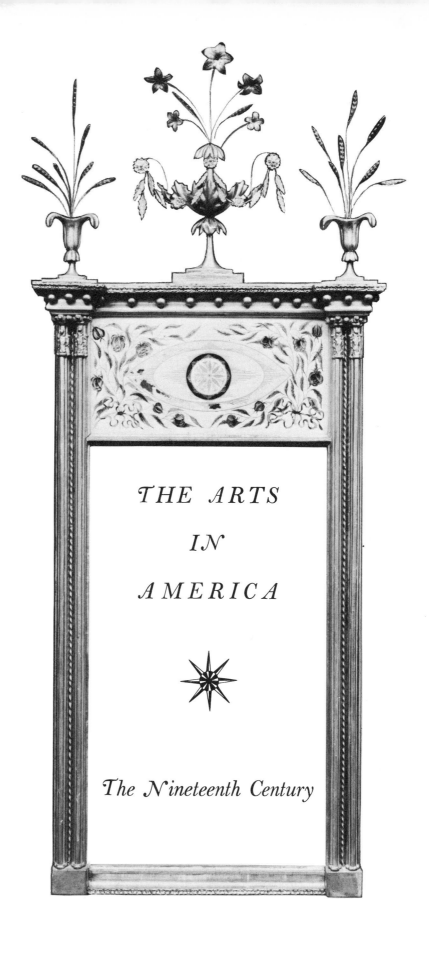

THE ARTS
IN
AMERICA

✵

The Nineteenth Century

PAT LYON AT THE FORGE, by John Neagle (1796–1865). *Courtesy,* MUSEUM OF FINE ARTS, BOSTON. PAINTING ON DEPOSIT FROM THE BOSTON ATHENAEUM, BOSTON, MASSACHUSETTS

# THE ARTS IN AMERICA

## *The Nineteenth Century*

WENDELL D. GARRETT     PAUL F. NORTON

ALAN GOWANS

JOSEPH T. BUTLER

*CHARLES SCRIBNER'S SONS*

*New York*

# CONTENTS

# LIST OF ILLUSTRATIONS

Pat Lyon at the Forge (*color*)                    FRONTISPIECE

## List of Illustrations

## List of Illustrations

## List of Illustrations

## List of Illustrations

## List of Illustrations

## List of Illustrations

# A CENTURY OF ASPIRATION

*by Wendell D. Garrett*

## THE COMPLETION OF INDEPENDENCE, 1790–1820

DURING the first three decades under the Constitution, Americans labored to create a new republican culture. Political independence, so nationalists argued, must be accompanied by cultural autonomy.

The cult of assertive nationalism of the spread-eagle sort was excessively strong between 1790 and 1820. The young nation spread its wings in the judicial nationalism of John Marshall's decisions and in the political nationalism of Monroe's challenge to the European powers. While economic nationalists pressed for a protective tariff and internal improvements, cultural nationalists called for the creation of a native, original culture. A great nation must have a great literature and great art and great architecture. This quest for cultural nationalism sought a way to use the resources of the American land, the American past, and American society to produce an art that was new, indigenous, universally beautiful, morally true, expressive of American ideals, and representative of the American spirit. The result of this strong nationalistic urge for self-expression was the beginning of an American point of view and an American style in art. American painters, poets, sculptors, architects, novelists, and playwrights did indeed achieve significant success, but not in the ways they had anticipated.

Refusing to copy British art and architecture slavishly, Americans turned to Rome and Greece for inspiration. There was, they believed, an analogy between the grandeur of the classical past and the optimistic future of the new Republic; Greek art and Greek democracy could serve as models for American art and American democracy. The harmony and proportions of neoclassicism in the nation's public buildings would give an impression of order, logic, and stability. Thomas Jefferson, the devout student of

Andrea Palladio, was most impressed by the Roman ruins of southern France, in particular by the Maison Carrée in Nîmes. Benjamin Latrobe, the distinguished early 19th-century architect, found his inspiration in classical Greece; after him the Greek Revival dominated American building for decades. Painters likewise found in the classical world a major source of inspiration; Greek and Roman art represented perfection both as form and design as well as an expression of a culture. West, Peale, Trumbull, and Stuart represented the "grand style" of this historical, classical school of painting. Though their work was derivative and reflected English trends, and at times depended on the artificialities of an overblown style, they did however practice a factual and concrete directness: generals were painted in their authentic uniforms and Indians were not idealized.

But a revolt against neoclassicism was stirring among the second generation of artists and architects, a significant circumstance that revealed the divided character of American culture. The fervent search for an American style, the scramble for individuality, the discovery of Nature as a superior source of inspiration, the compulsion of a young culture to break with the past—all these led American cultural life of this period into a perplexing dilemma. Artists, architects, and writers were influenced by a steady tension between the necessity for tradition and the necessity of creating a "native" art, the need to imitate and the need to express an American style. Two very powerful forces—cultural nationalism and romanticism—were to alter significantly the form and content of what was created in the early years of the Republic.

Insofar as Americans conceived of that culture as completely distinctive and entirely different from anything England and Europe had produced, they deluded themselves. A "native" and "original" culture was not so readily to be brought into being. Before the Revolution, America was too new, too raw, too poor to be able to train, to teach, or to afford artists and writers in anything like the style achieved in contemporary Europe. The absence of a long, cultivated tradition, of schools of art, of artistic and literary communities, of musical and scientific centers for the exchange of learning and ideas, relegated America to the backwash of European cultural achievement. In spite of the promise of an exciting revolutionary culture, resources were lacking to translate exhortations and slogans into a reality; after many years of hesitant experiment the culture of the colonists had remained derivative and provincial. Americans might be familiar with the manners and tastes of London, but in the end the pressure of a provincial situation and the tests of utility became decisive: portraiture had to be realistic; literature and scientific knowledge useful; architecture and furniture functional.

By the end of the Revolution the achievements were meager, yet American confidence in the future of their culture was strong. During the critical period of the 1780's faith alone sustained that optimism; as Henry Adams later pointed out, each man knew that "every stroke of his axe and hoe made him a capitalist, and gentlemen of his children." Leaders like Jefferson emphasized again and again that "it is impossible not to be sensible that we are acting for all mankind." "We feel," he wrote of himself and his generation, "that we are acting under obligations not confined to the limits of our own society." Education, among other forces, would in time enable Americans to equip a new generation with the culture worthy of a republic.

Yet there remains the paradox that the Americans who led in the rejection of Europe were themselves intellectuals deeply indebted to European books and ideas. There is the example of Jefferson himself: no American was more powerfully influenced yet less bound by the rules of European architecture. Americans soon discovered they could not altogether cut themselves off from their roots and free themselves from cultural dependence on Europe, especially England. While they rejected Europe, the act of rejection was also one of carry-over, and the act of revolt was itself an expression of the European consciousness.

In another sense, certain of their efforts were more successful. Conditions in the New World and loosened ties with Europe exerted an influence toward change, and the culture of the new nation revealed a tendency to make significant modifications in what it borrowed. America would prove to be a testing ground; within the civilization transplanted to the New World the seeds of a new society were sprouting. Free of the choking weeds of outmoded habits, some European ways and cultural traits would wither, some would strike root, still others would change and adapt to the new environment. The budding of American consciousness was already in evidence before 1776; under the forcing frame of the Revolutionary era and the Confederation period, cultural nationalism burst into full flower. The upheaval of the war itself had social as well as political consequences, stimulating tendencies in the culture to develop new and distinctive features. St. John de Crèvecoeur, French-born commentator on American frontier life and social forces, perceived this theme as early as 1782 when he asked the penetrating question, "What then is the American, this new man?" He gave his own answer, "*He* is an American, who, leaving behind him all his ancient prejudices and manners, receives new ones from the new mode of life he has embraced. . . . Here individuals of all nations are melted into a new race of men, whose labors and posterity will one day cause great changes in the world."

Men and women who referred to themselves as Americans rather than as transplanted Europeans were conscious of the change. This sense of difference and separateness produced a fervid American national spirit. In so expansive an era, some Europeans found this aggressive mood both crude and bumptious. The Duc de Rochefoucauld-Liancourt, touring in the 1790's, thought there were too many Americans who were "sure nothing good is done, and that no one has any brains, except in America." Noah Webster reminded his countrymen that "we ought not to consider ourselves as inhabitants of a particular state only, but as *Americans*." An American, he went on to say, "as soon as he opens his lips, should rehearse the history of his own country; he should lisp the praise of Liberty and of those illustrious heroes and statesmen who have wrought a revolution in her favor."

As Jefferson remarked later, "The European nations constitute a separate division of the globe . . . they have a set of interests of their own in which it is our business never to engage ourselves. America has a hemisphere to itself." The influence of distance and the new American environment slowly, yet pervasively, worked their alchemy upon European forms brought to the new country. By 1800 this culture was native to the place;

in a number of ways what Americans would be for generations to come was settled in the course of these early national years. After 1800 when the line of settlement moved westward within the United States and when larger numbers of non-English immigrants flooded the cities and hinterlands, this sense of separateness, so well expressed by Jefferson and others, swiftly increased.

### THE SPREAD OF SETTLEMENT AFTER THE WAR OF 1812

THE existence of empty land was a fact of primary—indeed almost dominant—importance in the development of American society through the 19th century. "So vast is the Territory of North America," Benjamin Franklin prophesied as early as 1751, "that it will require many Ages to settle it fully; and, till it is fully settled, Labour will never be cheap here, where no Man continues long a Labourer for others, but gets a Plantation of his own."

Land does not make a people; but few would argue with the contention that the conquest of the gargantuan continent with ax, plow, and factory became both an expression and a determinant of the American character. Early in the history of the Republic, abundant land was placed at the disposal of the people. It seemed to the British traveler Morris Birkbeck in 1817 that the entire country "was breaking up and moving westward," along the Hudson-Mohawk valleys, or down the Ohio, or on the Cumberland and Wilderness roads in a double-pronged invasion of the Northwest and the Southwest. John C. Calhoun was saying in the same year, "We are greatly and rapidly—I was about to say fearfully—growing." Free land was a powerful magnet to the native American and the immigrant European alike.

It was the West that drew them on; the West that was a challenge and terror all in one. Here was a vast continent to be discovered, explored, cleared, populated, built up, and energized; and here was the restless, vigorous, expansive spirit of Americans on the move. They moved frequently, and they moved everywhere within this thinly populated nation.

Here was a bold setting for a venture in social construction, and before long the cultural silhouette began to bear some relation to the environmental silhouette of the landscape. Since the beginning, irresistible territorial ambitions and the sense of mission which gripped Americans have been crucial images in the national mind. Scott Fitzgerald has called this continental image "the last and greatest of all human dreams; for a transitory enchanted moment man must have held his breath in the presence of this continent, compelled into an aesthetic contemplation he neither understood nor desired, face to face for the last time in history with something commensurate to his capacity for wonder."

In 1804, the novelist Charles Brockden Brown, exhilarated by the Louisiana Purchase, scorned those who had nagging doubts and fears about indiscriminate westward expansion: "We may be sure that, in no long time, it [the United States] will stretch east and west from sea to sea, and from the north pole to the Isthmus of Panama." A popular Fourth-of-July toast made in Waterville, Maine, in 1815 boasted: "The Eagle of the United States—may she extend her wings from the Atlantic to the Pacific; and fixing her talons on the Isthmus of Darien, stretch her beak to the Northern Pole." The later expansionist slogan "Manifest Destiny" became the most popular way of expressing this notion of America's divinely intended mission to incorporate all of its adjacent lands—the desire for territory essential to the completion of our "natural boundary." Americans entertained so many territorial ambitions that they seemed to the French Consul General De Beaujour to want "nothing less than to devour the whole of North America." And this was only the springtime of American territorial ambitions; summer was still to come.

At the beginning of the 19th century the United States was an overwhelmingly rural society. All of the great events which agitated American life between 1790 and 1830, with the exception of the War of 1812, were almost exclusively internal and domestic. The population in 1790 was fewer than four million people, of whom three-quarters of a million were Negroes; 82 per cent of the total white population was of English stock. For the next forty years, until the "Atlantic Migration" of the 1830's, immigrants were slow in coming, largely because of the long series of wars sweeping over the Continent. Immigration in the three decades between 1790 and 1820 averaged only about 4,000 or 5,000 a year. But the natural increase in the number of inhabitants more than compensated; by 1820 the population had mounted to almost 10,000,000. In 1790 only 200,000 Americans lived in towns or cities of 2,500 or more, and only three per cent in cities of 8,000 or more inhabitants. In 1800 there were only five cities of more than 10,000 people: Philadelphia was the largest with 70,000, followed by New York with 60,000, Boston with 25,000, Charleston with 18,000, and Baltimore fifth with 13,000. By 1830 both New York and Philadelphia had passed 150,000, while the great surge westward led to the spectacular, even faster, growth of new towns and cities. Even though the spread of western settlement had a rural base, town life sprang up almost immediately in the newly opened regions. Pittsburgh became the gateway to the whole Ohio Valley; there the flow of goods and people brought the city a great commercial prosperity. Other regional centers of trade developed in Cincinnati, Cleveland, Lexington, Louisville, and St. Louis. Public land was abundant and available, and by the 1820's a jagged line of settlement extended west of the Appalachian Mountains between the Canadian border and the Gulf of Mexico.

But the landscape on this line of settlement was not a wholly comfortable sight; indeed, it was frightening to many. The wilderness seemed hostile and savage; it was strange, untidy, uncompassable. Artists depicted it as "that wilder image" on canvas. This formidable landscape—mountains, forests, rivers, plains—presented obstacles to expansion and settlement; it was something men sought to escape or destroy. Plain experience taught men that nature could be disorderly, cruel, and downright dangerous and capricious—capable of killing a man in an unguarded moment. The prevailing 18th-century concept of nature as a friendly power, manifesting a generous deity, with permanence, stability, balance, law, and order, underwent significant modifications in the American environment. On the frontier, one very practical, urgent challenge was to find out about it, tame it, and use it.

In an indirect sense—not only in the decorative and aesthetic sense but in the ways that the total physical environment related to human living —the American landscape helped to shape the American national character. By reason of their frontier, transatlantic, and isolated position, Americans tended to accept some and reject certain other patterns of belief and aspects of romanticism. This was a period of transition and contradictions, in which the great unified pattern of thought inherited from the 18th-century enlightenment became less clear and certain. The European concept of nature and the accepted generalizations about man began to lose coherence after 1790 in the face of confusions and contradictions of the frontier experience. Experiences with the Indian were too recent and tragic for him to be seen as a "noble savage." How did one explain disease, death, fetid swamps and scorching deserts, earthquakes and other natural catastrophes if nature was supremely orderly and benevolent? So long as one dealt with nature in the abstract and viewed the wilderness at a comfortable distance, one could find in it assurances of order and divinity; but in the early 19th century as men pushed out the lines of settlement, it was not so easy to be serenely confident of this accepted pattern of thought.

In the settlers' way of talking, in their pictures, and in their buildings the boundaries of artistic and linguistic propriety became as vague, fuzzy and casual as those of geography. Language was characterized by a general looseness and grew by the unauthorized improvisations and verbal extravagances of everyday speech. Enormous panoramic paintings celebrated the grandeur, the variety, and the color of an exotic continent. In upstart western towns, spontaneous innovations by builders with but few of the traditional skills necessary to meet the housing needs of an impatient migratory people, led to the "balloon-frame" house. A people on the move, in constant motion, seeking their fortunes in the wagon companies going west, in the transient mining camps, in the frontier towns, or busting the prairie sod, required arts that were swift, immediate, spontaneous, direct, with a freshness of impression. No one tradition could hold up for long here. Patronage depended not on an indulgent aristocracy but on a tight-fisted audience that applied the tests of utility, relevance, vividness, and fidelity to the subject. Thus, the opening of the Western frontier subtly influenced the style of what was built and painted and the content of what was written and created.

### THE AMERICAN SYSTEM AND THE BIRTH OF INDUSTRY, 1800–1850

POLITICAL and cultural independence had taught Americans the importance of developing the economic strength of the nation. Business enterprise and competition, however, were largely dormant at the end of the Revolution. Americans found themselves outsiders in a world of exclusive trading systems; the currency was unstable; and the new nation continued to look to England and Europe for manufactured goods and markets for commercial crops. Few knew how to organize large business enterprises. After the economic turmoil of the Confederation period, people turned in desperation to the government for help in 1789. They expected the new Constitution and the strengthened state governments to provide efficient instruments for solution of the nation's economic difficulties. Eloquent spokesmen, such as Alexander Hamilton and Tench Coxe, were urging Americans to surrender local self-sufficiency for greater specialization and for a national exchange of commodities. They argued that their fellow citizens had to diversify the economy, to separate manufacturing from agriculture, and to remove the factory from the home. In their mercantilist assumptions about the proper organization of commerce, they identified their own interests with those of the whole country and requested vigorous government action to further trade.

After 1790 the country struggled with serious obstacles to development. America was predominantly an agricultural economy, an agrarian polity, and a rural society. Provincialism was intense. Roads were few and in abominable condition; communication between the larger cities was slight, and between towns and villages it was even more limited. Turnpikes and canals were just beginning to be built. There were no railroads, telegraphs, or telephones. News traveled slowly. Most men outside of the towns and cities were farmers. They made many of the articles needed for domestic and personal use; only occasionally would a trip to the local merchant in the nearest village be necessary for hardware, cloth, spices, gunpowder, china, and glass. If the farmer was located far from a village, he might rely on chapmen or peddlers. More often he dealt with the local craftsmen who had special skills, tools, and designs—blacksmiths and braziers, pewterers and silversmiths, coopers and cordwainers, tanners and dyers, cabinetmakers and upholsterers, brickmakers and housewrights—each of whom in his own town or region commanded a small market and held a virtual monopoly of the services required by rural communities and their household industries.

By 1800 Americans could dream of unlimited possibilities: of the application of water- and steam-driven machinery to production, of the West rich with unexplored natural resources, of the gains possible from favorable legislation both state and national, of great capital to be raised by means of corporations, and of maritime wealth from neutral trade among the warring nations of Europe. The early decades under the Constitution did witness a substantial growth in the productive system, although not along the lines anticipated in 1789.

Before 1800 the responsibility for success or failure in the craftsman's struggle against nearby competitors rested squarely on the master craftsman. He had to train and educate his apprentices and journeymen. He kept books, designed the products, and handled the sales. Nearly all manufacturing was done in the craftsman's own shop, where he was aided by apprentices, servants, and journeymen. More often than not the average household establishment had no journeymen, their place being taken by wives, children, and other members of the family. This system made it easy and natural for widows to continue their husbands' businesses. There was no type of small-scale enterprise without its female entrepreneurs, and that these female activities were taken as a matter of course shows the essential family character of business enterprise.

A number of factors conspired in this period to limit manufacturing to a single household. Lack of power machinery, of course, was crucial. Another limitation on size was the smallness of the market. Only a very few skillful entrepreneurs succeeded in developing export trade to other cities. The supply of labor remained extremely scarce through this period. The English rule of a seven-year apprenticeship had to be relaxed to four and even three years in many cases; even so, masters continually advertised for apprentices and runaway servants, and sometimes even offered bonuses in clothing and supplies at the completion of the term. After men had served their apprenticeship to acquire the necessary hand skills, it was unusual for them to have access to much capital for setting up a new shop. For that reason many shops and businesses became hereditary proprietorships, sons taking over the trades and the equipment of their fathers. These men owned their own tools, processed their own raw materials, and sold their own finished products in limited areas.

In view of the scattered character of settlement in the new nation, particularly west of the Appalachians, the absence of adequate transportation facilities had economic implications, at once enormous and vital, for the craftsman and artisan. With such great distances, it meant that his surplus goods had only local, and therefore limited, markets unless the interior could be provided with improved transportation. And so long as the market was restricted, there would be restraints on the expansion of production and the accumulation of wealth. Yet, the value of their skills in a local, noncompetitive market had given artisans and craftsmen a strong position in the economy. The cabinetmaker or cooper or silversmith had alone been able to make the products available for sale in his community, and he had a large measure of control over the price he obtained. It was the transportation revolution that, in the end, destroyed his comfortable security.

The growth of the country in size and numbers, and the extension and improvement of transportation facilities, were making distribution the key to profits in the early decades of the 19th century. Every sector of the economy felt the effects. By producing goods beyond the needs of their immediate communities, new factories and industries were destroying local crafts and manufacturing monopolies in many towns and villages, thereby forcing farmers to be dependent upon outside sources for goods and services. As improvements lowered the cost of moving goods from one part of the country to another and as new markets opened, merchants were able to distribute substantial quantities of goods, drawing upon the most efficient and cheapest producers. The artisan no longer had the local market to himself, but had to compete both with imports and with the least costly national output. As merchants began to get orders from outside their bailiwick, they hired master workmen and journeymen to produce goods exclusively for the new trade. These growing possibilities for large-scale production damaged the status and independence of individual working-men. From an independent employer, therefore, the master craftsman was reduced to a wage earner who supplied commodities which the merchant capitalist would sell in the national market.

In this expanded and highly competitive market artisans felt seriously threatened; they simply were not able to increase the output to meet the demands of the economy. They could not halt the improvements and the slow spreading of the factory through the land. As the division of labor and mass-production techniques became the fundamental principles of industrialism, they reduced the emphasis upon special skills of handicrafters; the highly trained artisans were forced to work beside beginners doing monotonous tasks in the noise and dust and under the increased strain and discipline of the factory system.

By the early 1830's, journeymen had lost their special status and suffered changes in their standards of living. For twenty years there had been a steady decline of wages, culminating in the depression of 1837–1839 that left one-third of the working population of New York City unemployed. In the New England mills, wages generally fell thirty to fifty per cent between 1839 and 1843. In this decade the same amount of labor that had once produced a comfortable subsistence for the craftsman or artisan or mechanic and his family was inadequate to maintain his standards. His only alternatives were increased effort and longer hours, or the reduction of his wants. Industrial workers became frustrated and struggled to understand the character of the change that was already largely accomplished by 1840. Labor newspapers complained that the condition of the worker was growing worse; that he was becoming more and more dependent on capital; that his resources were being curtailed; and that a new uncertainty over wages and employment had entered his life. The realization of the conspiratorial enormity of this change gave rise to much of the unrest and agitation of the period. Trade unions were formed and riots and strikes broke out.

The decline in the status and wages of the craftsmen, artisans, and mechanics evoked in the 1820's and 1830's a rising volume of protest against monopolies and the growth of corporations which affected the workman adversely. Some directed their grievances against the spread of chartered "monopolies" in transportation and banking, and organized trade unions among the depressed handicrafters. Others turned to politics with the organization of the American Working Men's Party in Philadelphia during the short depression of 1828–1829. But these labor movements and political parties were sensitive to the fluctuations of the business cycle and were rarely successful except for brief periods. Soon many workers fell prey to the utopian schemes of middle-class liberals such as Robert Dale Owen and Fanny Wright. But most of these schemes failed almost as soon as they began, finding no place in an expanding industrial economy. Workers found they could not halt the "improvements"; they could only escape toward the frontier.

Mechanics and craftsmen found an outlet in the newly opened areas of the nation. Coming as they did from the older sections of the country, they brought established patterns of life, clinging to whatever they could of their early lives, accommodating themselves only reluctantly to the strange environment across the mountains. They did not often become farmers. Usually they settled and worked at their trades in the new towns where the lag in transportation offered them some security until the railroad caught up with them. They were to remain a disenchanted and unsettled element in the population.

## POPULAR CULTURE IN A GREAT DEMOCRACY, 1830–1860

IN the years between 1830 and 1860, Americans made it quite plain that theirs was to be an equalitarian and open society. Andrew Jackson, whose character and affiliations defined the terms of the new democratic upsurge, became the spokesman for many people who sought to widen the democracy they had inherited from an earlier generation. Upon retiring from the presidency in 1837, he told the people in his Farewell Address that they should "Never for a moment believe that the great body of the citizens of any State can deliberately intend to do wrong." Faith in the infallibility of the common man's judgment became the sun around which American political thought and action revolved. This upsurge in the democratic faith was most striking in the deliberate expansion of the suffrage: property was removed as a limitation to voting; governors became popularly elected instead of being chosen by state legislatures; the judiciary in some cases was subjected to popular election; and states found it necessary to submit their constitutions to the people for ratification. The floodgates of democracy were opened and it was possible for any group or class to participate in government. Jackson's denunciation of monopoly in the tariff and his action in the bank wars confirmed him in the role as tribune of the people. During his presidency Old Hickory earned the loyalty of a large national following both as spokesman for the expansive impulses of the period and as symbol of the natural frontiersman capable of standing up to foreign and domestic aristocrats. He was the first President to capture the imagination of the common people; they saw themselves and their aspirations reflected in him.

Indeed, it might be said that the democratization of politics, the expansion of economic opportunity, and the diffusion of social power were only some of the more obvious signs spelling out the rise of the Common Man; the democratic spirit was apparent throughout society and significantly modified the forms through which Americans expressed themselves. Their culture—the new thoughts and the way people stated them to one another—differed in form and content from that of the preceding, Jeffersonian generation. In the new American society there was a collapse of the taste standards of the European societies from which Americans had come. The principle of social equality made impossible the European idea that the lower classes were to derive their tastes from above, with either an aristocracy or a republican élite acting as arbiter. Most Americans prided themselves on having become liberated from aristocracies, in matters of taste as well as in matters of politics. Their popular culture—the culture of the many rather than of the few, of the masses rather than of the classes— reflected in its art, literature, music, religion, education, and science the values of the common man rather than those of an aristocratic or republican élite, and often deliberately differentiated itself from élite culture. They held that creativeness is not the monopoly of the professional artist and that much of the energy of art comes from the experience of simple, anonymous people. An untutored talent in poetry or a "primitive" in paint- ing may come up from the submerged population. "You are in a country," wrote the novelist James Fenimore Cooper to the sculptor Horatio Greenough, "in which every man swaggers and talks, knowledge or no knowledge; brains or no brains; taste or no taste. They are all *ex nato* connoisseurs, politicians, religionists, and every man's equal and all men's betters." The popular culture of this new generation was, therefore, less coherent, less restrained, less rational, than that of the National period, but the common men who imbued it with force were developing a culture that expressed their aspirations. Its excesses and its very considerable achievements were indications of the tensions under which American artists, architects, and writers labored as they groped for an "American style" in a shifting, expanding, highly mobile nation.

"I love liberty," John Randolph of Roanoke once exclaimed, "and I hate equality." America is a democracy, but the inner tension between the two poles of the democratic idea in the hurly-burly age of Jackson was never more passionately described than in Randolph's sentence. By the decades of the 1830's and 1840's, when the principle that governments rest upon the consent of all the governed reached its flood tide of influence, scores of foreign travelers toured America, dutifully recording their im- pressions of the popular culture: all seemed agreed that the United States was the great experiment in democracy. They were particularly impressed with the gap in manners between the Americans and the Europeans. The comments of Charles Dickens on the materialism of American life and the grossness of manners that flowed from it are now classic. Alexis de Tocqueville's judgment gives a better perspective: American manners, when compared with a more rigidly stratified society, were on the rough side, but had the ease of an equalitarian society. He observed that democratic societies like America were "ardent, insatiable, incessant and invincible" in their passion for equality. "They will endure poverty, servitude, barbarism, but they will not endure aristocracy." Even though the prickly Mrs. Trollope in her famous book on *Domestic Manners of the Americans* (1832) had said of the American people, "I do not like their principles, I do not like their manners, I do not like their opinions," she did admit that opportunities were here for all: "Any man's son may become the equal of any other man's son, and the consciousness of this is certainly a spur to exertion." She was particularly shocked at the male habits of tobacco chewing and spitting, at the execrable theater behavior of both sexes, at the silent bolting of food in public eating places, and at the rudeness both of women and children. Anthony Trollope, trying to heal the wounds his mother's book had caused, was able to add very little in the 1870's that could correct her picture of the 1830's. He agreed with her about American "lower orders" who did not know their position, yet he had a grudging admiration for people who scorned subservient manners and demanded respect for what they were as persons.

The opportunities open to Americans constantly replenished the reservoir of American faith in equality. Harriet Martineau thought she saw unlimited horizons for the lowly in America: "An artisan may attain to be governor of the state, member of Congress, even President," she said. Expressions of this sentiment were blatantly and continuously proclaimed: "The equality of Man is, to this moment," wrote the British traveler Alexander Mackay in 1842, the "cornerstone" of American society. "It is extremely seldom," he continued, "that the willing hand in America is in want of employment." As Emerson observed, "America is another word for opportunity." Particularly when compared with European social conditions, this country opened economic vistas for every man.

These opportunities were reflected in how well the average citizen lived. When Francis Grund toured this country, he was much impressed by the dwellings of skilled laborers: "On entering the house of a respectable mechanic in any one of the large cities of the United States," he remarked, "one cannot but be astonished at the apparent neatness and comfort of the apartments, the large airy parlors, the nice carpets and mahogany furniture." He concluded that "the laboring classes in America are really less removed from the wealthy merchants and professional men than they are in any part of Europe." Harriet Martineau recalled: "I saw no table spread, in the lowest orders of houses, that had not meat and bread on it. Every factory child carried its umbrella; and pig-drivers wear spectacles." Other observers remarked on the notable absence of beggars, although there were poor in America, to be sure, particularly in crowded urban settings. The German immigrant Francis Lieber wrote home: "In America there is no peasant. . . . He is a farmer, and may be rich or poor; that is all the difference." This breadth of opportunity contributed to the general looseness of class lines. Majority rule was invested with a kind of sanctity and the common people came into their own as political and cultural arbiters and participants. It was in the course of these years that the Democratic Dogma, as Brooks Adams called it, was pushed to its outer limits.

The whole period of the "great experiment" in Jackson's America was one of change. The steamboats and canals, the new railroads, the revolutionary factories, the growing cities were at once causes and symptoms of the upheaval through which the old order was passing. New influences, partly emanating from Europe and partly indigenous, were at work. The very intellectual underpinnings of the eighteenth-century Enlightenment were being knocked out. The ideals of the previous age—urbanity, precision, reason—were under attack from the Romantic cult of the natural, the simple, and the ordinary. The straight lines and unadorned surfaces of Georgian and Greek Revival architecture seemed cold, unfeeling, and formal to admirers of the natural. Wide-spread acceptance of a romantic view of nature was significant for American popular culture, for it was believed that nature revealed its truth and beauty not to a limited few but to the mass of men. Culture was the common attribute of all people; reason, education, and taste in external forms and historical styles were not necessary to appreciate the finest creations of life. Nature and the individual—the wilderness image and the rise of the common man, the two great themes of the nineteenth century—turned painting in this period to landscape and portraits. The celebration of these themes in ante-bellum America by painters of ranging talent and varied schools was surprisingly fertile, bounteous, and exuberant; moreover they enjoyed a sustaining audience and environment until the introduction and popularity of the daguerreotype. Fashionable portraitists built their clienteles in the large cities; others made annual tours to the growing cities looking for jobs; and men of lesser talents toured the small towns and frontier settlements with their colors and brushes seeking commissions. "By and by," grumbled old Gilbert Stuart, "you will not by chance kick your foot against a dog-kennel but out will start a portrait painter." "When I was in America," the British art critic Anna Brownell Jameson wrote of a trip made in 1838, "I was struck by the manner in which the imaginative talent of the people had thrown itself forth in painting: the country seemed to me to swarm with painters."

There was a place for art in every home, for every man was worthy of it. A painting over the fireplace was as much a necessity as a Bible on the table. American portrait painting was prolific; at the same time, landscape acquired an autonomous value in painting: no longer was it simply the background for portraiture or historical events, but rather the focus of visual attention. The noted lecturer George W. Bethune wrote in 1852, "Especially within the last ten years, large advances have been made and Art has fairly begun to flourish among us." James Jackson Jarves, as an art critic and collector in the fifties and sixties, observed that "it has become the mode to have taste." Writing in 1905, the painter-critic Samuel Isham reported that aging artists who could remember the mid-nineteenth century "look back at it through the years as to an Eden, the like of which cannot occur again." The absence of rigid class lines and the rapid growth of society confirmed in popular opinion the shared quality, if not the superiority, of this popular culture. The genre painter William Sidney Mount reflected the point of view of the Native School when he urged his fellow artists, "Paint not for the few but the many." A number did by painting landscapes of unspoiled nature, the wilderness image (or as Thomas Cole named one of his paintings, *The Arcadian or Pastoral State*), on cluttered canvases, combining, often paradoxically, romantic idealism and the realism of "minute portraiture." They turned for inspiration less to the classical fine arts traditions abroad than to the vernacular, native traditions at home. By 1860, common men, who had imbued their culture with force and had developed a culture that expressed their aspirations, lived through an era when the distinctive configurations of a recognizably American art took shape.

### THE TRIUMPH OF ROMANTIC IDEALISM, 1830–1860

THE romantic reaction against the critical and skeptical temper of 18th-century classicism represented a revolt of individualism against authority, of emotionalism against rationalism. The romantic reaction meant a re-affirmation of those solemn, noble, and worthy elements in human nature, of the goodness and the greatness of man, which were denied by the critical intellect but affirmed by the responsive heart and the sympathetic imagination. While classicism emphasized the rational order and design of creative intelligence, the romantic sensibility found the divine spirit permeating all things and worshiped Nature as the sustainer and guide of life. Romanticism argued that man was primarily influenced by what he experienced. Romanticism, in short, represented a new way of thinking and living for Americans who recognized in the age of Andrew Jackson that there were differences between themselves and their Jeffersonian predecessors. While the old order was being attacked, modified, and discarded, a new order was proposed and inaugurated by Emerson and his followers. And even though few Americans followed Emerson the whole way to pantheism, his popularity as a writer and lecturer revealed a widespread acceptance of transcendental views.

On the surface at least, the popular faith in progress reached a high peak, reflecting the democratization of society, the opening of the West, and the spreading effects of the Industrial Revolution. By 1860 it was clear to all that the republican, agrarian order of the past had been replaced by a democratic, industrial society. Everyone in all classes felt the impact of this change to some degree. Unquestionably this optimistic concept and expression of progress had a profound effect in securing the triumph and popular acceptance of romanticism, but it represented only one side of the coin. Romanticism reflected the optimism of the idea of progress, but it was also characterized by the pessimism of nostalgia.

Living in such a dynamic, free-wheeling society in the full tide of radical change left many people clinging to a bundle of paradoxical ideas and attitudes. The combined effect of a dissolving tradition of thought and a new scientific conception of man and nature drove many sensible minds into a mood of frustration and doubt. The decline of the influence of Christianity and the prospect of atheism had implications that were menacing; this introspective focus on the spiritual condition of man at mid-century caused widespread sufferings of conscience. Out of a sense of loneliness and isolation, a mood of depression and despair, grew an emotional longing for earlier conditions—a nostalgia for a lost world of simple youth. The image had its basis in memory, for most urban Americans during the Industrial Revolution had either grown up in the country or in a town small enough for ready contact with the rural environment. Though this generation never ceased to look forward to a new period of firm convictions and established beliefs, it lived in the meantime uncomfortably between two worlds, one dying and one struggling to be born.

A large part of the public, living through a period when doubt was undermining the eternal verities and when the traditional framework of thought was breaking down, reacted to their age with hope and dismay, optimism and anxiety. If nostalgia (as we shall see) was a continuous undercurrent of American life and thought between 1830 and 1860, it achieved its effects beneath the surface of a widely professed faith in progress. Perplexity gave birth to an anxious will to believe. Sensitive observers, particularly Transcendentalists, were soon aware that a reconstruction of thought was now a prime necessity. Heretofore the concept of "Nature and Nature's God" had been formal and mechanistic; now Nature came to have a new meaning and fascination. In the United States—an immense, unexplored, bountiful continent—a romantic sense of wonder was

22

turned upon Nature. The natural was viewed as the "authentic" and "essential" in man and his universe—a reality that the layers of civilization had covered over. Romanticism opened immense vistas to the imagination of artists and writers. At the same time, it was possible for many Americans to adopt romanticism without fully accepting its philosophy or understanding its implications.

The rise of romanticism in America with its emphasis upon the individual, the subjectivity of experience, the validity of the emotions, and the worth of the lowly and primitive, was obviously germane to a heavier emphasis on the intrinsic worth of the common man. Thus painters and writers turned to the study of the simple, the humble, the familiar in human life. The great tide of settlement pouring westward and the national experience of the frontier became the themes of a whole group of artists. Scenes of political campaigns and elections where a vigorous democracy aroused the excitement and passions of rural folk were worthy of our best painters' efforts. The impetus to understand and record the vast spectacle of this new land was explicit in the themes of realistic landscapes and genre of this period and impelled artists to paint what was before their eyes with passion and delight. Beginning with Allston and Audubon, a school of talented painters, represented by Cole, Durand, Catlin, Quidor, and Kensett, who turned their eyes to Nature and the unspoiled land emerged around 1830. "The painter of American scenery has indeed privileges superior to any other: all nature here is new to art," Thomas Cole proudly wrote. Following Cole's lead, Durand and others established what has since been called the Hudson River school of painting. Its earliest adherents found noble subjects for their brushes in the vistas of the Hudson, as well as in the mountain country of New York and New England. The untamed loneliness and the solemn beauty of the American wilderness came to have for them a new meaning and fascination. Nature became a vision of magical beauty and terrifying power.

The wilderness, which earlier had seemed hostile and savage, now concealed and could reveal the mysteries and beauties of the universe. The varieties of landscape ceased to be mere obstacles to settlement and mountains, forests, plains, rivers became wonders worth visiting because they stirred the emotions. Nature was observed in its kinder aspects, tame, gentle—and no longer as a primeval, frontier foe. Men now sought neither to escape nor destroy the wilderness, but to make it a part of their lives. By the 1850's, romantic painters had developed a faith in Nature that was triumphant; Nature was strange, picturesque, fantastic, and wonderful, yet beyond the reach of human powers to comprehend. In this context, landscape painting drifted into the representation of moral allegories; it became the vehicle for a message capable of teaching the observer. The American public had also discovered Nature and its appetite for landscape painting seemed inexhaustible.

Genre painting, with its hearty emphasis on the anecdotal and on human-interest elements, its glorification of everyday experience, and its meticulous brushwork, was another expression of the romantic movement. American genre subjects were almost entirely indigenous: earthy scenes and unflattering pictures of strong-jawed, toothless flatboatmen; farmers nooning; drunken voters and politicians; the roguish housewife; sweet, contented old men; the reflective Negro farm hand. Artists like Mount and Bingham cast over their canvases a gentle tone and glow that showed the American people at their best. Far from being crude or uncomplimentary, these mellow scenes reflected the rise of the common man and his popular art—an art of enthusiasm and delight, of humor and graceful style, of observation and affection, of vivid expression and subtle luminosity, of a romantic realism so simple and transparent as to seem artless.

During the 1860's and 1870's, coinciding with and partly resulting from the terrible tragedy of the Civil War, romanticism slowly declined and deteriorated into sentimentalism, triviality, and historical anecdote. This change in taste was reflected in Leutze's long series of historical and melodramatic pictures and in Huntington's fancy confections of sentiment. With the startling exception of Winslow Homer, painters of American life failed to have anything vital to express at the time of the great rebellion. Trivia and sentiment blinded them to the revelant, dramatic issues and themes of the Civil War. In the mounting crisis were all the elements of an American Iliad of panoramic dimensions—the swift movement of armies, the picturesqueness of the doomed plantation society, the gallantry of

Robert E. Lee and the wizardry of Stonewall Jackson, the tragic destiny of Lincoln. But painters somehow missed the point in the afterglow of romantic realism; the climate of the decade was not favorable to American imaginative life. The war and its aftermath were ugly and painful; they led to what Ruskin called "Purism," an idealization of life which created an unreal world of sentimental beauty.

## NOSTALGIA AND THE INDUSTRIAL REVOLUTION, 1830–1860

IN the turbulent age of rising capitalism and national expansion, it was clear to all, from the President to the worker watching the power loom, that technological progress was effecting immense social and economic upheavals. The disorder caused by the mechanization of American industry was compounded by social problems resulting from the rapid growth of American cities. The machine transformed the very appearance of the visible world. Tireless, efficient, requiring only the cheapest unskilled labor to tend it, the machine was the creator of industrial wealth. Machine production of large quantites of goods also created great distribution areas in which were mobilized banking, retail, and transportation centers. There were now entire landscapes created by the machine: slag heaps, large brick factories, and mills and houses for the factory workers. The visible scars in both the city and the countryside disturbed many Americans and began to shake their faith in the concept of progress.

Agricultural simplicity had been left somewhere far behind and agrarian individualism had been lost—or so it seemed to critics and crusaders in the 1850's—in a wilderness of greed and oppression, stocks and bonds, cutthroat competition and growing monopoly. There was a widely shared conviction that corporations and banks, monopolies in design if not altogether in fact, with their juggling of stocks and currency, their sinister manipulations of public men, their anonymity and inviolability, were conspiring to seize the government—to transform it into a mechanism of tyranny, pillage, and corruption. America had been at one time the hope of the oppressed. But to achieve a high level of prosperity, mill owners and promoters herded cheap labor into factory towns and created the slums of great cities. Laborers were housed in crowded hovels, forced to work for next to nothing and to wear out their lives digging ditches, tending machines, doing the menial tasks of industrial society. American businessmen were ready at any cost to make mine, forest, field and river yield richer and richer tribute to new machines. "The machine in the garden," the despoiling intrusion of factories and railroads on the beauty of the land, was hailed by some prophets as evidence of social progress. Unabashed by the change and social dislocations of the Industrial Revolution and the spread of the factory system, Northern businessmen looked upon their era as one of progress; progress without poverty, wealth without want.

But others were offended by the materialism of a changing America, offended by the dilemmas posed by industrialism, and were, as a result, desperately at odds with the magnificent optimism of industrial leaders who fought among themselves for the spoils of the land. They felt a deep-seated, agrarian, romantic longing or "cultural homesickness" for the values of the Old Republic. Lured backward as they were by their nostalgic image of the past and their bitter protest against the conditions of the present, radicals and others turned with longing to their lost youth, to the lost agrarian Eden, to the republican America of the early years of the 19th century. They feared the looming drift of their own era; the noise and smoke of factories and locomotives, the misery of the immigrants and cheap labor swarming into crowded cities, the concentration of monopoly powers into the hands of private individuals, the increase of social evil as a partner to the accumulation of wealth. The age was deeply torn between the gloomy despair of nostalgia and the bright belief in progress, the ideal of the Old Republic of little government and stoic self-sufficiency and the material lures of a new society of acquisitive capitalism. The American landscape now displayed factories with their machines, great cities growing greater, and recent immigrants who had never shared the shaping frontier experience. On canvas the sylvan landscapes of the romantic school provided one form of protest against the pitiless extinction of the past by the Industrial Revolution. Emerson thus described his country in 1844: "In America, out of doors, all seems a market, in doors, an air-tight stove of conventionalism."

26

Reformers who deplored the way in which rampant industry and corrupt politics were defiling the traditional virtues of America sought through a galaxy of reform measures to recast society totally and improve humanity. Forty years of feverish agitation after 1820 aimed to purify society and to relieve men of imperfections. The reformers' haste for improvement drove them to social change, just as haste for settlement thrust them westward. The reform impulse was as broad as life itself: diet and dress were subject to it, housing and sex, medicine and peace, economics and politics. Under the leadership of Emerson, Phillips, Garrison and Parker, Bryant, Leggett, Owen, and Greeley, in the 1840's and 1850's (especially in New England) there was a great intellectual and religious awakening, driven by the conviction that the whole course of human history was one of inevitable and endless progress; at the same time, this froze a substantial number of Americans into a mood of nostalgia. Prohibitionists, abolitionists, feminists, public educationalists, evangelists, prison, diet, and dress reformers—all wrote letters, essays, books; held meetings, conventions, debates, and lyceums. For a time they made a great noise and caused a great tumult, but hardly altered the course of Northern business and society.

The aggressive reformers, however, in their crusade uncovered one of the great flaws of the Republic: the slavery in which part of its population lived. But, it was clear, slavery was not just another object for reform. It was the greatest moral and social issue confronting Americans. The persistence of bondage in the South slowly but with certainty created a gulf between the South and the rest of the country. Southern culture gradually acquired a character and identity of its own, shaped largely by the plantation and the defense of slavery. When war in the 1840's put great new territories in the Southwest at the disposal of the country, the problem of whether these areas were to be slave or free opened a serious and inescapable crisis. The impact of that crisis on American society—resulting in savage fighting on the battlefields that left victor and vanquished alike exhausted—then and for the future was at once devastating and enduring.

## THE TRAUMA OF THE CIVIL WAR, 1861–1865

A MILLION casualties were counted before the eleven seceding states of the South finally admitted defeat in their efforts to establish an independent republic. The Civil War required the recruitment of the whole society, civilian as well as military, and it was expensive in terms of mortality, money, the destruction of materials, and the devastation of the country. Battle casualties were heavy but more died of disease behind the lines and in the prison camps than were killed at the front.

The Civil War was not only a testing of the American people as a nation; it was a watershed in their history. In both the North and South, men had blundered into the conflict without a full reckoning of the consequences. When the war broke out, the South was growing in wealth, proud of its culture, and brimming with promise for the future. By the late 1850's Southerners had come to believe that their "peculiar institution" would endure and spread. But by 1860 the strain of accommodating the differences between the sections of the country destroyed the political party system. Politicians, bigots, and extremists in the North and South stirred up a bewildered generation with hatred and hostility. Under these circumstances, particularly without unified party policies and without other mechanisms of compromise, the nation, politically rudderless, drifted helplessly into full-scale war.

This was total war against the people and economy of the South. As the losses indicate, it was primarily an infantry war, in which artillery and cavalry played important but secondary roles. Because of the fire power of massive armies and the increasing effectiveness of the blockade, the Confederacy was prostrate and helpless before the conqueror by the end of the war.

The price of suppressing the rebellion was high; the South returned to the Union an impoverished section. The destruction of the ante-bellum civilization introduced social and economic problems that were to burden generations to come. The destruction of the southern economy was the most tangible and lasting result of the war. The emancipation of the slaves, the breakup of the plantation economy, and the shortage of ready cash occasioned the development of the pernicious lien system. Under this system a farmer gave a lien or legal claim on his crop to creditors in order to obtain seed, supplies, and equipment with which to work his land. Merchants who gave credit demanded cash crops and saddled the region during the Reconstruction period with one-crop agriculture and its attendant evils; sharecropping and crop lien by tenants would last into our times. The multitude of problems attending reunion and manumission delayed reconciliation for many years and produced scars which are not yet entirely healed. As the people bound up the wounds of war and made the transition to peace in their effort at Reconstruction, they learned to what extent political considerations, social dislocations, economic interests, and the war's abundant legacy of bitterness had changed their society and their character as a people.

## THE FRAGMENTATION OF INDUSTRIALIZED SOCIETY, 1865–1890

THE era of Reconstruction was essentially anticlimactic, descending from the sharp tragedy of Lincoln's assassination to a blurred ending in weary abandonment. The Radical Republican majority in Congress imposed its will on President Andrew Johnson and punished Southern contumacy by instituting a comprehensive system of military rule that lasted a decade in some states. These were the years of Negro-Carpetbagger government under army protection, of lawless reprisals by the dreaded Ku Klux Klan, of wholesale corruption in public life—the dismal closing phase of the sectional conflict. Yet the period was also one of significant beginnings, when the powerful thrust of industrialization and economic change after 1865 carried North and South alike into the modern industrial world. By 1890 the United States had ceased to be primarily an agricultural nation producing raw materials for the more advanced European economies; it became one of the world's great manufacturing powers. Gigantic factories supplied a mounting share of the national wealth and capriciously poured great fortunes into the hands of individual entrepreneurs who assumed the risks and rewards of managing capital and credit. Expansion became the dominant motif of American society and the American economy in these decades.

But it was the mass of laborers who bore the heaviest share of the costs of industrialization. Workers were available in abundant numbers for all the tasks the entrepreneur set them, but were unable to demand rewards that corresponded to their efforts. Hardships in the lives of the most deprived sector of the labor force were the price the United States paid for industrial expansion. This pool of available labor kept expanding through immigration. Nine million immigrants came to America between 1880 and 1900; eastern and southern European types predominated, and the industrial centers were their destinations. By 1890 fully sixty-eight per cent of the population had been born abroad, and another ten per cent were the children of foreign-born. Within the shop and factory they did most of the unskilled work, whereas the skilled jobs and minor administrative positions were reserved for native white Americans. The wedge of racial discrimination was thereby driven into the labor force, setting overbearing small bosses on the top and rebellious foreigners resenting their social inferiority at the bottom. Under these desperate working conditions of racial antagonism, insecurity of employment, monotonous work, loss of personal contact, industrial accidents, and slum housing, the gulf broadened between employees and their employers, and led directly to the rise of militant unionism, to political interference, and to radical reform movements. Rarely was the ascent from rags to riches possible for immigrants; deep social divisions among the population widened the gap between them and native Americans. The transformation of the economy through the introduction of the machine was exacting a shameful human toil. Fragmentation became the outstanding characteristic of an American society wherein industrialization was producing such widespread social disorder. The growing difference between life in the harsh factories and in the gilded palaces raised incisive questions about the inevitability of the process. Reality began to erode the bright premise of the myth of success in the case of most American immigrants.

One of the most striking results of the expansion of industrial enterprise after the Civil War was the great increase in the numbers and wealth of the upper classes. An entirely new aristocracy of "self-made" men was created within a generation, and so rapid was its ascent to power and riches that few members of this new class received any training in the social responsibilities of great wealth. Prosperous merchants and planters of an earlier day with $100,000, who set modest standards of elegance and public virtue, were replaced by new industrial magnates and railroad barons who enjoyed annual incomes—untaxed—of more than a million dollars. By 1890, the Vanderbilts were worth $300,000,000, the Astors $250,000,000, and Andrew Carnegie, Marshall Field, and Jay Gould had all risen above the $100,000,000 mark. There were also 3,000 "ordinary" millionaires. Americans regarded these amazing figures with admiration, envy, and a little mistrust.

Had these vast accumulations been earned by the exercise of traditional virtues? These gigantic personalities were the first to admit that they controlled wealth through brutal competition. It was a commonly accepted belief that the proper concern of American industrialists was to keep their profits rising and their costs falling, free of outside interference, through pools, trusts, monopolies, and trade associations. It did not matter that relentless, cutthroat competition reduced efficiency in business and encouraged colossal waste of natural and human resources. Those who failed were believed to be either less able or less prudent.

The growth of such fortunes and the spread of industry throughout the land lent credence to the old belief that in America opportunities were almost unlimited and that material success was a sign of virtue. Andrew Carnegie was one of the most articulate preachers of the cult of success of the period; it was, after all, part of the American Dream that promised success to every poor, hard-working, frugal American boy. It was John D. Rockefeller's opinion that no matter how poor some persons might be, they possessed "infinite possibilities. They have but to master the knack of economy, thrift, and perseverance and success is theirs." Carnegie wrote, "The millionaires who are in active control started as poor boys and were trained in the sternest but most efficient of all schools—poverty." And he held up as models of the successful man (besides himself) other leaders in manufacturing, finance, and merchandising who now held the mace of authority: those who rose from the ranks of the thrifty, shrewd, and practical clerk or mechanic, to leadership. Boys in the cities saw the stately mansions of these great men, saw their princely carriages, their gigantic offices and stores. They read how these leaders of business society had acquired their rewards, and the ambitious set out to emulate them. Thus the ideals of our business leaders became the ideals of the great majority of the people.

This worship of success—the popularizing of the "bitch goddess success," as William James caustically phrased it—this striving for wealth and position, so typical of the period, left its mark on Americans. The money of the new millionaires gained recently from speculation and grimy factories, from coal mines and oil fields, seemed slightly tainted; their dollars lacked the respectability of the more modest fortunes of old, well-established families. Their passion for work, their claw-and-fang tactics, their lust for wealth brought them rewards, but they still longed for respectability and status. The would-be aristocracy of the titans and robber barons, unwilling to justify itself by money alone and unable to do so by birth, made taste the symbol of its position. Ostentatious demonstration of their success through the construction of imitation palaces filled with paintings and statuary, books and manuscripts, furniture and *objets d'art* was the easiest means of gaining recognition for what they had become and obliterating the recollection of what they had been.

The worship of success, therefore, reinforced a crude materialism in late 19th-century America. The competition for riches and rapid accumulation of fortunes produced new elite groups and exerted an enormous influence over American taste between 1865 and 1890. They attempted to win recognition as the new élite by patronizing a borrowed culture from Europe which they believed would sustain their pretensions to aristocracy.

BORROWED CULTURE IN THE AGE OF EXCESS, 1870–1890

So it was that culture became a symbol of status for the possessor in an industrial society that was deeply divided and rapidly changing. Old families lacked the institutional resources to enforce firm standards of belief or behavior, an appropriate etiquette or sense of rank. The men grown wealthy from building the industrial machine who decided to construct new homes, churches, museums, libraries, and colleges could not find any fixed standards of what was appropriate in architectural style and had, therefore, to arrive at their own values. They turned to high-priced architects like McKim, Mead and White for Renaissance palaces, and to Henry Hobson Richardson for Romanesque villas. These massive arched structures in brick and stone, often embellished with ornamental columns and courts, and lavish in the use of space, impressed the onlooker with the regal qualities of their residents or trustees.

Rich Americans spent more money on art during the thirty years after 1880 than had ever been spent by a similar group in the world's history. Having made their fortunes, the American captains of industry ransacked European galleries and estates. But more often than not collecting was entrusted to dealers or agents, shrewd businessmen themselves, who sought maximum commissions by handling the most reliable goods from Europe at the highest possible prices. John Pierpont Morgan never bothered to inspect the Vermeer for which he paid $100,000. Old masters, first editions, and rare antique furniture had the greatest worth; tested by time and in short supply, they were likely to increase in value and had a gratifyingly aristocratic appearance. Paintings were, however, the primary object of their pecuniary piety: paintings were symbols of a place in society, a badge of position, rather than a means of enjoyment or enlightenment. Most Americans, as a result, came to think of paintings as something in a museum or a rich man's house, removed from their lives.

As the gulf between official culture and popular culture widened, the creative personalities of this country suffered the dilemma of not being able to locate an audience either among the hollow élite or among the untutored populace. American writers and painters, in particular, were cut off from their audience and regarded as outsiders. At best Americans regarded them as a luxury in their culture. Where once the American artist had to wage the Emersonian fight for self-reliance and for freedom from a sense of provincialism, the main fight now was for acceptance in a culture that

33

valued conspicuous wealth and pretentious display. Business leaders of the United States never developed the imagination and breadth of view necessary to an enlightened ruling class. The very qualities that had brought them financial success were such as to make them least concerned with social and cultural welfare. The result was that most of these businessmen shirked their responsibilities or delegated them to underlings who dared not risk any innovations—a situation that proved deadly to the patronage of the arts in late 19th-century America. While American painting, sculpture, and allied disciplines in the decorative arts languished from lack of appreciation and subsidy, the expenditures of the rich went to purchase the "gilt-edged securities" of foreign art.

Lord Bryce, the most eminent foreign commentator on the United States of his generation, catalogued several reasons why the country was not more creative in art, literature, and science. Life was so restless and held so many distractions that it did not afford those "hours of comparative tranquility" in which great creations usually germinate. Most of the nation's energy went into subjugating nature and into progressing materially. These interests monopolized even men's thoughts and conversations, to the detriment of literature and art. Men of leisure, feeling out of place, were "wont either to make amusement into a business or to transfer themselves to the ease of France or Italy."

What were artists and writers to do? They were repelled by the crassness and money-making preoccupation of their country, but they were drawn at the same time by its vigor and natural beauty. To embrace or flee? Thoughtful men of the time were ambivalent about their country. In 1876 Thomas Eakins began teaching anatomy without pay at the Pennsylvania Academy of the Fine Arts. He was forced to resign in 1886 over a scandal ensuing from his asking a nude model to pose for an art class. John Singer Sargent, Henry Adams, and Henry James fled to Europe. Winslow Homer fled from society to the Maine coast, to paint the wildness and beauty to be found outdoors. Albert Pinkham Ryder retreated to a life of solitude and filth, painting the unworldly subjects of the Bible, of Shakespeare, of Wagner. These retreats and flights abroad to a European apprenticeship were of some value to American artists, but the surrender

34

and the effects of being cut off from the currents of their place and time were often destructive; for the flight into himself has usually led the artist to obscurity rather than depth. Yet if this split between the indigenous and the cultivated arts, the accepted and popular cultures, had its dangers for the careers of American artists, it also had its strength. Popular culture by the 1890's had performed a great ground-clearing function by breaking the monopoly over taste that the élite arts had held so long. In literature and painting, the desire to describe the life of common men was part of a successful revolt against the formal rules of the borrowed, official culture.

## THE REVOLT AGAINST FORMALISM, 1890–1900

REGENERATIVE forces combined in the 1890's to produce a cultural flowering in the United States and to lay the foundations for new trends in American creative thought. Revolt was in the air and what the future would bring no man could foretell. Confident that they had the ability to set aright the social and economic injustices inherited from the preceding decades of the 19th century, Americans launched a virtual crusade on all levels of government and society to revitalize democracy, to bring the economic machinery under their control, and to find an answer to the twin evils of special privilege and poverty.

Agrarian unrest and discontent took shape in a new progressive faith in political action; the adoption of the Populist platform heralded the coming triumph of a new reform movement. A revolution in the theory and practice of education was getting under way and gaining wide acceptance through the progressive theories of John Dewey. The social gospel movement within urban Protestantism began to prevail over the divisive forces within religious institutions. In philosophy William James conceived a new system, pragmatism, in which the truth or value of an idea or act was measured by its workability and its consequences. American journalism was transformed and became a vital force in the lives of the masses. A new literary movement, naturalism, was beginning to make its first impression on American writers in the 1890's. New poetic forms emerged with themes

celebrating the homely and common aspect of life. And in American painting and architecture there were signs of vitality and a new vision.

The decade of the 1890's was filled with the efforts of a younger
generation of artists to break away from the genteel tradition and the
decorative direction of eclecticism and cosmopolitanism of an older generation to a new realism. Between the demise of romanticism in the 1870's and
this new movement of realism at the end of the century, an uncertain mood
of imitativeness prevailed and American painting passed through a troubled
period of disintegration. General prosperity and easy travel made it possible for painters to study in Europe the prevailing trends of academic
constructions and decorative harmonies of lyrical sentiment. Out of their
reaction against the naturalism and romanticism of the generation of the
1850's they turned to a style of decoration and charm—the cult of aesthet-
icism—rather than to one of native vitality and power. Their wealthy
patrons also traveled and learned to admire and collect the work of fashionable Paris painters; patrons with such advanced tastes soon began to prefer
European paintings over American. The profession of painting in America
suffered a disastrous setback as a result, and became by the 1890's a
poverty-stricken pursuit for most aspirants. As Samuel Isham wrote in
1905: "When the younger men went abroad to study, they found it was
not possible for a man to live by it, even if he were talented, well taught,
and hard working." By the last decade of the century, painters, and indeed
the whole country, were in an uncertain, imitative mood. Henry Adams
observed in 1903: "The painful truth is that all of my New England generation . . . [was] in actual fact only one mind and nature. . . . Self-distrust
became introspection—nervous self-consciousness—irritable dislike of
America, and antipathy to Boston. . . . Improvised Europeans, we were,
and—Lord God!—how thin!" These efforts during the gilded age to link
our painting with that of Europe became characterized by a destructive
attitude of dependence, a return to colonial status in the arts, and a loss of
self-reliance.

Reacting against the fashionable modes and taste in painting, a small
number of individualists revolted and painted life with zest from their own

point of view as they saw it. The new realism movement used luminous colors, strongly emphasized brushstrokes, and a marked command of expressive movement in its impressive creations—Homer's images of roaring seas and harsh northern solitudes; Eakins' impressive sports scenes of rowing, sailboating, and shooting marsh birds; Bellows' pungent scenes of prize fights, religious revivals, and swarming streets. The compelling impulse of these men was, out of their revolt against formalism, a desire to paint something uniquely American and rich in artistic significance. This creative ferment was not confined to painting. American sculptors, led by Augustus Saint-Gaudens and Daniel Chester French, were raising their art to a new technical eminence. In the field of architecture H. H. Richardson had demonstrated the new spirit of artistic expression in his rich, massive, vital, monumental buildings. Out of this decade of revolt and change within American culture, a new horizon was created for the arts in America. All thoughtful observers agreed at the turn of the century that one era was dead beyond recall and that a new epoch in America was just beginning.

# ARCHITECTURE

*by Paul F. Norton*

INTRODUCTION

CORRESPONDING to the long period of political consolidation of the United States between the Revolutionary War and World War I is the remarkable development of architecture from nearly absolute dependence upon the European background to the emergence of new American solutions to the problems of style and structure as illustrated in the work of Sullivan, Frank Lloyd Wright, and the great inventors and engineers like James Bogardus (skeleton construction), Elisha Graves Otis (the elevator), J. A. Roebling (bridges), and W. L. Jenney (skyscraper construction). As the new republic grew in size and political authority, it grew as well in its awareness of the need for cultural development. After all, no European nation of consequence was without its heritage of literature and the arts; and it was no mere gratification of personal whims that led Thomas Jefferson to visit many of Europe's famous monuments, to buy books and paintings, and to meet important contemporary European architects. He knew perhaps better than any other American that the new nation would not command universal respect with only shrewd commerce and political victory.

In arguing for acceptance of good design for the Capitol in Richmond, Virginia, Jefferson felt compelled to say, "But how is taste in this beautiful art [architecture] to be formed in our countrymen unless we avail ourselves of every occasion when public buildings are to be erected, of presenting to them models for their study and imitation?"

The hope held by the enlightened Americans for the future of the arts was rhetorically set forth by B. H. Latrobe in his anniversary oration to the Society of Artists of the United States in 1811:

*The taste for the fine arts when it shall become a national taste, will be as permanent as the national language. It will not be a fashion set by a Charles, or a Louis XIV; it will be a law to which the economy of our legislatures will bend, and heroic actions will not go unacknowledged, because a statue or a monument requires an appropriation of money.*

To show fully how these hopes were realized is the purpose of this book.

A broad glance at 19th-century American building reveals a continuous application of past styles to contemporary construction without particular thought as to the appropriateness of a style to the function of the building. The word "style" in architecture means the continuous use of a group of forms and shapes for the construction and decoration of buildings in more or less the same manner over an extended period of time. A re-use of such a group after a lapse of time constitutes a "revival" of a style. As in late eighteenth-century England where a choice of style became less and less a matter of practicality and more an adventure in romanticism, American architecture prompted by English example became increasingly diversified, often to the point of exoticism. English, French and German architects had catered willingly to a demand for buildings intended to excite the imagination by constructing architectural glimpses, so to speak, of the past or physically distant.

Placed in the midst of urban architectural surroundings dating back for hundreds of years, or in vast parks guarded by great oaks and beeches, copies of Greek and Roman temples, or Chinese pagodas and tea houses, or the reflections in stone of Gothic chivalry and religion, were easily accepted as a proper part of European culture. But there is this difference, that neither the Yankee builders and western frontiersmen, nor their hardheaded industrialist followers, were captivated by romantic imagery as strongly as their European forebears. A Gothic house could resemble in some detail a mediaeval one, but for an American, brought up in a tradition of struggle for survival, this Gothic styling was a matter of suitable decoration rather than a way of providing a refuge in mediaevalism like Horace Walpole's extravagant Gothic house, Strawberry Hill. Nor did the average American financier expect his Greek Revival bank to excite feelings of classical beauty and democracy, so much as he believed that those strong Doric columns would suggest Athenian security, confidence and wealth.

Although 19th-century architecture is unthinkable without its reliance upon past styles, it is nevertheless a very different sort of thing. Contemporary architects were quite aware that, desirable as it may have been to emulate ancient builders, the problems of modern living could not be satisfactorily solved without adjustments in design. Obviously a Greek temple could not serve as a Christian church unless modified, nor was a Gothic church plan adaptable to provincial Protestant use without numerous changes. Less radical revisions were required to reconcile Gothic house design to 19th-century needs, but what source could provide the right façade for a railroad station? As the century proceeded this kind of problem be-

*Plate 1.* SEDGELEY, on the Schuylkill near Philadelphia, 1799. Demolished. Designed by B. H. Latrobe for William Crammond, Philadelphia merchant. As the profession of architect was not yet well regulated, Latrobe could not compel the builder to let him supervise construction. Latrobe said afterwards of the house, "I have been disgraced both by the deformity and expense of some parts of the building, because after giving the first general design, I had no further concern with it." This drawing by Latrobe presumably represents the house as he wished it. Original watercolor by B. H. Latrobe. *Courtesy,* FAIRMOUNT PARK COMMISSION, PHILADELPHIA, PA.

came more and more acute, until it was finally resolved after a series of bold moves on the part of several architects to release themselves from the aesthetic bondage imposed by the past.

The confusion resulting from the architect's inability to choose adroitly from old sources and the client's naiveté as to appropriate style is nicely illustrated by the application of one style, namely Gothic, to almost any and every type of construction. Thomas Jefferson planned "A Gothic temple or portico" for Monticello in 1807, Latrobe built the first Gothic house in America in 1799 (*Plate 1*), and Trinity Church was erected in the same style in New York at about the same time (1788–90). Variations on these early themes appeared frequently in the middle years of the century, and as tall commercial buildings became essential in cities these too were given decorative pointed arches. From this time on there were no barriers to using Gothic—even the Brooklyn Bridge of 1869 had its quaint Gothic-arched stanchions (*Plate 88*), and the Agricultural Hall for Philadelphia's Exposition of 1876 meaninglessly boasted pointed arches and Gothic spires.

That the best specimens of 18th-century architecture in America are aesthetically fine is not owing so much to the architectural training of the builders as to their good sense of proportion, their educated clients' interest in good workmanship, and their foresight in following rather closely the available builder's guides and architect's books. The books commonly consulted were mainly English publications by Gibbs, Swan, Paine, and others.

In the 1790's a new breed of designer appeared—the professional architect. All in the first generation were foreign born. All were trained by apprenticeship to important English and French architects or had studied in foreign schools of architecture. Their arrival meant a new, imaginative approach to the problems of designing, and a new method of training young men to the profession. This is not to say that these architects did not consult Stuart's *Antiquities of Athens* and other authorities, but that they used their sources creatively.

As the profession of architect became recognized, the architects themselves began to exert standards of performance by compiling cost analyses for construction and setting fees for designs and superintendence. This codification of rules for the profession led rapidly to the foundation of architectural associations in the 1850's lending further stature to the group. Finally came the architectural schools which, with their own high standards of aesthetics and professional practice, helped immeasurably to make the United States the architectural leader it has become in the 20th century.

While the architects were responsible for the changing appearance of city streets and country estates, the new emphasis on industrial expansion made necessary another profession, that of engineer. Early in the century a man could call himself both architect and engineer, sometimes selecting his title depending upon which talent best exemplified the immediate activity. B. H. Latrobe, for instance, called himself architect or surveyor while working on the Capitol in Washington, and signed his name as engineer while superintending work on the Delaware and Chesapeake Canal. William Strickland assumed both titles as surveyor of the town of Cairo, Illinois. Engineers were called upon to build canals and steamboats, then railroads and train sheds, and both of these modes of transportation demanded the building of bridges. Later in the century the complexities involved in erecting skyscrapers and other huge edifices inextricably bound the engineer to the building industry to the point where the important architectural firms always employed men with engineering training, and frequently the engineer was a senior partner as in the firm of Adler (engineer) and Sullivan (architect), and Holabird (engineer) and Roche (architect).

While architectural style, the solution of engineering problems, new innovations in equipping buildings (for example, elevators, ventilating systems, fire-proofing), and improved professional conditions are the most noticeable areas of change during the 19th century, it should not be forgotten that architecture continued to be considered as a fine art. No architect of merit thought otherwise. Yet what each architect in turn believed to be an aesthetic improvement over his predecessors was not always that; more likely it was a change in aesthetic point of view as a response to the demands of an advancing industrial civilization. As one looks back over the century with this thought in mind, it is clear that Robert Mills, Strickland and other architects at the beginning of the century designed buildings as admirable and beautiful as any at the end of the century. In other words, the aesthetic standards may have changed, but the results were not necessarily an improvement. While 19th-century architects kept up with the construction needs of their society, made numerous innovations,

*Plate 2.* STATE CAPITOL, RICHMOND, VIRGINIA. 1785–1789. Designed by Thomas Jefferson with the assistance of Clérisseau. The plan (*Plate 3.*) shows Jefferson's first conception; that it correspond closely to the plan of a Roman temple. The final version is less temple-like; office windows intrude, exterior half-columns become flat pilasters, the portico is one column less in depth, and the general decorative effect is less rich. Most of these changes were imposed by the need for economy. The projecting wings are not a part of the original design. PHOTOGRAPH BY WAYNE ANDREWS

and were inventive and ingenious to a high degree, their minds were never freed from the influence of the past. In the 20th century architects have escaped from the past; the question may still be asked whether the result is aesthetic progress or change?

FROM BUILDING TO ARCHITECTURE (*circa* 1785—*circa* 1825)

THE definition of architect implies at the least a knowledge of the profession and a natural gift for creating good design. The difference between amateur and professional in the field is that the amateur possesses less knowledge for lack of architectural education and continued practical experience. How do we account for the fact that in the 1790's and early 1800's so many good buildings were erected from the plans of men falling into the category of amateurs? Each amateur is perhaps an individual case. Thomas Jefferson (1743–1828) relied upon his sense of good taste developed through individual study and European travel, coupled with the selection of competent carpenters and masons. His famous design for the Capitol at Richmond, Virginia (*Plate* 2), in the basic form of a Roman temple,

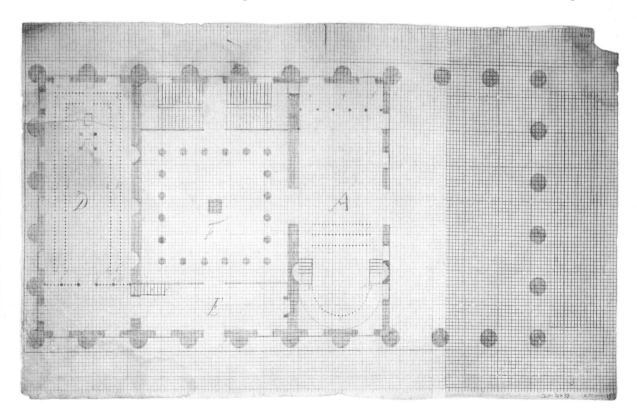

*Plate 3.* PLAN OF VIRGINIA STATE CAPITOL as Jefferson first conceived it. *Courtesy,* MASSACHU-SETTS HISTORICAL SOCIETY, BOSTON

resulted from his being entranced by the sight of the ancient Maison Carrée at Nîmes, France. According to his own account he sat before this best preserved of Roman temples for hours on end, enamored of its beauties, "gazing . . . like a lover at his mistress." When it came to making the actual plans for the Capitol, requested by the Virginia legislature, Jefferson sought the help of the French architect, Charles Clérisseau. As designer of his own home, Monticello, near Charlottesville, Va. (*Plate 4*), he consulted the time-honored pages of Palladio's books on architecture first published in Italy in 1570. Here he found inspiration for both his first and second designs, the latter being a subdued imitation of Palladio's Villa Rotondo at Vicenza, fused with elements of English Palladianism from Lord

*Plate 4.* Monticello, Charlottesville, Virginia. 1770–1809. Designed by Thomas Jefferson. A romantic hilltop retreat where Jefferson spent several months each year even while Secretary of State and President; it was also his place of retirement overlooking the town in which his last architectural achievement, the University of Virginia, came to fruition. photograph by wayne andrews

Burlington's Chiswick House. At both Richmond and Monticello the deviations from the prototypes are highly significant. The Capitol had to be adapted for a new non-religious use, and Monticello, though serving the same purpose as its ancestors, that of the country retreat, had to conform to the simpler scale of Virginia life and was built of brick—a material by its size suggesting less monumentality than stone. Late in life, Jefferson turned once again to architectural design. He had long since recognized the need for more institutions of higher learning, so when the chance came, he conceived a group of buildings linked by passageways to form a closely knit academic village. This was the University of Virginia (*Plate 5*). The focus of his plan was on a central, domed building serving not as a chapel as one

*Plate 5.* ROTUNDA, UNIVERSITY OF VIRGINIA, CHARLOTTESVILLE, VIRGINIA. 1822–1826. Conceived and mainly designed by Jefferson. Each pavilion enclosing the lawn before the Rotunda was designed as a different example of classical architecture. The space within the domed Rotunda could contain a perfect sphere, like its prototype the famous Pantheon in Rome. Jefferson's serpentine walls (one brick thick) connect the pavilions and living quarters on the lawn with a second set of dormitory buildings behind. PHOTOGRAPH BY WAYNE ANDREWS

might expect, but as a library—the heart of the institution. Again Jefferson sought help from his architectural books, also from Dr. William Thornton, a notable amateur, and, more significantly, from B. H. Latrobe, a professional.

*Plate 6.* GARDNER (WHITE-PINGREE) HOUSE, SALEM, MASSACHUSETTS. 1804–1805. Designed by Samuel McIntire for John Gardner. Although the door and windows are spaced with perfect regularity on the façade, the interior planning makes rooms of various shapes depending upon specific needs, and there is an ell at the back as kitchen. The house was deeded to the Essex Institute in 1933 and has been restored. PHOTOGRAPH BY WAYNE ANDREWS

*Plate 7.* GARDNER (WHITE-PINGREE) HOUSE, SALEM, MASSACHUSETTS. 1804–1805. Fireplace in front drawing-room. The idea of delicate surface decoration comes from Robert Adam, while its particular use is McIntire's. The motifs, displayed classically, are often Americanized as here in a Classic bowl of American fruit, the sheaves of wheat in the corners, and elsewhere the American Eagle. PHOTOGRAPH BY WAYNE ANDREWS

Unlike Jefferson, Samuel McIntire (1757–1811), was a specialist in only one area. He was a very good woodcarver and builder of houses. He selected designs from the usual set of guidebooks and skillfully adapted them to the materials available in New England where he worked exclusively. His clients were generally of the merchant class whose success in no small way made possible the increasingly splendid architecture built along the eastern seaboard. Although McIntire's houses properly belong in the Georgian era, his late ones, like the Gardner House, Salem, Mass. (*Plates 6* and *7*), are markedly changed in style and show the influence of English Regency work. McIntire dispenses with the clutter of classic decoration and leaves a clean, orderly brick façade broken only by two marble stringcourses. The handsome ovoid portico gives just enough accent to the entrance. The elegance of the interior is reflected in the fireplace with its array of delicate Classic ornaments—Adamesque swags, winding vines around half columns of the Composite Order, and key mouldings; and, as if to show his allegiance, a sheaf of American wheat in the frieze above both columns where a Roman might have placed the ubiquitous tripod. Without McIntire's distinctive genius for erecting such superbly proportioned houses, Salem, and New England in general, would be architecturally much less well endowed. He did not, however, feel compelled to change his style yet again with the coming of Classicism.

McIntire, untutored, untravelled, was a natural woodcarver and builder of distinction, but not an architect. Nor was Samuel Blodgett, Jr. (1757–1814), who built one of the first large commercial structures in America, the Bank of the United States in Philadelphia (1795–97) (See *The Arts in America: The Colonial Period*, New York, 1966, *Plate 85*). However, this is really a large Georgian house made to fit banking requirements, not a redesigned classical temple. Beyond this, Blodgett did little of architectural significance.

The energetic Dr. William Thornton (1759–1828) was a man of many accomplishments. He had received a medical degree from the University of Edinburgh (1784), travelled on the Continent, and lived on a plantation in Tortola, V.I., before entering an architectural competition for the Library Company of Philadelphia. That he won the competition without doing any more than consulting some books on architecture is a tribute to his genius. He later won another competition, after some unusual circumstances, for the Capitol in Washington, but his plans could not be built, nor could he produce the requisite working drawings. This awkward situation was only resolved by hiring a professional architect, Stephen Hallet, to revise the plans and direct construction. We may admire Thornton's ingenuity, yet recognize that when a predicament of this sort could arise it was time that professionals took over the field of architecture.

Whether Charles Bulfinch (1763–1844) qualifies as a professional architect is questionable, even though he designed a large number of buildings and was entrusted with continuing the erection of the Capitol in Washington after Latrobe resigned. Bulfinch neither went to an architectural school nor was apprenticed to an architect. He, like Jefferson, was well educated and had travelled extensively in Europe, but much of his life was spent non-architecturally in Boston where he was employed in various civic duties. His buildings, though correct, are generally uninspired and fit better stylistically with late Georgian rather than with the progressive Greek and Roman revival architecture. Best known are the state houses in Hartford and Boston (*Plate 8*), the Harrison Gray Otis houses in Boston, and the Maine State Capitol, Augusta.

The greatest city-planning and architectural project of the budding republic was the development of the Federal City (as it was then called) out of the swamps along the Potomac. To some it appeared an absurd enterprise; to those with more vision, an opportunity to unify the states politically by forming a physical center and erecting buildings to realize this concept. The first session of Congress governed by rules of the Constitution assembled in New York, but only to wait upon the preparation for their removal to a neutral ground between North and South. Significantly, the first four professional architects to emigrate to America were employed in succession on this enterprise. None was completely successful in coping with the misunderstandings, intrigue and outright dishonesty prevalent in the Federal City. Land proprietors and speculators fought viciously, streets were mainly mud, lodgings were dirty and difficult to find, and had it not been for the level-headed, unselfish work of George Washington, Jefferson and a few other dedicated men, it is unlikely that the city could have become a seat of government in 1800. Not that the city was fully prepared by that date, for it could still be described as a wilderness by John Davis who came to hear Jefferson's inaugural address. "When I had heard the speech of Mr. Jefferson," he said, "there was nothing more to detain me among the scattered buildings of the desert."

*Plate 8.* STATE HOUSE, BOSTON, MASSACHUSETTS. 1795–1798. Designed by Charles Bulfinch immediately after returning from his trip to Europe in 1785–1787, but not completed for another decade. There are elements of Chamber's Somerset House in the Strand, and of Adam ornament. Recent additions have spoiled the total unity of the building. Comparison shows how very few changes were made between the original design (*Plate 9.*) and the finished work. The Corinthian columns were of wood and only replaced this decade. PHOTOGRAPH BY WAYNE ANDREWS

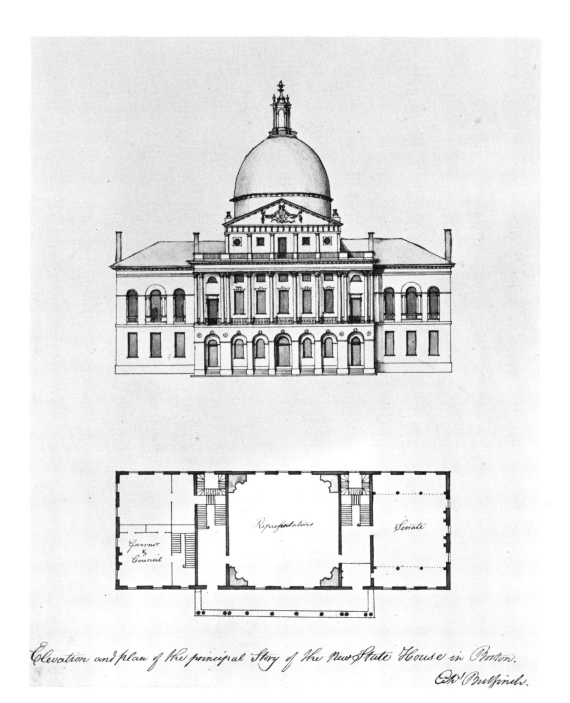

*Elevation and plan of the principal Story of the New State House in Boston.*

*Chs. Bulfinch.*

*Plate 9*. BULFINCH'S DRAWING of the front elevation of the Massachusetts State House. *Courtesy*, STOKES COLLECTION, PRINTS DIVISION, NEW YORK PUBLIC LIBRARY

The peculiar plan of Washington (*Plate 10*) with its maze of streets cutting through the city at odd angles was in fact the well-conceived design of Pierre Charles L'Enfant (1754–1825). He was a Frenchman who had studied art at the Académie Royale in Paris. In 1776 he enlisted in the American Army and became a lieutenant of engineers.

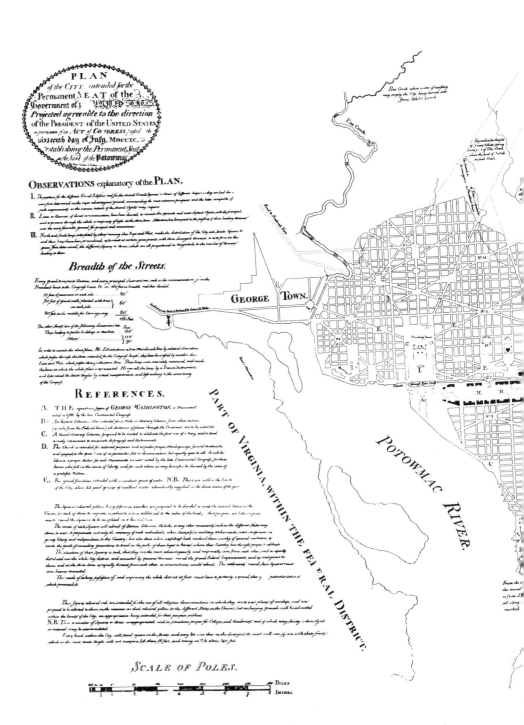

*Plate 10.* PLAN OF WASHINGTON, D. C. 1791. Designed by Pierre Charles L'Enfant. The Mall, with Capitol to the east and President's House on an extension to the north, was a suggestion of Jefferson's. The street arrangement is said to owe much to Evelyn's plan for London after the great fire (1666) and to the extensive garden planning at Versailles. The attractive canal through the Mall has long since disappeared. *Courtesy*, NATIONAL ARCHIVES, WASHINGTON, D. C.

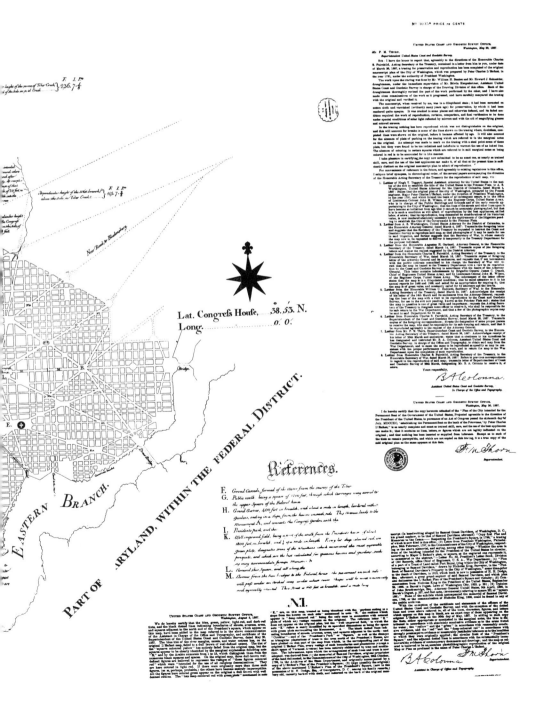

*Arts in America*

When in 1791 Washington wanted someone to prepare a plan for the Federal City, he asked L'Enfant. He designed the city, with the help of plans of various European cities given to him by Jefferson, as a grid cut through at angles by broad avenues. L'Enfant, not without pride, said that "the plan should be drawn on such a scale as to leave room for that aggrandisement and embellishment which the increase of the wealth of the Nation will permit it to pursue at any period however remote." Although many of the city lots carved out by this system were inconveniently of

58  *Plate 11.* CROSS-SECTION OF THE HALL OF REPRESENTATIVES, CAPITOL, WASHINGTON, D. C., 1804. Designed by B. H. Latrobe. This version was actually built and used by Congress before the fire of 1814. The shape in plan was a rectangle with attached semicircles at each end, replacing the oval plan drawn by Thornton as a compromise between oval and semicircle. Latrobe had wished to conform more closely to Greek precedent, so when he redesigned the same room after the fire he persuaded the authorities to accept his semicircular plan. This second hall is now Statuary Hall. *Courtesy,* DEPARTMENT OF PRINTS AND DRAWINGS, LIBRARY OF CONGRESS, WASHINGTON, D. C.

myriad shapes, the transportation needs of the future were admirably served until the present time.

When it was discovered that L'Enfant, who was also expected to make designs for the Capitol building, only "had them in his head," Jefferson suggested a competition. As mentioned earlier, the competition was won by Dr. William Thornton and the construction begun by Stephen Hallet (flourished 1782–1795). Hallet, another Frenchman, was trained as an architect and quite able to superintend the construction of a building as large as the Capitol. Without permission, however, he extensively modified Thornton's design to suit himself. When this was discovered, Hallet was summarily dismissed and disappeared from the scene. The painter, John Trumbull, who was residing in London, having heard of the difficulties in Washington, sent over the young, gold-medal graduate of the new school of architecture of the Royal Academy; namely, George Hadfield (1767–1826). Within two years Hadfield was also forced to resign. His architectural taste was of a high order, as may be seen from the few other buildings he designed, like Arlington House, Arlington, Virginia, but his temperament could not endure the frustrations of working in Washington. Finally President Jefferson hired Benjamin Henry Latrobe (1764–1820), recently arrived from England, as surveyor of public buildings in Washington. In this position he completed the south wing of the Capitol, only modifying the interior design (*Plate 11*), and he gained approval for changing the central part of the building to resemble the domed Roman Pantheon. Begun as a Georgian design, the Capitol was fast becoming neo-classical, and shortly would serve as a model for the interior arrangement and exterior appearance of many state capitols built in the next few decades.

Latrobe was indeed most instrumental in promoting the popularity of the Greek Revival, a style which lasted well into the middle of the century in the Midwest. Along with its almost indistinguishable sister, the Roman Revival, this style accounts for practically all the best buildings designed between 1800 and 1840 anywhere in the country, and is at the basis of the exploitation of classical decoration on a more monumental, even grandiose scale at the end of the century. Latrobe acquired his architectural training in London as an apprentice to the shrewd and accurate Samuel Pepys Cockerell. His taste was formed by study of the great architectural books then being published with engraved measured drawings of Greek and Roman antiquities (*Plates 12* through *15*), and by his close observation of the works of Sir John Soane. What made Latrobe easily acceptable in

*Plate 12*

60

*Plate 13*

*Plates 12 through 15.*
TEMPLE ON THE ILISSUS, facade (*Plate 12*)
and a detail (*Plate 13*), from Stuart and Revett,
*Antiquities of Athens* (1762), Vol. I, Chap. II.
The book was published in time for Latrobe
to have referred to it while designing his
Bank of Pennsylvania. *Plates 14 and 15*, also
from the *Antiquities of Athens*, (Vol. I, Chap. IV)
show the Choragic Monument of Lysicrates at
Athens and a detail. Latrobe referred more
than once to these plates, and the entire monument
became an essential part of several buildings by
Strickland and others. PHOTOGRAPHS, *courtesy*
ART DIVISION, THE NEW YORK PUBLIC LIBRARY

Plate 14

Plate 15

61

America as an architect was not only his ability to design, but his character as an intelligent, well-educated gentleman of many accomplishments. He knew Latin, Greek and several modern languages, was musical, and wrote with uncommon literary skill. It is no wonder that his time was fully occupied designing houses and public buildings in a country little used to the cultural or architectural standards of England, but very desirous of attaining such standards.

The building most satisfying to its designer was Latrobe's Bank of Pennsylvania in Philadelphia (*Plate 16*), unfortunately demolished about 1871. Its pleasingly proportioned, Greek Ionic porticoes and low, Roman, vaulted dome like that of the Pantheon, are features here superbly com-

62    *Plate 16*. BANK OF PENNSYLVANIA, PHILADELPHIA. 1798–1800. Designed by B. H. Latrobe for Samuel M. Fox, president of the bank. Latrobe made a little sketch for Fox while on a brief visit to Philadelphia. Seven months later he was much surprised and pleased to hear that his design had been accepted. Compare the portico with the Temple on the Ilissus (*Plate 12*). The low dome, like that of the Pantheon, covers the banking hall and lights it through an *oculus*. One of the first buildings in America (the old Philadelphia jail was earlier) to use vaulting to create an interesting interior space. Original drawing by B. H. Latrobe. *Courtesy*, THE COLLECTIONS OF THE MARYLAND HISTORICAL SOCIETY, BALTIMORE

*Plate 17.* "Old West," Dickinson College, Carlisle, Pennsylvania. 1803. Designed by B. H. Latrobe, although he did not see the finished building until he made a western trip to Pittsburgh in 1813. Original plans are in the possession of the college. These show that the building was erected almost exactly as planned (*Plate 18*), except for the curious mermaid weathervane, the product of some local craftsman. PHOTOGRAPH BY PAUL F. NORTON

*Plate 18.*
Original Sketch by Latrobe for "Old West," Dickinson College. *Courtesy,* THE COLLECTIONS OF THE MARYLAND HISTORICAL SOCIETY, BALTIMORE

bined. Architecture as beautiful as this could only act as a stimulus to the art of building. In 1803, after a disastrous fire, Latrobe drew plans for a new building for Dickinson College, Carlisle, Pa. (*Plate 17*). Partial to educational institutions, he only charged for the actual cost of hiring his draughtsman. Unlike earlier educational buildings in America, "Old West,"

*Plate 19*. ROMAN CATHOLIC CATHEDRAL OF BALTIMORE, MARYLAND. 1804–1821. Designed by B. H. Latrobe for Bishop Carroll of Baltimore. Undecided as to which style would most please the diocese, Latrobe made both Gothic and Roman designs. Before the project was completed he had made a long series of designs, many of which are still preserved by the Archdiocese of Baltimore. The Roman design was chosen, though Latrobe preferred the Gothic. (See *Plate 20*.)
PHOTOGRAPH BY WAYNE ANDREWS

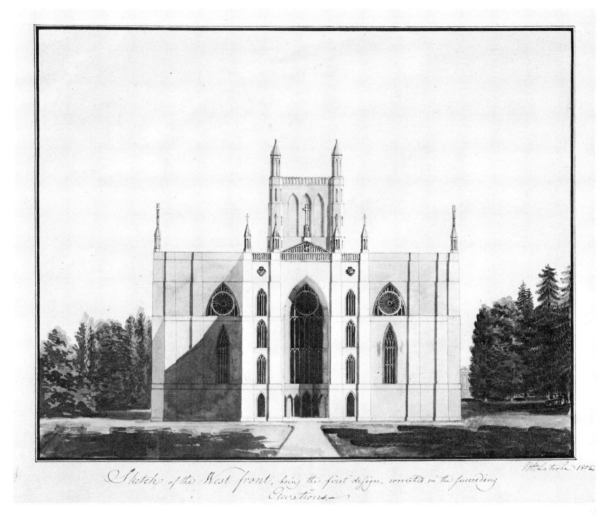

*Sketch of the West front, being the first design, corrected in the succeeding Elevations*

*B. H. Latrobe 1805*

*Plate 20.* Sketch of a Gothic Design for the Baltimore Cathedral. *Courtesy*, Architectural Records Collection, Smithsonian Institution, Washington, D. C.

as it is called, was designed with its corridor on the west side for weather protection with rooms to the east. It also has the more advanced idiom of the splendid central arch with echoing smaller arches in the wings. The Baltimore Cathedral (*Plate 19*) design was also an act of generosity on Latrobe's part. Again he asked only for enough money to cover his expenses, even though this was a very large architectural project. When in Italy in the 1780's, Latrobe had admired the Roman Pantheon; and the Cathedral—with the same basic elements of Corinthian portico and dome

65

over the main room—recalls successfully, without copying, its ancient counterpart.

The construction of churches became a major enterprise along the eastern seaboard as the towns and cities increased in population. Generally the larger churches demanded the use of an architect. No mere builder could have built the Baltimore Cathedral nor designed so expertly the

*Plate 21.* SAINT MARY'S CHAPEL, BALTIMORE, 1807. Designed by Maximilian Godefroy for Father Dubourg, the head of St. Mary's College. The "Gothic" decoration of the façade fits reluctantly the pattern of a Roman triumphal arch. Perhaps Godefroy attempted to use Batty Langley's *Gothic Architecture Improved* . . . wherein such inconsistencies abound. Brick laid in Flemish bond gives a small-scale surface texture, not without its charm. Clustered brick columns, with totally-out-of-place modified Roman capitals frame the façade, while pointed niches are still awaiting their statues. PHOTOGRAPH BY WAYNE ANDREWS

numerous churches erected in the Classic and now the Gothic styles. Maximilian Godefroy, a French refugee officer, lived from 1805 to 1819 in the United States. He built a chapel in Baltimore (*Plate 21*) for St. Mary's College where he taught fine arts, and later he designed the Unitarian Church in Baltimore with a Roman dome. He, like Latrobe, worked in more than one style to meet the demand of clients not always willing to

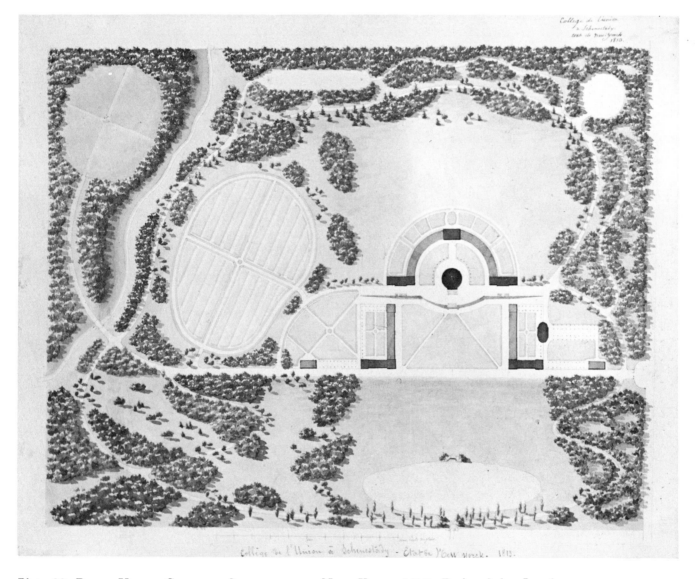

*Plate 22.* PLAN, UNION COLLEGE, SCHENECTADY, NEW YORK. 1813. Designed by Joseph Jacques Ramée. His work for the College included the general layout of the campus as well as several of its buildings. The name "Union" refers to a union of religious sects. By its charter the college may not have a majority of Trustees from any single sect. Original drawings are still in the possession of the College. Finding too few commissions in America after the War of 1812, Ramée left for his native France in 1817. *Courtesy*, SCHAFFER LIBRARY, UNION COLLEGE, SCHENECTADY

accept the architect's judgment, nor convinced of the correctness of any particular style.

Still another of the emigrés, Joseph Jacques Ramée (1764–1842) was responsible for the first plan of Union College, Schenectady, N. Y. (*Plate 22*), helping to meet the increasing need for educational institutions. One might expect a French-trained architect to have produced a formal plan in the manner of Versailles, but just at this time there was a vogue for the romantic informal English garden. The winding stream and meandering pathways are much like the gardens at Stowe and elsewhere in England. This self-conscious informality leads to the mid-century work of F. L. Olmsted, always a lover of nature well-groomed, but unspoiled. The accent of serpentine lines in the landscaping is in contrast to Ramée's college buildings planned as a crescent with extensions. The dormitories

*Plate 23*. DORMITORY, UNION COLLEGE, SCHENECTADY, NEW YORK. 1813. Designed by Joseph Jacques Ramée. Planned like an English country estate, complete in itself; future needs for expansion were unforeseen. Unlike Jefferson's University of Virginia, the central building of the campus was designed undoubtedly as a chapel, although when built (1858–1876) from the plans of E. T. Potter, it became a library. *Courtesy*, SCHAFFER LIBRARY, UNION COLLEGE, SCHENECTADY

(*Plate 23*) are not as exciting as Jefferson's at Charlottesville, though they are harmoniously grouped, and like Jefferson's, housed professors and students, and contain lecture rooms as well. They reflect earlier collegiate designing and something of the current French simplification of classical decoration as in the designs of Ledoux's Parisian custom houses.

The most important American architects of the second generation of professionals, were those young men trained in the office of Latrobe. To them he passed on a tradition of meticulous draughtsmanship, resourceful planning, and dedication to the enduring qualities of beauty inherent in classical design. Following the principles of classical architecture as laid down in Vitruvius's volumes written at the time of the Emperor Augustus, he taught them to perceive the beauty in extant buildings and to acknowledge the modifications in Classic principles made by the great architects of the Renaissance. A young architect with natural talents and a close apprenticeship to such a master could expect a bright career in the new nation.

One of these young architects, Robert Mills (1781–1855), followed this very formula leading to fame in the profession. Born in America, Mills was really the first native professional architect. He sought advice about his career from Jefferson who recommended him to Latrobe with whom he worked for several years. Practically all his designs, excepting the Washington Monument in Washington, D. C., which is of course an obelisk, are classical, either by direct inheritance or through the lineage of Italian and English Renaissance designs. Mills's most ambitious commissions were in Washington—the Treasury Building (*Plate 28*) for one, the Patent Office, and the Old Post Office, but these are products of his mature years. Mills was well satisfied to pursue beauty and convenience by making ancient ornament fit modern needs. In an essay on the progress of architecture in Virginia he wrote that, "I have always deprecated the servile copying of the buildings of antiquity; we have the same principles and materials to work upon that the ancients had, and we should adapt these materials to the habits and customs of our people as they did to theirs." The best of Mills's early work is in South Carolina, the state of his birth, and may be represented by the First Baptist Church, Charleston (*Plate 24*), where he gave particular attention to the play of clean surfaces and shadows which is both classic and typical of the architect. Latrobe's work had necessarily been confined mainly to the linear strip of land stretching from Washington to Philadelphia, whereas architects of the new generation were able to influence building taste far beyond these limits as more communities became affluent and territories became States.

While Mills was a hard worker even in his apprentice days, another pupil of Latrobe's, William Strickland (1788–1854), son of a carpenter, began by being indolent and irresponsible. But after he conquered his early faults of character he reached just as high an architectural peak as Mills, and in one contest took the prize away from his mentor Latrobe, much to

*Plate 24.* FIRST BAPTIST CHURCH, CHARLESTON, SOUTH CAROLINA. 1819–1822. Designed by Robert Mills. Built of brick covered by stucco and roofed with slate. The architect unabashedly called it "the best specimen of correct taste in architecture of all the modern buildings in this city." For a decade Mills carried on a brisk business in Charleston before leaving for Washington in 1829. *Courtesy,* HISTORIC AMERICAN BUILDINGS SURVEY, WASHINGTON, D. C.

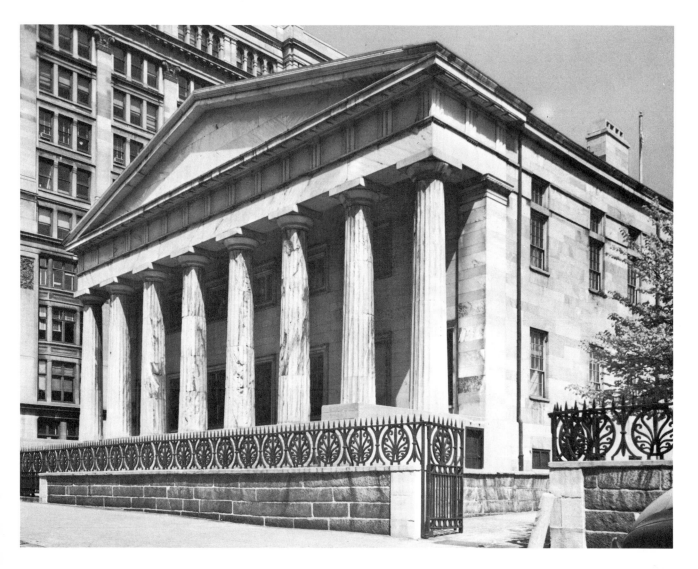

*Plate 25.* SECOND BANK OF THE UNITED STATES, PHILADELPHIA. 1818–1824. Designed by William Strickland. The porticoes were taken rather directly from Stuart and Revett's *Antiquities of Athens*, the engraving illustrating the Parthenon. As a consequence of its use as a bank, the building only slightly resembles a Greek temple, and it lacks the subtle curvature of its prototype. At right angles to the axis of the porticoes is a tunnel-vaulted banking room. The building served later as a customs house, and is now a part of the Independence National Historical Park. PHOTOGRAPH BY WAYNE ANDREWS

the latter's dismay. This was in the competition for the Second Bank of the United States, Philadelphia (*Plate 25*). Its design owes much to Latrobe's teaching and indeed can hardly be distinguished from his manner, except that the proportions are less well handled and there is a lack of inventiveness in treating the flanks. Similarly the Naval Asylum (later the United

States Naval Home) at Philadelphia (*Plate 26*), is not an inspired building. The open air piazzas for the ill, juxtaposed with the noble Ionic portico, make the latter seem superfluous and out of scale. That Strickland had comparatively few large commissions is probably owing to the backward state of commerce in Philadelphia in the 1820's and because he worked on many other kinds of projects such as canals, monuments, maps, and so forth. One of Strickland's non-architectural activities was to travel through England and Scotland at the request of the Pennsylvania Society for the Promotion of Internal Improvement. The purpose of the trip was to

On Stone by J. C. Wild.                                                                              Printed by J. Collins.

U. S. NAVAL ASYLUM.

PHILADELPHIA.

*Plate 26.* NAVAL ASYLUM (UNITED STATES NAVAL HOME SINCE 1879), GRAYS FERRY ROAD AT 24TH STREET, PHILADELPHIA, PENNSYLVANIA. 1826–1829. Designed by William Strickland. The attic story and dormer windows added later (1848 and 1870's). The piazzas are supported by 88 iron columns resting on granite piers. The marble Ionic columns of the portico were modelled on those of the Temple on the Ilissus (*Plate 12.*) as portrayed in Stuart and Revett's *Antiquities of Athens*. Lithograph by J. C. Wild. PHOTOGRAPH *courtesy*, GEORGE B. TATUM

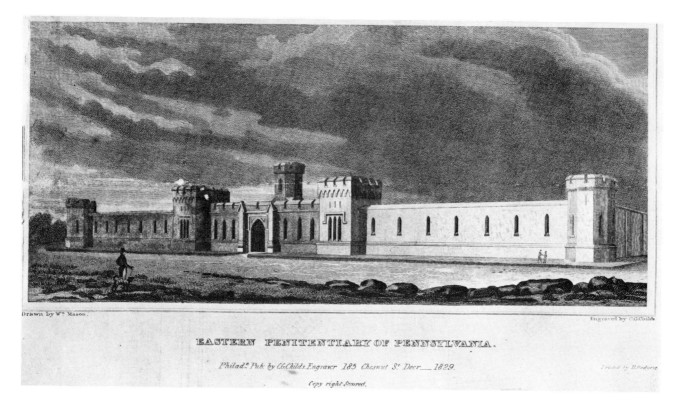

Drawn by Wᵐ Mason.  Engraved by C.G.Childs

EASTERN PENITENTIARY OF PENNSYLVANIA.

Philadᵃ Pub. by C.G.Childs Engraver 185 Chesnut St Decr___1829.

Copy right Secured.

*Plate 27.* EASTERN STATE PENITENTIARY, PHILADELPHIA, PENNSYLVANIA. 1829–1836. De-signed by John Haviland. This prison is the first in the country to be designed on the radiating wheel principle. All corridors leading to each wing of cells could be visually controlled from the center. The intent was that each prisoner should have an individual cell, thus eliminating some of the indecencies of multiple confinement. From *Reports of the Inspection of the Eastern State Penitentiary of Pennsylvania* (1831). PHOTOGRAPH, *courtesy,* NEW YORK PUBLIC LIBRARY

strengthen trade, transportation and manufacturing in the city by bringing useful information from abroad.

The full force of the Gothic Revival was not felt in America until the middle of the century, nevertheless significant beginnings of it appeared in the early decades. John Haviland (1792–1852) must be counted among those who were bold enough to use the style even though there were no ancient examples at hand to serve as a stylistic guide, nor any books to study with good engraved plates of the best European Gothic buildings. Havi-land's knowledge of the Gothic, like Latrobe's, must have been carried mainly in his head. He was born in England, and did not come to America until 1816. His training had been in the office of the classicist James Elmes. Although the majority of his designs in America were Greek Revival, his best known work is the Eastern State Penitentiary at Philadelphia (*Plate 27*) whereon fortified Gothic turrets abound, recalling nothing of the beauty of a mediaeval cathedral but rather the heavy, solid strength of fortifications. His success here gave him several other penal commissions and some notoriety in Europe, as the Eastern State Penitentiary was visited from across the Atlantic by several observers who considered it a model of ingenuity and humane imagination.

## MID-CENTURY REVIVALS (*circa* 1825—*circa* 1860)

THE success of the first architects to use the Classical Revival theme prompted a host of contemporaries to follow their lead. As each new

*Plate 28.* EXTERIOR OF THE TREASURY BUILDING, WASHINGTON, D. C. 1836–1842. Designed by Robert Mills. The first building to serve as a Treasury was built by George Hadfield, but it was destroyed by fire twice. The next Treasury was also burned. Mills thus took pains to make his design fireproof. Sixteen oxen were brought to the site to raise the 34 monolithic columns into place. Although Mills requested the columns be of granite, the cheaper freestone was purchased. All the columns had to be replaced by granite in 1909. *Courtesy,* HISTORIC AMERICAN BUILDINGS SURVEY, WASHINGTON, D. C.

State entered the Union, architects were on the spot to build a Capitol and other public buildings, and for the next four decades nearly all of them chose to emulate Latrobe, Strickland, and Mills. But the Classical Revival, now emphasizing more the Greek than the Roman, was essentially an architecture of stone since the only remaining ancient examples were of that material. In order to meet the requirements of American society the elements of the style had to be converted into wood, far cheaper and more plentiful here than in Europe. Furthermore, the popularity of the style made it desirable for a multiplicity of building types, including the ordinary house. It is no surprise then to find the architects consulting English books devoted to Classical design, nor to have the first American book on the subject, Asher Benjamin's, *The Country Builder's Assistant*, first published in 1797, go through several editions up to 1805. Benjamin wrote other books including *The Practical House Carpenter, Being a complete development of the Grecian orders of architecture* (six editions and many reprintings from 1830 to 1857); and numerous authors added more titles on the same theme.

By 1825 Latrobe had already died, but Mills and Strickland were yet to reach their mature periods. These two men, along with Ithiel Town (1784–1844) whose career as a significant architect commenced late, led the rest in taking most of the important public commissions and many private ones until the younger architects emerged as supporters of the Classical style. Mills came to Washington in 1830 and from then to the end of his life was involved in various projects for the Federal Government. Of these the Treasury Building (*Plate 28*) is the most important. It was a vast project costing $1,500,000 to complete. The architect's original plans called for a façade along 15th Street of 500 feet. Only the colonnade of 336 feet was finished before Mills's death. The idea for the colonnade of thirty-four Ionic monolithic columns undoubtedly comes from the Greek *stoa*, where also financial business was transacted. This building, along with Mills's Patent Office and the Old Post Office, prominent in the Washington landscape, were regarded for many decades as proper standards for government architecture.

The later work of William Strickland tends toward experimentation
with styles other than Classic in areas of design unfamiliar to him, and
consequently his successes were fewer. In many ways Strickland's best
building is the Philadelphia Exchange (*Plate 30*) where he adapted a complex set of requirements (reading room, post office, rooms for commerce, insurance offices, and Strickland's own architectural office) to an odd-shaped
site. The exuberant classical shapes, including a replica on top of the
Choragic Monument of Lysicrates in Athens (*Plate 14*), are combined with

76

a flare for the dramatic. Luckily it will be preserved as part of Independence National Historical Park. Strickland's worst monument is the ludicrous State Capitol at Nashville, Tennessee, (*Plate 31*) where he attempted futilely to represent the Acropolis in Athens, reinterpreting its major building, the Parthenon, as a center of statesmanship. Its lack of dignity in proportion, its ineffective tall cupola pinning the building down like a beetle on a specimen board, and its lack of the requisite delicate detail make the Tennessee Capitol a failure. It is partially redeemed by serving as a source —followed often by other architects, sometimes with greater success—for a temple design reorganized as a state house.

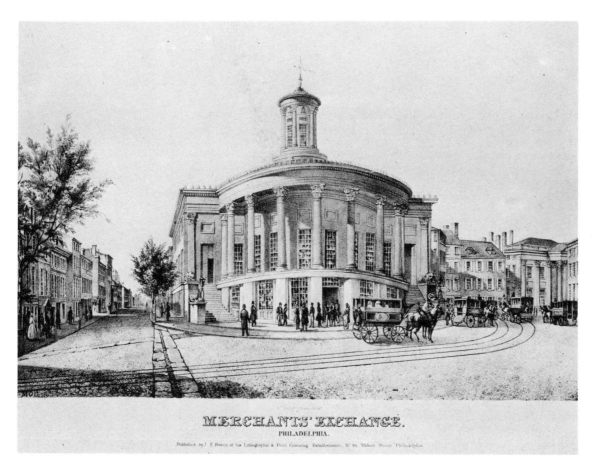

MERCHANTS' EXCHANGE.
PHILADELPHIA.

Published by J. T. Bowen at his Lithographic & Print Colouring Establishment, N° 94 Walnut Street Philadelphia

*Plate 30.* EXCHANGE BUILDING, PHILADELPHIA, PENNSYLVANIA. 1832–1834. Designed by William Strickland. The Corinthian capitals were carved by two Italian sculptors, Peter and Philip Bardi. At a banquet for the 140 workers after the placing of the capstone, the architect was toasted as: "William Strickland, the architect of the Merchant's Exchange. He will realize the boast of the ancient emperor. He found us living in a city of brick, and he will leave us in a city of Marble." This prediction fell somewhat short of the mark, though the Greek-revivalists tried their best. LITHOGRAPH, *courtesy*, THE COLLECTION OF THE LIBRARY COMPANY OF PHILADELPHIA

77

The Greek Revival movement was given great impetus when Ithiel Town (1784–1844) at the age of forty turned decisively to ancient architecture for his major inspiration. This was when he designed the Eagle Bank at New Haven, Conn. (*Plate 32*) in 1824. The bank soon failed

*Plate 31.* STATE CAPITOL, NASHVILLE, TENNESSEE. 1845–1853. Designed by William Strickland at a total expenditure of $925,639.02. The building is 239 feet long and 112 feet wide at the ends. The Ionic Order of the Erechtheum was copied (but without its subtleties) for the porticoes. The architect died in 1854 and was interred in the north entrance wall of the basement. His son, Francis W. Strickland, was appointed to complete the details of construction. PHOTOGRAPH BY WAYNE ANDREWS

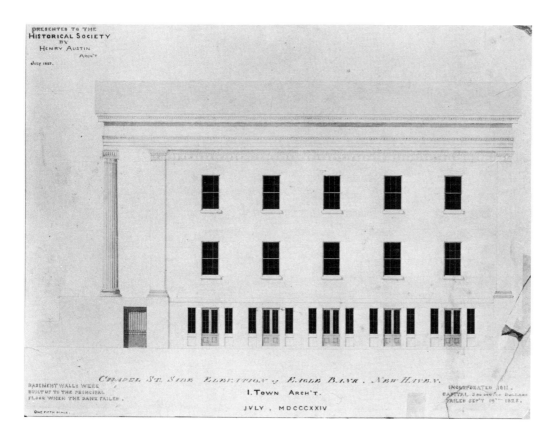

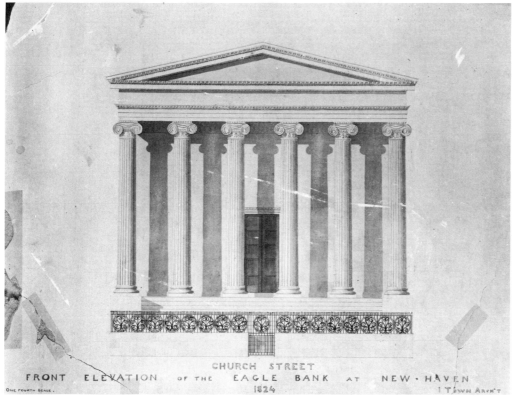

*Plate 32.* EAGLE BANK, NEW HAVEN, CONNECTICUT. 1824. Designed by Ithiel Town. Built only a little above the foundations, it was demolished in 1832 after the bank had failed. Original drawings, *courtesy,* NEW HAVEN COLONY HISTORICAL SOCIETY, NEW HAVEN, CONN.

80    *Plate 33.* STATE CAPITOL, RALEIGH, NORTH CAROLINA. 1833–1840. Designed by Ithiel Town. A new capitol has replaced this building which is retained as a state museum. David Paton acted as clerk of the works, since Town could not be on the spot to supervise construction. Scottish stone masons were imported under Paton's direction. Total cost of the building was $530,684. The plan is in a cross form 160 feet (north to south), 140 feet (east to west), and 97½ feet high. The material is granite quarried nearby. Although mainly Greek decoration on the interior, there are some Gothic details. *Courtesy,* LIBRARY OF CONGRESS, WASHINGTON, D. C. PHOTOGRAPH BY FRANCES B. JOHNSTON

and what had been built was demolished—nevertheless, the preserved drawings show that it was a building based upon the superb Ionic Order of the Erechtheum in Athens. Then in 1829, Town asked Alexander Jackson Davis (1803–1892) who was already in his employ to become a partner. The famous firm claimed distinction as the first to attempt "to form a partnership for the transaction of [architectural] business," on a professional basis. For the next fifteen years until Town's death in 1844, the firm handled a large amount of work and produced some of the finest buildings of these decades. Davis continued to practice for another thirty years. The firm built several state capitols; among them the one at Raleigh, North Carolina (*Plate 33*), where the precisely cut stonework, so characteristic of their style, is a delight to the eye. Here the Greek Doric Order is raised aloft in a non-Greek manner and serves as the entrance accent for the main bulk of the building which is not at all templelike, but rather harks back to Latrobe's solution for the central section of the Capitol at Washington, even to the octagonal base for the circular dome.

Davis, who referred to himself as an "architectural composer," inviting comparison with less skilled draughtsmen, gradually dominated the style

*Plate 34*. SAMUEL RUSSELL HOUSE, MIDDLETOWN, CONNECTICUT. 1828. Designed by Town and Davis for Russell, a wealthy merchant whose fortune was amassed from trade with China. The house was bought by Wesleyan University from a descendant of the original owner. Six columns for the façade were taken from the Eagle Bank, New Haven. (*Plate 32.*). PHOTO-GRAPH BY WAYNE ANDREWS

adopted by the firm, while Town's inventive mind kept up with trends in construction, and his immense library of 11,000 volumes helped both men maintain close contact with Europe through written sources. The firm's classic ideal in residential design is summed up by the Samuel Russell House, Middletown, Conn. (*Plate 34*). Clear and simple, except for the ornate Corinthian colonnade complete with fluting, the house justifies the reputation of its architects. The serenity and nobleness attained here has seldom been equalled by other architects using this style.

*Plate 35.* "ANDALUSIA," ANDALUSIA, PENNSYLVANIA. 1836. Portico designed by Thomas Ustick Walter, for Nicholas Biddle. Walter, son of a bricklayer and builder, entered Strickland's office at fifteen, gave up to study painting and science, and later re-entered Strickland's office for a year before practicing on his own. The portico was added on the insistence of Biddle after the banker's trip to Greece in 1806 where he became enamored of Greek culture. PHOTOGRAPH BY WAYNE ANDREWS

A possible rival to the perfection of Town and Davis houses is the colonnade added to "Andalusia" at Andalusia, Pa. (*Plate 35*), by Thomas Ustick Walter (1804–1887). Built for the financier and Aegean traveller Nicholas Biddle, it was the combined wish of architect and client to copy the Theseum in Athens as closely as materials would allow. The proportions of the temple are nicely preserved in the colonnade, entablature and pediment, their painted whiteness even rivalling the brilliant, sunlit Greek temple. But the little box full of rooms behind the colonnade is

*Plate 36*. GIRARD COLLEGE, PHILADELPHIA, PENNSYLVANIA. 1833. Designed by Thomas Ustick Walter. As with his own house, Nicholas Biddle, whose will provided funds for the erection of the building, determined what its dimensions should be, and that it should take the shape of a Greek temple. There had been a competition for a design, and Walter's design was not at all like the finished building; the will of the client was imposed on the architect after he had been selected to be the architect. In this case, one may be glad that the client had his way, because the result was magnificent. PHOTOGRAPH BY WAYNE ANDREWS

inappropriate for a classic colonnade, as it fails to carry the theme of the Doric Order to a satisfying conclusion. The weakness, as always with the revival of classical architecture, is in bringing the exterior into functional harmony with the interior. Two irreconcilable exteriors—one classic, the other Georgian—could not be fused comfortably as the interior is derived from English domestic and the colonnade from ancient religious usage. Nevertheless, viewed from a distance, Andalusia conveys much of the clarity and sheer beauty of an Athenian temple.

*Plate 37.* THE CAPITOL, WASHINGTON, D. C. 1793–1830. Additions in 1851–1865 were by Thomas Ustick Walter. The competition for the extension of the Capitol was held in 1850 and the prize divided among four contestants as the judges could not decide that any one design had the highest merit. The Senate instructed Robert Mills to make new plans using ideas from the others, but President Fillmore thought otherwise and appointed Walter as architect. *Courtesy,* HISTORIC AMERICAN BUILDINGS SURVEY, WASHINGTON, D. C.

Girard College in Philadelphia (*Plate 36*), also by Walter is, like Andalusia, temple-inspired, though with this difference—the architect could leave out the distracting windows and, like the Greeks, use a flat wall against which the Corinthian colonnade proudly stands. The single large entrance door responds to the dignity and scale of the colonnade.

The unavoidable consequence of the increase in territory and population of the United States made the Capitol (*Plate 37*) in Washington inadequate for its purpose. The Senate voted for a competition to make an addition to the building. Several architects submitted designs before the deadline of December 1, 1850, but President Fillmore declared the Senate's competition unlawful and appointed Walter, one of the competitors, as architect in June 1851. The new wings and central dome are nicely scaled to each other, but unceremoniously overpower the old building. The fake stone dome is most effective rising from the dark pile, floodlit and sculptural at night.

The Gothic style was assimilated less easily than the Classic by Americans, who associated their democratic way of life with antiquity rather than with the feudal concepts of mediaeval society. Only for churches was Gothic readily acceptable. Although domestic and commercial examples of the style were built in increasing numbers during the thirties and forties, it was the urban churches which became architecturally outstanding.

Richard Upjohn (1802–1878), born in England and apprenticed to a cabinet-maker and builder, arrived in America as late as 1828. He was aware more than other American architects of a recent upsurge in the use of Gothic in England concurrent with a movement to bring back to the church the liturgical rites formerly performed. The English Ecclesiologists, as they were called, loved ritual and believed that the only suitable style for ritualistic observance was the Gothic. After all, what other style could they associate as well with the "piety" and "virtue" of the Middle Ages? Consequently Upjohn's first major commission was to rebuild Trinity Church, New York (*Plate 38*) in suitable Gothic. The tall spire, at first a landmark on Manhattan because of its great height (279 feet), is now dwarfed by crowding skyscrapers. The mediaeval features are all present,

*Plate 38.* TRINITY CHURCH, NEW YORK. 1839–1846. Exterior view and the original drawing of the façade. Designed by Richard Upjohn. The previous church on the site (built 1788–1790) was a modest Gothic edifice. Weakness in the walls and roof required it to be razed. The new church copied in many respects the architect's earliest church, St. John's, Bangor, Maine (1836–39). A deep chancel and raised altar were in keeping with the adjustments in church design recommended by the Cambridge Camden Society (later the Ecclesiological Society). The cost of the church was over $100,000. The original drawing of the façade is used by *courtesy* of THE AVERY LIBRARY, COLUMBIA UNIVERSITY, NEW YORK CITY. The photograph of the exterior is from *New York Landmarks* by Alan Burnham and is reproduced by permission of THE MUNICIPAL ART SOCIETY OF NEW YORK

86

the pointed arch, finials, crockets, stained glass windows, hammer beam rafters, steeply pitched roof, and yet something prevents it from appearing ancient. Perhaps it is its crispness owing to lack of aging, but more likely it is the building's lack of relation to its ornament. Each Gothic detail is superimposed, like lace on an old Valentine, on an essentially flat wall surface instead of fusing with it. A. J. Davis used nearly the same manner for his great extravaganza Lyndhurst (*Plates 39* through *41*) on the Hudson River. Davis and others building in Greek Revival Style composed horizontal, balanced, axial designs, whereas the Gothic lent itself to irregular, asymmetrical, vertical planning. The latter qualities are here exploited to create a model of the picturesque. The drawings Davis made (*Plate 39*) show how carefully studied is his informality. Few customers could resist the charm of his presentation drawings. Delamater Cottage (*Plate 42*) further up the Hudson, also by Davis, is a marvelous example of what the Gothic revival became in vernacular wood construction throughout the east and midwest. Thousands of little cottages like this were built with many, if not all, the decorative features strewn across the front of Delamater Cottage. Barge-boards at the eaves cut with a jig-saw, pointed windows with mouldings of complicated ornament, small leaded windows, and wall battens nailed upright to imitate the verticality of mediaeval structures—all this had strong appeal as a welcome contrast to the restraint of Classical order.

In 1846, the same year Upjohn finished Trinity Church, his younger contemporary, James Renwick (1818–1895), completed Grace Church, New York (*Plate 44*), in Gothic not unlike his rival's, except that Renwick chose to adopt late rather than early Gothic forms and crowned the tower with an uneasy spire. It is less of a fairy castle than Upjohn's because the decoration is better integrated with the structural members. This was the first for Renwick of a whole series of remarkably well-designed churches.

Although the Classical Revival and then the Gothic were by far the most popular for all types of buildings, and particularly for important public buildings, during the several decades before the Civil War, other

*Plate 39*

88

*Plates 39–41.* LYNDHURST, TARRYTOWN, NEW YORK. 1838–1865. Designed by A. J. Davis, first as a romantic, Gothic, country mansion, he later enlarged it to become an enormous pile of grayish Sing-Sing marble. Davis's earlier client was General William Paulding, sometime mayor of New York City. A nextdoor neighbor was Washington Irving in his "nookery." Additions almost doubling its size were made for George Merritt, New York merchant. *Plate 39*, is Davis's 1838 drawing for the structure; in *Plate 40*, we see his 1865 conception. *Plate 41*, shows the west elevation of Lyndhurst. The drawings are reproduced by *courtesy* of THE METROPOLITAN MUSEUM OF ART, NEW YORK (HARRIS BRISBANE DICK FUND, 1924). The photograph of the exterior is from the NATIONAL TRUST FOR HISTORIC PRESERVATION, WASHINGTON, D. C.

89

more exotic styles were gradually introduced. These newer styles had less to recommend them as serious attempts to recapture vestiges of past culture in architectural form; they satisfied instead a thirst for the unusual, the opulent, the symbol of status in society, and spoke only too eloquently of capitalist prejudices arising from steady industrial expansion. The substantial house of Colonial days was but a cottage in comparison with those built by the wealthy in the 1840's and 50's. Thus Davis built a

*Plate 42.* DELAMATER COTTAGE, RHINEBECK, NEW YORK. 1844. Designed by A. J. Davis, for Henry Delamater, a local banker. Startlingly different from contemporary Greek Revival houses, this playful piece of delicate wooden frippery could have been suggested to Davis by plates in A. J. Downing's *Cottage Residences* (1842), or other of Downing's books. Davis collaborated with Downing in his *Architecture of Country Houses* (1850) by drawing many of the illustrations. PHOTOGRAPH BY WAYNE ANDREWS

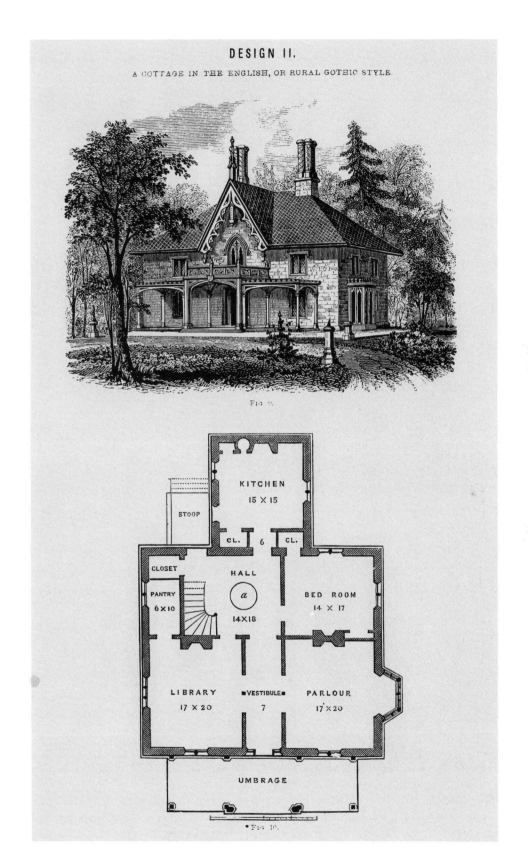

DESIGN II.

A COTTAGE IN THE ENGLISH, OR RURAL GOTHIC STYLE.

Fig 9.

KITCHEN
15 × 15

STOOP

CL.  6  CL.

CLOSET

HALL

PANTRY
6 × 10

a

14 × 18

BED ROOM
14 × 17

LIBRARY
17 × 20

VESTIBULE
7

PARLOUR
17 × 20

UMBRAGE

Fig 10.

Plate 43. ILLUSTRATION OF A DESIGN PROPOSED IN A. J. DOWNING'S *Cottage Residences*, 1842.

91

*Plate 44.* GRACE CHURCH, BROADWAY AND 10TH STREET, NEW YORK. 1843–1846. Designed by James Renwick. This was the architect's first commission, won in a competition at age 25. He had previously worked mainly as an engineer. The first spire was temporary and of wood. It was replaced later with the present stone spire. Photograph reproduced from *New York Landmarks* by Alan Burnham with permission of THE MUNICIPAL ART SOCIETY OF NEW YORK

mansion for Electus Backus Litchfield, the railroad magnate, in Brooklyn (*Plate 45*). The architect imported the Italian manner, manifested by towers, turrets, wide-spreading eaves and round-headed windows in groups of two or three, like the villas of the Tuscan countryside.

At Sag Harbor, Long Island, the carpenter-architect Minard Lafever (1798–1854) built the First Presbyterian Church (*Plate 47*) in an agonizing Egyptian style. Granite of the Nile is replaced by white-painted clapboards, reducing the scale seemingly to that of a doll house. The battered (that is, inward tilting) façade walls imitate those of the pylon or entranceway to an Egyptian temple. The logic of design was that a church, like a temple, is also a place of worship. Originally a spire rose from the center ringed with an unlikely Greek colonnade and with gradually narrowing unidentifiable shapes supposedly representing a mariner's spy-glass. In contrast to Lafever's playful use of Egyptian style, Henry Austin (1804–1891) of Connecticut used the austerity of an Egyptian pylon for his gateway to a Christian cemetery on Grove Street, New Haven (*Plate 48*).

Fantastic as it may seem, Samuel Sloan (1815–1884) of Philadelphia persuaded his client Haller Nutt, a plantation owner, to build an Oriental dream house called inappropriately "Longwood," in the deep South at Natchez, Mississippi (*Plate 49*). It was built of brick laid in an octagonal plan, and the protruding ornaments of wood are enthusiastically cut as brackets, pillars and Moorish arches. Its onion-shaped dome lends further picturesqueness to the whole as does the luxuriant Spanish moss hanging from neighboring trees.

Still dominating the architectural scene before the Civil War, though gradually succumbing before pressure to introduce more variety and exoticism, was the sedate, dignified Greek Revival style now spread throughout the country in all its glory. Every community had its proud sample, like "Belle Grove" at White Castle, Louisiana (*Plate 51*) or less ambitious residences like the Brooks House in Marshall, Michigan (*Plate 52*). Marshall, settled in 1831 while Michigan was still a frontier territory, was built up quickly. It improvised on the planning adopted in the east for small

*Plate 45.* LITCHFIELD HOUSE, BROOKLYN, NEW YORK. Designed by A. J. Davis. With his brothers, E. B. Litchfield manipulated railroad interests extending across the entire country. He built this house just before the financial panic of 1857, and was forced later to sell part of his estate to the city of New York. Both the city and Litchfield gained by the deal, as the portion sold became Prospect Park, a much-needed public recreation area. The house and surroundings are now preserved as a part of the park. *Courtesy,* LONG ISLAND HISTORICAL SOCIETY, BROOKLYN, NEW YORK, from the original photograph (*circa* 1870) in the possession of the Litchfield Family.

towns by using a central common and principal public buildings grouped around it. Because of being built all at one time, and probably because of a genuine interest on the part of its citizens, Marshall can boast a harmony of architectural style rarely found in sprawling midwestern towns.

The only structures not entirely under the spell of Classicism or other revival styles were those satisfying the needs of an industrially expanding society; namely, railroad stations, bridges, mass housing and factories. Even these structures often bore the signs of revivalism as a nod to tradition in their use of cupolas, pilasters, and so on, while exerting their basic vigor of design in solving the new problems of spanning and enclosing great spaces and meeting the demands of mass production.

*Plate 46.*
DETAIL FROM THE LITCHFIELD HOUSE, BROOKLYN, NEW YORK, showing native motif in the ornament of the capital. Photograph reproduced from *New York Landmarks* by Alan Burnham with permission of THE MUNICIPAL ART SOCIETY OF NEW YORK

The lead in railroad construction, as with the steam engine itself, was taken by English engineers. Americans following quickly on their heels were building their first railroads by 1829, but the volume of traffic was relatively small, permitting railroads to function perfectly well without large stations.

*Plate 47.* FIRST PRESBYTERIAN (OR WHALERS' CHURCH), SAG HARBOR, NEW YORK. 1843–1844. Designed by Minard Lafever. Ship's carpenters were employed, perhaps accounting for some of the woody details like the whalers' blubber spades in rows above the eaves. The spire fell during the hurricane of 1938. Lafever's several books on architecture, like *The Modern Builder's Guide* (1833, and often re-published), replaced the older, less pertinent English guides. PHOTOGRAPH BY WAYNE ANDREWS

By the 1850's the one or two tracks entering stations had to be doubled or trebled, and from this time on major cities built stations with transverse spans accommodating greater and greater widths. The Philadelphia, Wilmington, and Baltimore Railroad depot at Philadelphia (*Plate 53*) required

*Plate 48*. GROVE STREET CEMETERY, NEW HAVEN, CONNECTICUT. 1845–1848. Designed by Henry Austin. The brown battered walls, the symbol of the sun-god, the cavetto cornice, and the Nile plant columns are reminiscent of Egyptian style, though stones were never cut by Egyptians to these specific shapes nor combined for an entrance gateway in this particular manner. Austin worked in the office of Ithiel Town where the elder architect's famous library would have acquainted him with Egyptian ornament. PHOTOGRAPH BY WAYNE ANDREWS

98     *Plate 49.* "LONGWOOD," NATCHEZ, MISSISSIPPI. 1860. Designed by Samuel Sloan, for Haller Nutt, who had visited Egypt with his family mainly to observe the growing of cotton. Sloan had published as early as 1852 in his *The Model Architect* (Vol. II, pl. 63) a house very similar to this (see *Plate 50.*) so the idea was waiting for Nutt to approve of. In Sloan's *Homestead Architecture* (1861), he published a view of Longwood, commenting upon it as "a remembrancer of Eastern magnificence which few will judge misplaced as it looms up against the mellowed azure of a Southern sky." The Civil War stopped construction. Nutt died shortly thereafter and the house was never finished. PHOTOGRAPH BY WAYNE ANDREWS

a train shed 150′ wide in 1851, while Chicago's Great Central Station (*Plate 55*) had trusses reaching 166′ across many tracks. Since the problem of spanning was mainly one for engineers, there was little concern with harmonizing functionally the interior train shed with the street façade, at least until the end of the century.

Bridges were built for railroads, and railroads as connecting links for industry. Manufacturing companies built their structures to house machinery basic to mass production and to store goods. Industrialists bent on economy of construction and the accruing of large incomes had minimal interest in decorating the source of their wealth. Nevertheless, quaint bits of ornament appear sometimes on the early factories. More appealing, perhaps, is

*Plate 50.* Engraving of a House of the Longwood Type from Samuel Sloan's *The Model Architect*, 1852.

the robustness, the sheer fascination, of a wall with thousands of glass panes. Even the anonymity of a group of factory buildings—like children's blocks designated and differing only by number or letter—has its appeal, each unit a part of an industrial castle fortified by the sale of equally anonymous products boxed in multiples like the buildings from which they

*Plate 51.* "BELLE GROVE," NEAR WHITE CASTLE, LOUISIANA. 1857. Designed by Henry Howard for John Andrews of Virginia who moved to Louisiana and built this plantation on a grand scale. The interior was furnished with European furniture, tapestries, etc.; the grounds included extensive gardens, a race track, and various outbuildings. Rivalling in beauty many an English country estate, it now stands derelict owing to a fire of 1952 which burned the interior and exterior parts made of wood and plaster in fragile imitation of stone. PHOTOGRAPH BY WAYNE ANDREWS

emerged. Holyoke, Mass. (*Plate 56*) is typical of towns making the effort to cope with the enormous new burdens of industry. Holyoke's factories for the manufacture of cotton goods and paper cluster neatly along the three levels of canals fed by the Connecticut River supplying power and water in inexhaustible quantity. Along with heavy concentrations of factories came the

*Plate 52.* HAROLD C. BROOKS HOUSE, MARSHALL, MICHIGAN. 1840. Designer unknown, though attributed to Richard Upjohn. It was built for Jabez Fitch of New York and is one of the three earliest houses still standing which date from the decade of the town's foundation. Characteristic of provincial examples of the Greek Revival style is its irregularity. There are an uneven number of Ionic portico columns and no central doorway, and the high triangular pediment resting lightly on a too-heavy entablature contains a window composition beyond description. The walls are of brick painted white and the columns of wood. *Courtesy,* HISTORIC AMERICAN BUILDINGS SURVEY, WASHINGTON, D. C.

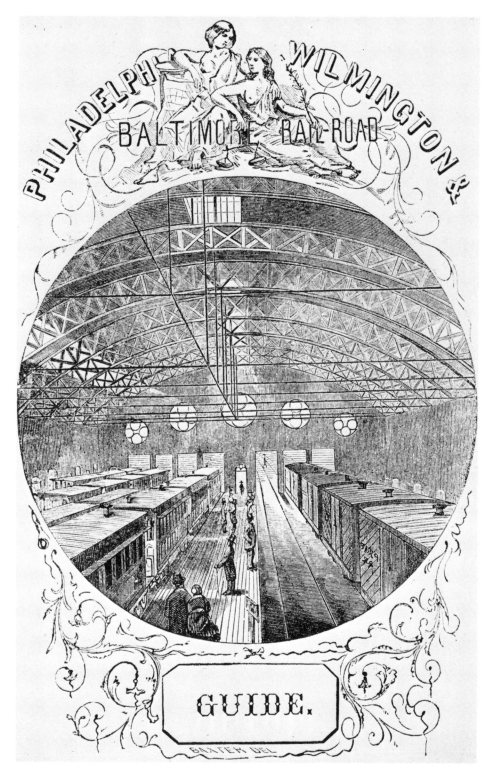

102     *Plate 53.* PHILADELPHIA, WILMINGTON AND BALTIMORE RAILROAD DEPOT, PHILADELPHIA, PENNSYLVANIA. 1851–1852. The shed was constructed by using the wooden lattice truss, patented by Ithiel Town in 1826 and 1835 for highway and railroad bridges. This truss, bolted together in unlimited multiple units, made possible the continuous span allowing a flood of light through glass interstices and adequate weather protection. From C. P. Dare, *Philadelphia, Wilmington & Baltimore Railroad Guide*, Philadelphia, 1856. REPRODUCED BY *courtesy* OF THE YALE UNIVERSITY PRESS from *The Railroad Station* by Carroll L. V. Meeks

*Plate 54.* MODEL OF LATTICE TRUSS FOR BRIDGES DEVISED BY ITHIEL TOWN.
PHOTOGRAPH, *courtesy* SMITHSONIAN INSTITUTION, WASHINGTON, D. C.

desperate need for mass housing nearby. Often the companies themselves
supplied housing for their own gain, but too frequently in the cheapest
possible way. The mill housing at Graniteville, South Carolina (*Plate 59*),
though plain and unassuming, is far more substantial and attractive than
that which was normally built throughout America.

As the decades passed, the architect designing with imported styles
found more and more styles to copy—and even ways of grafting more than
one style onto a single building. The license of self-expression, an over-
indulgence in weird combinations of architectural elements, eventually
reached a point of absurdity. While this phase of uneconomic, doubtfully
aesthetic, sometimes imaginative, and wholly amusing architecture gradually concludes, the stronger, less architectural, but dynamic use of the inventions of engineers and scientists in building construction emerged as the ele-
mental force which motivated the work of the architectural leaders in the
decades from 1860 to 1885.

103

*Arts in America*

## THE RICHARDSONIAN ERA (*circa* 1860–1885)

FOR his book *The Beauties of Modern Architecture* published in 1835, Minard Lafever drew forty-eight plates, thirty-two of which were "original" variations on Greek orders and other decorative motifs, the remainder scale drawings of parts of actual Greek buildings. Thirty years later his narrow concept of "Beauties" and "Modern" was quite inadequate to de-

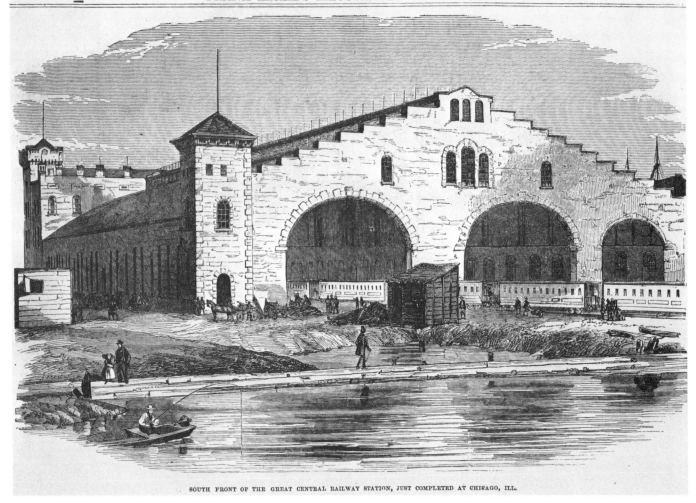

SOUTH FRONT OF THE GREAT CENTRAL RAILWAY STATION, JUST COMPLETED AT CHICAGO, ILL.

*Plate 55.* GREAT CENTRAL STATION, CHICAGO, ILLINOIS. 1855–1856. Designed by Otto Matz (1830–1919) using a truss patented by William Howe in 1840. The truss is wood except for vertical tension pieces of wrought iron. Trained in Germany at the Berlin Polytechnic Institute, Matz migrated to America and at 24 became "architect" to the Illinois Central Railroad. While this station was less than satisfactory as architecture, it served its utilitarian purpose exceedingly well for many years. From *Frank Leslie's Illustrated Newspaper*, August 30, 1856. *Courtesy,* NEW YORK PUBLIC LIBRARY

scribe the wide variations in architectural style introduced from Europe and Asia. For in that brief span of time there had arisen in every town and city the most unusual, often ungainly, architectural creations ever built in America, disparagingly referred to by later critics as Victorian, Reign of Terror, General Grant, Gingerbread, and the like. The best architects, like leading painters and sculptors, are almost invariably aesthetically far ahead of their time, so their work must await the approval of future

*Plate 56.* LYMAN FACTORIES, HOLYOKE, MASSACHUSETTS. 1849–1850. These factories were for the manufacture of cotton fabrics. George W. Lyman was one of two treasurers of the Hadley Falls Company, builders of the dam, canal system, factories and boarding houses. The laborers, mainly Irish, Scottish and English, worked eleven hours a day; children under twelve were by law not allowed to work more than ten hours per day. This view is reproduced from *Picturesque Holyoke.*

generations. Thus it was in the Richardsonian Era. Architectural exoticisms of considerable merit were introduced on the American scene before 1860, but without receiving serious attention. Whereas after 1860, the exotic of the past became not only acceptable but commonplace. What at first was tentative, experimental, and generally derided became sought after and aesthetically correct. The cycle then keeps repeating itself as more daring architects search for new designs to replace those fast becoming stereotyped.

*Plate 57.* AMOSKEAG MILLS, MANCHESTER, NEW HAMPSHIRE. 1838–1915. Practically all the mills were designed and built by company engineers. Cotton was manufactured first at Manchester in 1805. In 1831, some Boston financiers reorganized the manufactury and it became the Amoskeag Manufacturing Company until 1936. The first important mill was built in 1838; by 1860 seven main mills had been erected. Owing to a decline in business the company was separated into twenty independent industries. At the height of prosperity Amoskeag had sixty-four buildings and 17,000 workers. PHOTOGRAPH BY FRANK KELLY, MANCHESTER, N. H.

A gradual awareness developed among architects of the inappropriateness of continuing to borrow old forms without structural or symbolic justification. But in which direction should they go? How or where could they find new forms to replace contemporary stultification? One source of inspiration appeared in the new approach to design of three Englishmen: William Butterfield, R. Norman Shaw, and Philip Webb. Their highly imaginative adaptation, particularly Shaw's, of English vernacular and mediaeval elements led to creative designs of more than mere picturesque value. And their free use of derivative—not copied—decorative forms gave a freshness to their architecture which was quickly appreciated by their American contemporaries. Thus the finest architecture of the Richardsonian Era came to have two main ingredients: a highly creative use of past style;

*Plate 58.* MANCHESTER MILL NO. 1, AMOSKEAG MANUFACTURING COMPANY, MANCHESTER, NEW HAMPSHIRE. The 1844 part of the structure is seen at about the center of this view. PHOTOGRAPH, *courtesy*, NEW ENGLAND TEXTILE MILL SURVEY

and an exceptional emphasis of a variety of ingeniously combined building materials.

A view of popular architecture from Maine to California shows that wherever business flourished the majority of plans for town halls, city and resort hotels, and houses alike were those incorporating as many functionally unimportant appendages as possible. Built high into the air, these archi-

108

*Plate 59.* MILL HOUSING, GRANITEVILLE, SOUTH CAROLINA. 1845–1848. Architect unknown, but may plausibly be attributed to Edward Brickell White (1806–1882) of Charleston. St. John's Methodist Church, Graniteville (1848), is designed in Gothic by White. William Gregg established a textile mill here in 1845. He had previously made a small fortune as watchmaker and silversmith. Opposed to slave labor in the mill, he chose to hire many "poor whites," who benefited by his attitude and his care in the construction of good housing. There were about 100 Gothic cottages varying in size from 3 to 9 rooms and having an acre to an acre-and-a-half of land for each house. The architect may well have consulted Downing's *Cottage Residences*, 1842, for a design. (See *Plate 60.*) PHOTOGRAPH BY WAYNE ANDREWS

[Fig. 40.]

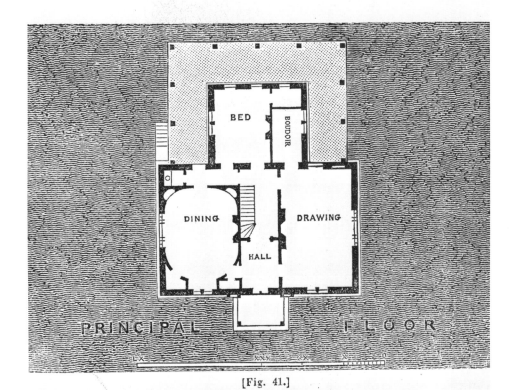

[Fig. 41.]

*Plate 60.* An Illustration from A. J. Downing's *Cottage Residences*, 1842, which may have suggested the design for *Plate 59*.

tectural monsters audaciously surveyed their menial older neighbors as though sheer bulk and lavish decor could compel the respect their wealthy owners coveted. Portland's Victoria Mansion (*Plate 62*), vertically accented and more pleasingly proportioned than most buildings of the period, rose well above adjacent houses. Its lofty Italian villa tower added a striking though superfluous set of belfry rooms, and the porch, with fully fluted Ionic columns, broadened the base of architect Austin's design while sheltering the large front windows from the glare of light and the gaze of the curious.

110    *Plate 61*. AMOSKEAG MILL HOUSING, MANCHESTER, NEW HAMPSHIRE. 1839–1848. Like the mills themselves, the housing (built intermittently from 1838 to 1920) was designed and constructed by mill engineers. Approximately three-quarters of those built still stand and are in constant use, though not all are now used for housing. Bricks were made at the site. The several different designs give variety to the whole group which is the largest anywhere in New England. Though simple and without much style, the proportions and general appearance are very satisfactory, as if the designer had looked hard at good Boston Colonial buildings. PHOTOGRAPH BY WAYNE ANDREWS

*Plate 62.* VICTORIA MANSION, PORTLAND, MAINE. 1859. Designed by Henry Austin for Rug- **111**
gles Morse (1816–1893). The owner, having acquired a fortune in the hotel business in New
Orleans, returned to his early home at Portland in 1856 and promptly built this brownstone
mansion for $400,000. The Civil War ruined Morse financially, so he had to give up his home.
The mansion had no tenants until 1895 when it was purchased by J. R. Libby, a local merchant. Giovanni Guidirini decorated the sumptuous interior (*Plate 63*). The first bathtub in Maine
was installed here, and one of the first furnaces. PHOTOGRAPH BY MASON PHILIP SMITH, PORT-
LAND, MAINE

*Plate 63.* INTERIOR, VICTORIA MANSION, PORTLAND, MAINE. *Courtesy,* THE VICTORIA MANSION, PORTLAND, MAINE

By the 1880's the country was filled with elaborate houses on the scale of Victoria Mansion. From the flat plains of Texas rose as many stylish residences as in the East. The sources of income which made possible their construction were different, but the appearance and intent of each was nearly the same, except for slight local variations. In Texas many houses are encompassed by broad porches on two levels and overhanging eaves giving protection from the sun. The Cameron House, Waco (*Plate 64*), is glutted with decorative brackets and indescribable ornaments fastened against a clapboard background. The low mansard roof does not quite cover all the protruding lower parts below nor does the octagonal mansard tower fit very comfortably on its base. It appears as though the builder had first tried an Italian villa design, then tempted by the none-too-subtle woodcuts in a builder's guide, superimposed the mansard roof, thereby gaining an extra highly ornate floor. Most amusing of all is the crown at the very top, glittering in the sun and not without its symbolic significance. The Bremond House, Austin (*Plate 66*), is surrounded by porches, crowded with cast iron ornament, and coyly covered by a low-swooping mansard roof.

That which suited Texans was equally approved of by Californians. At Redlands (*Plate 67*), for instance, the client allowed his (perhaps intentionally anonymous) architect to juxtapose three kinds of roofs, four patterns of siding, three different balustrades, and window openings of seven separate shapes. The better known Carson House, Eureka (*Plate 68*), is a bewildering mass of ornament used extravagantly on both interior and exterior in probably the most wilfully disordered array ever conceived—picturesqueness derived from chaos. Unique, unfettered, architecturally licentious, it is the epitome of the aesthetic expression of rampant industrial expansion.

What the individual desired for his own home is also reflected in the public buildings of the era. Like the private residences, the majority of the public buildings look much alike as they are grandiose, often rather crude in the use of ornament, overbearing, and expensive to construct. A good example is the Philadelphia City Hall (*Plate 70*), more than one hundred

*Plate 64.* CAMERON HOUSE, WACO, TEXAS. 1879. Designed by the Larmour brothers of Waco for William Cameron (1834–1899), a lumberman. Born in Scotland, Cameron attended college at Dundee. He came to the United States in 1852, became a construction foreman for the Missouri Pacific Railroad, and then in business for himself he sold ties and construction timber to the Missouri, Kansas and Texas Railroad, finally settling at Waco in 1878. By 1890 he is said to have owned 60 lumber yards, several saw mills, grain mills and elevators. The original plans (see *Plate 65.*) for the house are signed "Larmour Bros." There were several brothers, all practicing architecture, though W. W. Larmour was the head of the firm. The significance of the amazing crown on the roof can only be guessed at; perhaps the "king" of lumbermen. The house burned in 1965. *Courtesy,* AMON CARTER MUSEUM, FORT WORTH, TEXAS. PHOTOGRAPH BY TODD WEBB, SANTE FE, NEW MEXICO

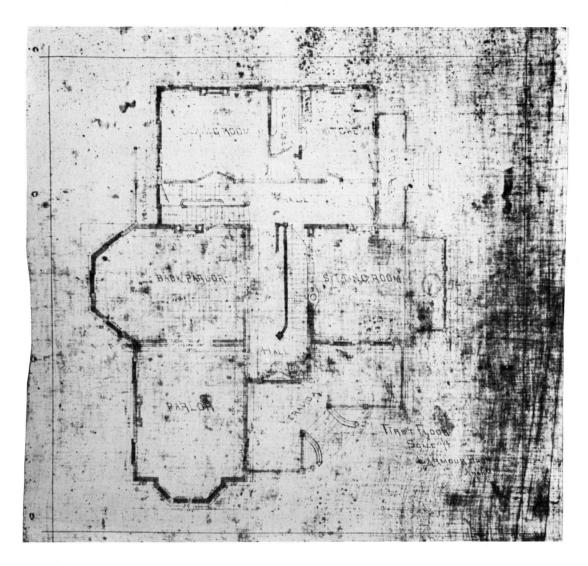

*Plate 65.* ORIGINAL PLAN FOR CAMERON HOUSE, WACO, TEXAS. *Courtesy,* PRO-
FESSOR DRURY B. ALEXANDER, SCHOOL OF ARCHITECTURE, UNIVERSITY OF TEXAS,
AUSTIN

years old and still very much in use. It cost more than $24,000,000 and
emulated the Louvre at Paris in using corner and middle pavilions with
raised mansard roofs and plentiful decoration of a blunt Classical sort.
And of its kind the notorious Grand Union Hotel, Saratoga Springs (*Plate
71*), catering to spa enthusiasts and patrons of the race track, fully
discloses with its endless hallways, immense shimmering dining hall, and
high arcaded porches sheltering the idle rocking-chair population, the rewards accessible to the rich.

*115*

Not to be outdone by other Eastern seaboard cities the Federal Government built its new State, War, and Navy Building in Washington (*Plate 72*), by borrowing, like the Philadelphia City Hall, the design from official Parisian architecture. The mansard roof sections, like pot lids on a stove, cover one of the most unnecessarily visually complex buildings ever erected. The endless coupled columns superimposed layer upon layer

*Plate 66.* BREMOND HOUSE, AUSTIN, TEXAS. 1886. Built by contractor George Fiegel for John Bremond. Bremond was the son of John Bremond, Sr., an early Austin merchant from New York. He inherited his father's business of general merchandising and groceries, and banking. Fiegel was from New Orleans. He built several homes for members of the Bremond family. He was builder as well as designer. The materials of the house are buff-colored brick with cream limestone trim. The roof is a variegated slate. The railings and other pierced decorations are of cast iron. PHOTOGRAPH BY TODD WEBB, SANTA FE, NEW MEXICO

are suffocating, boresome and aesthetically intolerable. It is not even picturesque, but it is a superb sample of planning for bureaucracy.

While government building continued to arrive at solutions for vast arrays of offices by resorting mainly to a multiplication of classical elements, colleges and universities reverted frequently to Gothic designs, as at Trinity College, Hartford (*Plate 73*), and tried to recreate by associative values

*Plate 67.* DAVID A. MOREY HOUSE, REDLANDS, CALIFORNIA, 1890. Owned now by Curtiss B. Allen. Morey, a cabinet maker, used the profits from citrus nursery stock for constructing his house. Elaborate panelling in the fourteen rooms reflects the owner's trade. No name has yet been coined to describe adequately this particular kind of design. Even though its excesses are legion, the house possesses a quality of composition hard to achieve while using such disparate elements.
PHOTOGRAPH BY PHILIP MARCH, *courtesy,* JOHN MAASS

the atmosphere of study and learning bred in the monastery and university of the Middle Ages. Yale, Princeton, Duke, and a host of other institutions building in these decades, each paid its tribute to past learning by erecting picturesque, Gothic residence halls, dining commons, libraries and even gymnasiums, though the rationale for building the latter in this style is obscure.

*Plate 68.* EXTERIOR OF CARSON HOUSE, EUREKA, CALIFORNIA. 1885. Designed by Samuel and J. C. Newsom for William Carson, a rich lumber merchant. James Ryan landed his ship here in 1850, shouted "Eureka," and then surveyed the area for a town. Through the nineteenth century business thrived owing to the plentiful redwood trees. Carson built his house next to his lumber yard. Most of the grotesque ornaments were brought from the East. PHOTOGRAPH BY WAYNE ANDREWS

*Plate 69.* INTERIOR VIEW OF CARSON HOUSE, EUREKA, CALIFORNIA. PHOTO-
GRAPH BY WAYNE ANDREWS

Each age has its dominating architectural personality. Michelangelo, Bernini, Inigo Jones, Wren, etc., during their lifetimes were acknowledged leaders. They influenced the work of their contemporaries often to the point of destroying what originality the latter may have possessed. The same may be said for Henry Hobson Richardson (1838–1886), a mighty figure in America from his first appearance as an architect in the late 1860's to the end of the century when his influence waned, giving way to new theories of functionalism. A first glance at Richardson's buildings may lead one to suppose he leaned almost entirely on a variety of styles from mediaeval Europe. Superficially this is true, for Richardson's personal style is un-

*Plate 70.* CITY HALL, PHILADELPHIA, PENNSYLVANIA. 1869–1881. Designed by John McArthur, Jr., with sculpture by Alexander Calder (37-foot figure of William Penn on top of tower), grandfather of the present artist by the same name. McArthur (1823–1890) was born and educated in Scotland. He made his home in Philadelphia and his reputation by building hotels and government hospitals. The tower is 548-feet high—at the time, the highest in the world. Alan Gowans says it "dramatized the new ideal of American destiny—no longer so much to be independent from Europe, as to consummate and embody the whole of the historical achievement of Western civilization." Engraving from F. Faust, *The City Hall, Philadelphia, Its Architecture, Sculpture and History* (Philadelphia, 1897). PHOTOGRAPH, *courtesy,* PHILADELPHIA CITY ARCHIVES

thinkable without the past. What makes it stand apart, not above influence though beyond copying, is that the problems he solved were not those of the Middle Ages. Had he tried to solve them by using the mediaeval formulas his successes would have been very limited. Richardson's earliest build-

*Plate 71.* GRAND UNION HOTEL, SARATOGA SPRINGS, NEW YORK. 1872. The original building was called "Putnam's Folly." Erected by Gideon Putnam in 1802. Small, though pretentious for its day, this early hotel was thoroughly renovated and enlarged in 1872 when A. T. Stewart of New York purchased the property. Stewart owned a department store in New York designed by John Kellum (1807–1871). It is possible that Kellum also made the design for the Grand Union. The immense building had a three-story piazza, a courtyard with a wide promenade porch on three sides, and the interior was lavishly decorated. This was the center for summer society; here Victor Herbert conducted concerts every day; and here in Saratoga the wealthy ostensibly cured their ills with warm spring waters while betting large sums on the races. PHOTOGRAPH BY WAYNE ANDREWS

121

ings were mainly copies of a distinct style, but as he grew in experience and forged his own architectural philosophy, his buildings, like his gay and energetic personality, became individual statements. Even his physical characteristics gradually became manifest in his designs. A German who had seen his work is purported to have said: "Mein Gott, how he looks like his

*Plate 72.* STATE, WAR AND NAVY BUILDING, WASHINGTON, D. C. 1871–1875. Designed by Alfred B. Mullett (1834–1890), who was born in England and brought to America in 1845. As Assistant Supervising Architect of the U. S. Treasury Department, he received many government commissions. Costing $12,000,000, a contemporary called it "an *almost* perfect specimen of architecture," thus suggesting that at least one other building came closer to the ideal. *Courtesy,* HISTORIC AMERICAN BUILDINGS SURVEY, WASHINGTON, D. C. PHOTOGRAPH BY RONALD COMEDY

own buildings," adding that "it was a great thing to be monumental." The burly, bearded figure, heavy in later years, naturally adapted the forceful, rugged shapes of the Romanesque style to his own purposes. And these purposes suited the rest of the country as well. In Richardson's work there is no frivolity, no sense of the luxury of the nouveau riche, no overloading with ornament, and no form ill-used or out of taste. The materials he chose were the best, the construction of laborious stonework and finely selected wood was also the best, and he unhesitatingly introduced the latest mechanical conveniences. His is not a style of magnificence, but of superbly combined form related effectively, without melodrama, to the building materials. In achieving this special unity of form and material, he secures a sense of composure, and his resourcefulness and boldness are unmatched by others in the two important decades of his career.

The problems attacked by Richardson were not confined to any particular type of building; in fact, he welcomed the challenge of variety and complexity, and, as avidly as a chess player devising tactics to thwart his opponent, he found solutions to architectural problems in many different areas. He designed, among other things, gas lights incorporating the supply tube as part of the decoration, an ice house, a lighthouse, and railroad cars and stations (*Plate 75*). All are stamped with his genius, and all emerge as highly satisfactory, though not the only, solutions. Richardson's earliest church designs were Gothic inspired, but his greatest achievement in religious architecture was Trinity Church, Boston (*Plate 76*), built like the pyramids for the millenium. This granite, multi-colored mass might have been a burden on the landscape. Instead, the bulk of the building is penetrated by a series of openings, large at the base and decreasing in scale at each higher level. The openings are surrounded by rusticated and patterned stonework which gives solidity and unity without decreasing the ornamental effectiveness. That the tower derives from the Cathedral at Salamanca and the entranceway from St. Trophîme at Arles is incidental to the total composition.

Typical of the prosperous New England industrial barons was the Ames family of North Easton, Mass. They had acquired a large fortune by the manufacture of shovels and later in railroad development, which they spent freely in building one structure after another at North Easton. The Library (*Plate 77*) is interesting as a rather simple, well-planned example of Richardson's use of rusticated granite and reddish Longmeadow sandstone, the latter as decoration juxtaposed with the magnificent chunks of grey stone. Although each stone in the walls is cut to a different size, the masonry work is so precise at the joints that the stones fit as neatly as the blocks in a Chinese puzzle. The stubby doorway with its all-inclusive arch is brilliantly suggestive in ornament of the piers of Durham Cathedral.

*Plate 73*. TRINITY COLLEGE, HARTFORD, CONNECTICUT. 1873–1880. Designed by William Burges (1827–1881), an English architect. He employed George W. Keller of Hartford (1842–1935) to supervise the work. The full grandiose plan was never finished—only a part of one quadrangle. Brown stone from Portland, Connecticut, was used for ornamental details which contrasts pleasingly with rusticated gray walls. *Courtesy*, TRINITY COLLEGE

*Plate 74.* Trinity College, Hartford, Connecticut. Drawing of original plan by William Burges. From R. P. Pullan, *Architectural Designs of William Burges*, London, 1887

By the time Richardson agreed to design stations for the Boston and Albany Railroad, he was in a position to accept whatever commissions he preferred, so one might wonder why he chose to design the insignificant little depots in the suburbs of Boston. That he did so is mainly because he was always attracted to an architectural problem associated with the progress of mechanics and industrialism. Though the stations were not in themselves mechanical, they represented the advance of transportation; furthermore, few architects had considered stations as worthy of their attention. They were purely utilitarian structures to hold a ticket office and baggage, and to

*125*

*Plate 75.*
These Three Drawings by H. H.
Richardson—of a proposed design for waterspout;
for a lantern; and for a gas-light in which the
tubing is an integral part—illustrate the architect's
interest in mechanical details. *Courtesy*, the
houghton library, harvard university

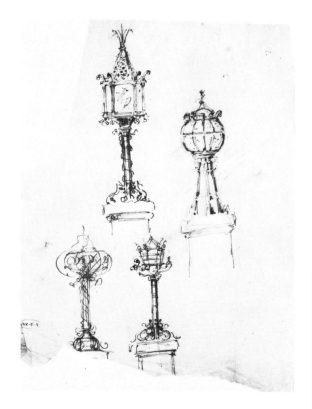

126

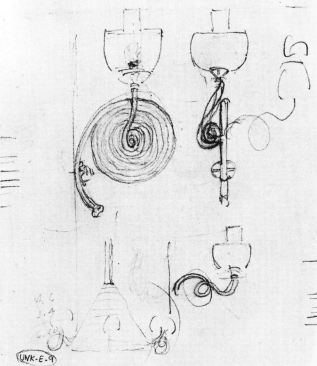

*Plate 76.* Trinity Church, Boston, Massachusetts. 1872–1877. Designed by H. H. Richardson. The irregular site demanded a plan of unusual shape. Richardson chose to adapt a kind of Romanesque plan with four arms almost equal in length and added a semicircular apse and vestibule. The great tower is supported by four enormous interior granite piers plastered over to form a group of shafts. The whole interior was plastered and painted to give richness of color under the direction of John LaFarge. The Milford granite is yellowish-gray and the trim of red Longmeadow sandstone, a color scheme already used by Richardson in his earlier Springfield buildings. The present entrance porticoes and cappings to the front towers are additions by Richardson's firm after his death. PHOTOGRAPH BY WAYNE ANDREWS

keep persons dry and warm while waiting for their train. But Richardson saw a chance to treat the stations aesthetically, as he did at Chestnut Hill (*Plate 79*), where his usual architectural vocabulary appears singularly

128  *Plate 77.* LIBRARY, NORTH EASTON, MASSACHUSETTS. 1877. Designed by H. H. Richardson as a memorial to Oakes Ames. As in Trinity Church, the stone here is Milford granite with Longmeadow trim. The low entrance arch is the first of its kind in Richardson's work, possibly suggested by Syrian churches. The roof is tile, except for the stone-covered tower. At the chimney end, the gable and part of the chimney itself have square-patterned stones as found in certain churches of Auvergne. Typical are the clustered arches over the main entrance and the strip of windows separated by short colonettes in the stack wing. The total effect is compact and harmonious. PHOTOGRAPH BY WAYNE ANDREWS

correct for the transition each passenger made from the light horse-drawn carriage to the heavy, cumbersome train.

The Allegheny County Courthouse and Jail, Pittsburgh (*Plate 80*), considered by Richardson himself as one of his best projects, one he wished to be remembered by, was ,hardly a new problem, but one which needed change and improvement in its solution by each succeeding generation. The courthouse is designed so that every room has outside light and is reached by

*Plate 78.*
FIREPLACE IN THE AMES LIBRARY, NORTH EASTON, MASSACHUSETTS.
PHOTOGRAPH BY WAYNE ANDREWS

an inside corridor lighted from the inner court. The façade tower, 250 feet tall, a vestige of mediaeval style, is given a new use as an intake duct for ventilation. Most remarkable are the highly polished materials in hallways, stairs and rooms. Appropriately the prison is less ornamental and heavier in form. No building was ever more rugged in appearance than this. Obvious to all is its function of security as an adjunct to the halls of justice across the "Bridge of Sighs."

The Glessner House in Chicago (*Plate 81*) is outwardly ominous, built as it is with rocks overly large in scale for a residence. More fitting in

*Plate 79*. Boston and Albany Station, Chestnut Hill, Massachusetts. 1883–1884. Designed by H. H. Richardson. The carriage approach is simple and excellently unified with the waiting room, whereas the train arrival platform is sheltered awkwardly. The great low entrance arch hooks the front pillars onto the main building and the continuous roof above as well. The side stone walls give further unity to this exceptional little building. Several other stations built for the same railroad are less imaginative, though all show Richardson's keen interest in developing architectural form appropriate to industry, transportation and business in an age much concerned with these matters. From *Henry Hobson Richardson and his Works*, by Mrs. M. G. Van Rensselaer, 1888. *Courtesy*, new york public library

*Plate 80.* ALLEGHENY COUNTY COURTHOUSE AND JAIL, PITTSBURGH. 1884–1887. Designed by H. H. Richardson as winner of a competition. The high granite walls penetrated by only a few heavy arched doorways and the bleak windows of the warden's house are rugged in the extreme. As a contrast to the indestructability of the jail, the courthouse is lightened by the many rows of rectangular and arched windows, the several turrets, and the tower. In this late building, the architect abandoned exterior polychromy using only rusticated gray granite. The unusual symmetry of the courthouse may reflect a change in Richardson's aesthetic, never to be developed by him, but carried out by his pupils McKim and White. PHOTOGRAPH BY WAYNE ANDREWS

a warden's house for a prison, the walls on the coachhouse side have small slits for windows, and the bulk of the stonework here is overpowering. On the shorter entrance side the windows are larger and set with almost Georgian symmetry except for the left side where the entrance to the court

*Plate 81.* GLESSNER HOUSE, PRAIRIE AVENUE AND 18TH STREET, CHICAGO, ILLINOIS. 1885–1887. Designed by H. H. Richardson for John Jacob Glessner, vice-president of the farm machinery company of Warden, Bushnell and Glessner. Early designs seem to reflect a new interest in Rennaissance and Georgian design, but these ruminations were happily set aside in the final effort. Foundations are of Joliet limestone, the superstructure of Wellesley granite, and the courtyard and walls of brick. Air conditioning was attempted by circulating air over blocks of ice in the basement before it entered the upper rooms. Montgomery Schuyler (1891) referred to the house as a "gargantuan freak," but more recent criticism finds it happily functional. *Courtesy*, HISTORIC AMERICAN BUILDINGS SURVEY, WASHINGTON, D. C.

lies. But even this façade has a forbidding look. Neighbors of Mr. Glessner were not happy with the result, believing the building an insult to their own more cultivated choices of style. In spite of the gloom, the house conveys a wonderful sense of the use of stone, direct, simple, and yet endowed with a superb architectural character. Richardson was in many ways doing his best work here. The interior of the Glessner House has less to recommend it, probably owing to Richardson's untimely death. Many of his other interiors, however, are beautifully composed with the use of finely polished oak and other rich dark materials as in the Paine House, Waltham (*Plate 82*). The

*Plate 82.* R. T. PAINE HOUSE, WALTHAM, MASSACHUSETTS. 1884–1886. Designed by H. H. Richardson, but not completed until after his death. The exterior is as bold and rugged with its boulder-finished turrets and elongated dormer as the interior is brilliant and precise in its use of richly moulded wood and peach-colored marble. Recently demolished. PHOTOGRAPH BY BERENICE ABBOTT

staircase is a work of art in itself as it winds its princely way to the floor above.

In the same year and the same city in which the Glessner House was erected, Richardson designed the Marshall Field Wholesale Store (*Plate 84*) as the complement in business structure to the mood of the house. What could be simpler than the basic concept of a rectangular shape with regularly placed openings, large at the base and smaller on the upper floors, supplying quantities of interior light. The exterior stonework, rugged and massive, forms a bulwark or protective shield, the walls gradually decreas-

*Plate 83.* DETAIL OF INTERIOR, R. T. PAINE HOUSE, PHOTOGRAPH BY WAYNE ANDREWS

ing in width and thickness as they rise. The rusticated surface is only relieved by one flat stringcourse, the more heavily rusticated arches, and a quaint pattern in the spandrels of the large arches of stones cut square and to much smaller sizes. Every device used to ornament this monumental

*Plate 84.* MARSHALL FIELD WHOLESALE STORE, CHICAGO, ILLINOIS. 1885–1887. Designed by H. H. Richardson. Destroyed about 1932 for replacement by a parking garage. The outer walls, those of the court, and the main inner walls were of solid masonry. Other piers and the floor beams were of metal. Although the building had a strong decorative influence on many of Chicago's tall buildings, it was itself only seven stories high. PHOTOGRAPH BY CHICAGO ARCHITECTURAL PHOTOGRAPH COMPANY

structure had been used before, but never in such a simple straightforward way. This was a building for architects to ponder and learn from.

While Stanford White (1853–1906) worked in Richardson's office he was entrusted with much decorative design for residence commissions coming to the older architect. Thus projects by Richardson often show the influence of White, as on the exterior of the Sherman House, Newport, R.I. (*Plate 85*), where the multi-material surface shifts to different textures on several planes, while the bulk shape and general outline is Richardson's. Because of the close association of White with Richardson for a number of years, the firm White joined in 1880—to be known as McKim, Mead and White—was in part the architectural inheritor of the professional brilliance of Richardson.

*Plate 85.* W. WATTS SHERMAN HOUSE, NEWPORT, RHODE ISLAND. 1874–1876. Designed by H. H. Richardson and Stanford White. Probably the plan and general form is Richardson's, while all the interior decoration and the elaborate, small-scale exterior ornaments are White's. PHOTOGRAPH BY WAYNE ANDREWS

It is highly relevant to take notice in this Richardsonian age of the men who were not trained as architects, but who nevertheless were structural creators and developers of the new materials of iron and steel. Early shapes given to metal were often those already in use in other materials. As techniques advanced in the manufacturing of metal, its application to structural problems increased and the tendency to imitate previous forms died out. James Bogardus (1800–1874), manufacturer of cast-iron for towers and walls, found he could produce not facsimiles of classic designs, but cast-iron shapes with decorative form at least derived from antiquity, or Gothic, or Renaissance models, any of which could serve as façades for stores and other commercial buildings where economy, durability and reasonable good looks were required. Popular in the 1850's in New York, Bogardus's scheme of construction spread to most of the large cities in the sixties and remained in vogue to about 1880. The cast-iron continued to be manufactured in New York and shipped by water to other cities. New Orleans has several fine examples still remaining like the former Bank of America (Krower Building; *Plate 86*) with Florentine Renaissance detailing. By the seventies even the great architects like Richard Morris Hunt (1827–1895) condescended to design with cast-iron fronts. Several of his buildings decorated Broadway (*Plate 87*).

More spectacular than store fronts in employing metal creatively were the new bridges, stations and exhibition pavilions. John Roebling's Brooklyn Bridge (*Plate 88*), though not the first to use the suspension method, was when completed the longest of its kind in America. Not ready to dispense with style altogether, even in what was essentially an engineering project, Roebling placed Gothic arches at each end as traffic entrances to a masonry pier which is remotely Egyptian and Classic. This should have made a weird appearance, and yet it does not. Somehow the proportions came out all right and the steel strands of suspension connecting each end of the bridge draw the vertical units together with unity and grace.

The art of spanning interior space cheaply with iron and glass, first developed in England and culminating in Paxton's famous Crystal Palace for the exhibition of 1851, was quickly learned and applied in America. Best

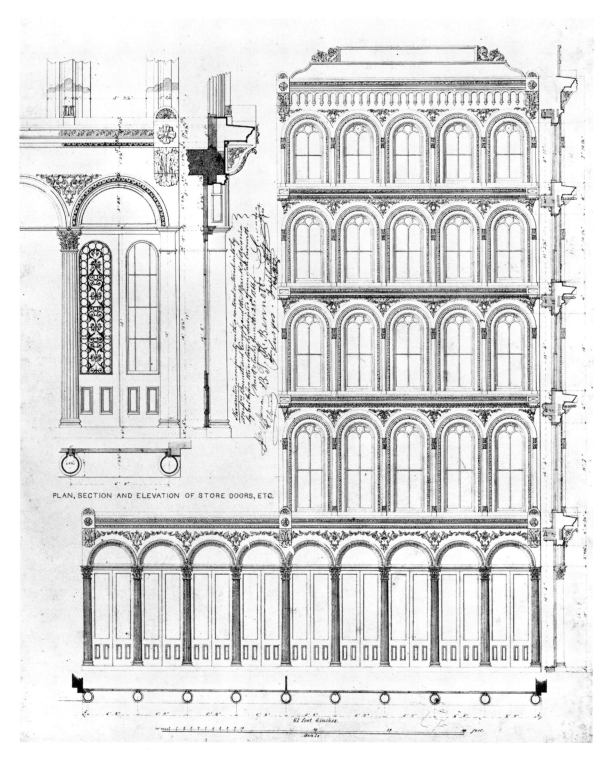

PLAN, SECTION AND ELEVATION OF STORE DOORS, ETC.

61 feet 6 inches.

*Plate 86.* KROWER BUILDING (FORMERLY BANK OF AMERICA), NEW ORLEANS, 1866. Designed by James Gallier, Jr., and Richard Esterbrook. This is a typical cast-iron façade of the era with a particularly graceful appearance. The design is inspired by Italian Renaissance buildings of the fifteenth century divested of their stony robustness and recomposed by New York architects of the 1850's and early 1860's. The iron was probably manufactured in New York and sent by boat to New Orleans. *Courtesy,* TULANE UNIVERSITY LIBRARY

known to New Yorkers was the old Grand Central Depot (*Plate 89*), now demolished in favor of the present station. The pedestrian entrance was an unfortunate combination of Italian Renaissance palace style topped with French mansard-roofed pavilions. The train entrance to the shed was an architectural fiasco with a misshapen Florentine church façade attempting to suppress or hide the great arch of the shed. The glory of the station was the shed itself: 600 feet in length, 200 feet wide, and 100 feet high, comparable in size to London's renowned St. Pancras Station (1863–65). A few years later Philadelphia had its International Exhibition (*Plate 90*) to celebrate the centennial of American independence. The main building was constructed entirely of prefabricated parts covering an enormous floor area. Today the decorative forms appear crude, while the structural plan, though primitive, looks ingenious as it spreads lightly across the exhibition floor.

*Plate 87.* HAMMERSLOUGH BROTHERS WAREHOUSE, NEW YORK CITY, 1873–1874. At 478–482 Broadway. Designed by Richard Morris Hunt. Not by any means the first cast-iron front in New York, but a good example of its continued popularity and of the decorative possibilities of this material. Hunt chose mainly classical motifs which, when attenuated because of the nature of iron, piled up in a most non-classical manner and, filled in with large panes of glass, are curious and quaint. Though much deranged, one supposes the original decorative inspiration is the Roman triumphal arch, but with a Mediaeval canopy shrouding it. The Ionic order is that of the *Temple of Apollo, Bassae*, published by C. R. Cockerell in 1860, just in time for Hunt to use it. PHOTOGRAPH, *courtesy*, PROFESSOR WINSTON WEISMAN, PENN STATE UNIVERSITY

*139*

140 *Plate 88.* BROOKLYN BRIDGE, NEW YORK. 1869–1883. Designed by John A. Roebling. The construction is based on suspension principles first used with metal cable by the French engineer Marc Séguin as early as 1824 for a bridge across the Rhone near Tournon. Four giant cables 16 inches in diameter support the road bed from two double-arched Gothic towers. Each cable has 5,541 steel strands. At least the towers are called Gothic because of the pointing of the arches; otherwise, there is little resemblance to anything Mediaeval. The central span is 1595 feet between two towers each 276 feet high. Roebling died while working on the caissons of the foundations in 1869, but fortunately his son, Washington Roebling, was able to finish the work.
PHOTOGRAPH BY WAYNE ANDREWS

Architects naturally give the first consideration to the design of the building itself, but they are also very conscious of the surroundings, for they are well aware that the setting is extremely important to the total aesthetic effect. Thus, where projects are large enough to warrant it, architects often collaborate with landscape designers. This joint effort, typical of mid-century practice, is particularly noteworthy in the case of a pupil of A. J. Downing, Frederick Law Olmsted (1822–1903).

*Plate 89.* OLD GRAND CENTRAL DEPOT, NEW YORK. 1869–1871. Designed by Isaac C. Buck-hout and John B. Snook for the New York Central & Hudson River, the New York & Harlem, and the New York & New Haven railroads. It fulfilled Commodore Vanderbilt's dream of erect-ing a station equal in size and grandeur to the famous English stations, such as St. Pancras, London. For economy and fireproofing they used iron painted white for the decorative features. The shed was kept clean by unhooking cars from the engine outside and letting the cars roll in controlled only by brakemen. *Courtesy*, PENN-CENTRAL COMPANY, PUBLIC RELATIONS AND ADVERTISING DEPARTMENT

141

His partnership with the architect Calvert Vaux, also Downing's pupil, in 1857 proved fruitful, first in winning the competition to design Central Park, New York City (*Plate 91*), and then in a large number of other municipal parks, educational and private grounds, and late in his career in the lake shore plans for the Worlds' Columbian Exposition of 1893 at Chicago. All these enterprises show Olmsted's preference for Downing's natural, informal landscaping inherited in turn from the English landscape school of the eighteenth century. Even the Columbian Exposition plan was basically meandering as it blended with Chicago's shoreline.

HAUPT AUSSTELL⁵ GEB.          EDIFICIO PRINCIPAL.          PALAIS DE L'INDUSTRIE.

MAIN BUILDING

*Plate 90.* MAIN EXHIBITION BUILDING, CENTENNIAL EXPOSITION OF 1876, PHILADELPHIA, PENNSYLVANIA. Designed by Henry Pettit and Joseph M. Wilson. Both Pettit and Wilson were trained as engineers, and this may account for the building's lack of interesting architectural details. It imitates the structural system of prefabricated parts of the London Crystal Palace Exhibition (1851) and, similarly, its length is related to the year of the exhibition (1876 feet). It was demolished at the end of the exhibition. This lithographic view is from *Centennial Portfolio* by Thompson Westcott (Philadelphia, 1876). *Courtesy,* NEW YORK PUBLIC LIBRARY

By 1885 the architectural profession in America had risen to prominence through the hard work, creative genius, and devotion of its members. Americans wanted the advantages of good architecture and were able and willing to pay for them. It would not be long before European architects would become aware of advances made in America which were ultimately to result in architectural influences re-crossing the Atlantic and in the emigration of enterprising architects of recognized ability who sought greener pastures in the New World.

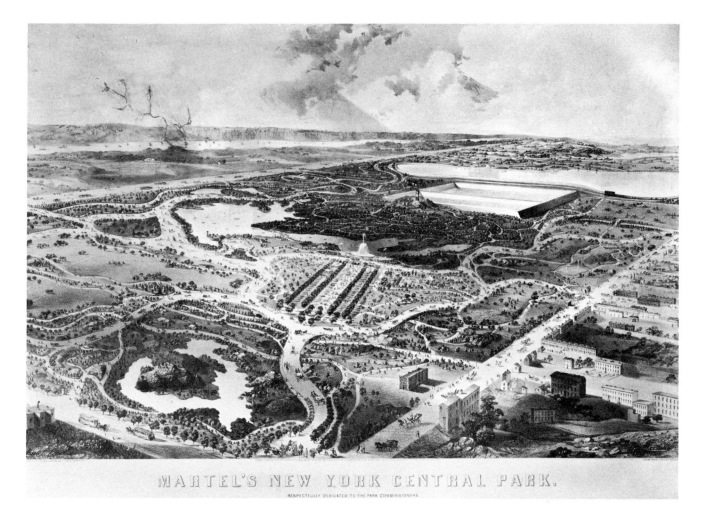

MARTEL'S NEW YORK CENTRAL PARK.
RESPECTFULLY DEDICATED TO THE PARK COMMISSIONERS

*Plate 91.* CENTRAL PARK, NEW YORK. 1857–1878. Designed by Frederick Law Olmsted and Calvert Vaux. The original idea was A. J. Downing's. Through his influence the New York public became enthusiastic about the project, but Downing died in 1852 before he had a chance to carry out his plans. *Courtesy,* STOKES COLLECTION, PRINTS DIVISION, NEW YORK PUBLIC LIBRARY

### THE BEGINNING OF FUNCTIONALISM (1885–1910)

IN the late works of Richardson there is something almost intangible which the next generation of architects was to sense and develop gradually into what has been called functionalism. The architects who relied most heavily on the master for their own style were not the ones who were sensing this intangible, they were merely the popularizers of so-called Richardson Romanesque. Among this large group were many very competent men, but few with the creative ability or courage to refine or improve upon Richardson's splendid use of materials and organization of interior space. Several, however, had his instinct for incorporating in their designs the latest mechanical inventions and newly manufactured materials. In fact, the skyscraper was made possible by just such inventiveness.

The first real skyscrapers (buildings twelve or more stories high and generally of skeletal construction) were built in Chicago in the 1880's, but their antecedents had appeared in New York and Philadelphia. In New York the first successful elevator, with a safety device, was installed by Otis in 1857. It was an essential invention for the skyscraper, though not the only necessary one. Philadelphia's Jayne Building of 1849 showed how style (in this case Gothic) could be applied to tall buildings. And the architect of the Harper Brothers Building in New York of 1854, essentially a Venetian palace grown large for commercial purposes, arrived unknowingly at a solution for the top of skyscrapers like those constructed thirty years later; namely, a flat roof over any number of identical floors below. William Le Baron Jenney's Home Insurance Building in Chicago (*Plate 92*) was the first to fulfill the conditions of being a skyscraper and was structurally a great credit to its designer. Jenney's skeletal construction consisted of a cage built of cast and wrought iron columns joined by wrought iron cross beams (steel beams above the sixth floor) bolted together. The walls for this metal frame were supported from floor to floor by the horizontal girders; and windows were plentiful for interior light. Brilliant as the engineering solution was, the exterior design reflects no unusual thinking. Jenney gave a pervasive Classical feeling to the two street façades by making vertical

*Plate 92.* HOME INSURANCE BUILDING, CHICAGO. 1884–1885. Designed by William LeBaron Jenney. Demolished in 1931. The exact source for Jenney's system of skeletal construction is uncertain, though it is apparent that many other engineers in Europe and America had already arrived at nearly the same solution—James Bogardus for his shot tower in New York; H. Fontaine for his warehouse at the St. Ouen Docks, Paris; Frederick Baumann in a pamphlet written on the construction of tall buildings (1884) which Jenney certainly saw; etc. Bessemer steel beams above the sixth floor were the first used for building construction. Exterior walls were of rusticated granite for the first story and brick with sandstone trim above. PHOTOGRAPH BY THE CHICAGO ARCHITECTURAL PHOTOGRAPH COMPANY

*Plate 93.* TACOMA BUILDING, CHICAGO. 1886–1889. Designed by Holabird and Roche. Demolished in 1929. Several technical innovations were incorporated here such as soil stabilization; water pockets and soft clay in the construction area are filled with cement. The footings for columns were really floating foundations of concrete 20 inches thick reinforced with I-beams. As in the Home Insurance Building, cast iron, wrought iron, and steel were used for various beams. Riveting for a structural frame was first employed here shortening the time of construction. Hollow, fire-proof tile arches supported the floors and encased all the columns. Carl Seiffert, engineer for the firm must be credited with some of the innovations. PHOTOGRAPH BY THE CHICAGO ARCHITECTURAL PHOTOGRAPH COMPANY

divisions with piers decorated like pilasters, and coupled pilasters at the doorway. Richardson's influence may be seen in the rusticated lower stories and in the series of arches at the top of the tenth floor which was originally the top floor. The addition of two more floors later did not improve the design, weighted down as it was by the complex cornice and balustrade.

While Jenney's revolutionary building was being constructed, Richardson designed and built his Marshall Field Wholesale Store (*Plate 84*). Of the two, Richardson's, though dependent upon masonry construction, is by far the more advanced; it plays an uncompromising chord, resisting the old forms and seeking something new.

The following year, in 1886, the firm of William Holabird (1854–1923) and Martin Roche (1855–1927), spurred on by the new freedom of construction allowed by the skeletal method, designed their Tacoma Building (*Plate 93*) with reduced wall surface and an immense increase in window area. This they accomplished by inserting a series of large bay windows projecting through the plane of the vertical wall support. This feature along with the attractive loggia at the top should have been enough. Adding horizontal bands of dubiously scaled Classical ornament was a fault they never fully corrected. But Dankmar Adler (1844–1900) and Louis Sullivan (1856–1924) in designing the masonry-constructed Auditorium Building (*Plate 94*) learned the virtue of simplicity and good massing from Richardson, and leaned heavily on his concept of decoration as expressed on the Marshall Field Wholesale Store, though without attaining the same degree of unity. No idle pilasters intrude upon Sullivan's design, while new features like the loggias at the entranceway and high on the tower surpass in interest Classical decoration which is always too small in scale for the immensity of tall 19th-century buildings. The fascinating new ornament created by Sullivan (*Plate 95*) was not just the outburst of a nonconformist, but joyous enrichment for an interior contrasting with the stubborn façade facing the hard city.

If the exterior of Sullivan's Auditorium Building is mainly Richardsonian, the interior is not; it is full-blown, gorgeous work of a very different kind unmatched in America for glittering brilliance (*Plate 96*). Ornamental effects which were at first only a means of brightening interiors and relieving the severity of exterior masonry soon became an obsession with Sullivan— a magnificent obsession. A building without ornament was for Sullivan lacking the intensity of life. His buildings had to be the fulfillment of a

148

*Plate 94.* HOTEL AND AUDITORIUM BUILDING, CHICAGO. 1886–1889. Designed by Adler and Sullivan. There were 400 guest rooms until Roosevelt College occupied the building in 1946. The main dining room was on the 10th floor with a view to Lake Michigan. The kitchen was curiously located over the stage to the theater, and held there by wrought iron trusses unrelated to the rest of the structure. There were also 136 offices. The theater, richly designed and well attended by Chicago crowds, was the first to be air-conditioned (air cooled by roof sprays). Designed for an audience of 4,237, it was possible to reduce the capacity by lowering ceiling panels. The acoustic properties, given much attention by Adler, are extremely fine. The room has recently been renovated after a long period of disuse. PHOTOGRAPH BY WAYNE ANDREWS

*Plate 95.*
ORNAMENT BY LOUIS SULLIVAN. A sketch from Sullivan's book, *A System of Architectural Ornament According with a Philosophy of Man's Powers*, Washington, 1924. Original drawings are at the Burnham Library, Art Institute of Chicago, Illinois. *Courtesy*, THE ART INSTITUTE OF CHICAGO

complete human desire. "We shall learn," he said, "to consider man and his ways, to the end that we behold the unfolding of the soul in all its beauty. . . ." This is what his mature buildings are: an embodiment of Sullivan himself. He loved strength and boldness of structure, but not without the enrichment of ornament. Both the Wainwright Building, St. Louis,

149

and the Guaranty Building, Buffalo (*Plate 97*), give expression of their skeletal structure through sturdy, vertical-masonry accents. Both are heavily decorated, the Guaranty Building having literally not a square foot of unornamented surface. It is hard to reconcile Sullivan's slogan "Form follows function" with his own designs where so much form is functionless orna-

*Plate 96.* HOTEL AND AUDITORIUM BUILDING, CHICAGO. 1886–1889. Sullivan's ornament, exuberant and derived in part from nature, is always appliqué. It fills panels, it covers arches, it cavorts around entrances and lower stories, but never is it integral to a structure. Divorce his ornament from its building and though the aesthetic effect suffers, the building stands as a structural unit. Books on Art Nouveau include Sullivan's ornament, but should they? European Art Nouveau may have some superfluous curves, but most of it is directed towards function and is not merely applied decoration. PHOTOGRAPH BY WAYNE ANDREWS

*Plate 97.* GUARANTY BUILDING (NOW PRUDENTIAL), BUFFALO, NEW YORK. 1894–1895.    *151*
Designed by Adler and Sullivan. It was their final commission as a firm. Much of the decoration, though still Sullivanesque, is attributed to the new designer in the office, George Grant
Elmslie. No other commercial building has ever received such an over-all pattern of lavish decoration. Some critics find the elongated proportions better for a tall building than the squatter
effect of the Wainwright Building in St. Louis. And at least one critic sees an "anticipation" of
Le Corbusier's pilotis or cylinders, upon which many of his buildings rest, in the cylindrical
piers at the ground level of the Prudential. PHOTOGRAPH BY WAYNE ANDREWS

*Plate 98.* MONADNOCK BUILDING, CHICAGO, ILLINOIS. 1889–1891. Designed by Burnham and Root. The south extension was added by Holabird and Roche in 1893 using steel-frame construction. This firm's return to surface decoration makes the addition seem older than its predecessor. The walls of Burnham and Root's building are stone at the base and brick above. There is no inner court as the building is very narrow allowing all offices an exterior view. Inside are cast-iron columns and wrought iron beams. Although it was unlike any building ever erected, its simple dignity was immediately accepted and still remains an outstanding achievement aesthetically and structurally. PHOTOGRAPH BY THE CHICAGO ARCHITECTURAL PHOTOGRAPH COMPANY

152

153

*Plate 99*. RELIANCE BUILDING, CHICAGO, ILLINOIS. 1894–1895. Designed by D. H. Burnham and Co. The top ten stories of steel-frame construction were put up in fifteen days. Remarkable for its large panes of glass with very thin mullions, this building's exterior wall is erected without visible load-bearing piers. The "Chicago window" used here is designed with a fixed, large, central pane with narrow side sashes. PHOTOGRAPH BY THE CHICAGO ARCHITECTURAL PHOTOGRAPH COMPANY

ment, unless a less literal view is taken; that is, that the function of form is in large measure to increase the totality of beauty.

The last tall building of masonry construction, and paradoxically the most radical in design, was the Monadnock Building (*Plate 98*), by the firm of Burnham and Root. Its walls, completely self-supporting, are massive at the base (72 inches thick), and there is no decoration on the surface from top to bottom. The explanation of this fundamental departure from the heretofore basic requirement of exterior ornamentation lies in a story told by Root's biographer, Harriet Monroe: "For this building Mr. Aldis, who controlled the investment, kept urging upon his architects extreme simplicity, rejecting one or two of Root's sketches as too ornate. During Root's absence of a fortnight at the seashore, Mr. Burnham ordered from one of the draughtsmen a design of a straight-up-and-down, uncompromising, unornamented façade. When Root returned, he was indignant at first over this project of a brick box. Gradually, however, he threw himself into the spirit of the thing, . . ." Little did they suspect that they were anticipating by thirty to forty years the delight architects would take in designing sheer, vertical-faced skyscrapers. This famous firm of Burnham and Root, caught up like so many others in the great building surge after Chicago's devastating fire of 1871, followed close upon the heels of the architects of the Tacoma Building with their own remarkable Reliance Building (*Plate 99*). In fact one might imagine this building to be designed by the same firm. In the Reliance, like the Tacoma, the bay window is exploited with broad plate-glass panes giving fine interior light. And they used skeletal steel construction, a commonplace by the 1890's.

In the last year of the century Sullivan contrived a very bold, rigid design for the Carson Pirie Scott and Co. Store (*Plate 100*). The only relief to the web of severe horizontal and vertical lines of the exterior is the curved corner. At first glance the impression given by this building is that of simple functionalism, whereas close observation reveals that each flat band of masonry is in reality composed of hundreds of stones, and is surrounded with an ornamental border. The window frames are covered with linear decoration, and the base of the building bristles with ironwork of a most luxurious kind.

*154*

*Plate 100.* CARSON PIRIE SCOTT AND COMPANY STORE (ORIGINALLY SCHLESINGER & MAYER DEPARTMENT STORE), CHICAGO, ILLINOIS. 1899, 1903–1904, 1906. Designed by Louis Sullivan and D. H. Burnham and Company. The earliest part is the nine-story, three-bay section on Madison Street (left in photo); then three, twelve-story bays on Madison and five on State Street; finally Burnham added five more bays on State Street. The magnificent exterior ornament of cast iron (see *Plate 101.*) is more luxuriant than on any other of his buildings and was designed in detail by George Elmslie who has said it was intended as "a richly flowing picture frame . . . to surround the rich ornate window displays." PHOTOGRAPH BY WAYNE ANDREWS

For the remainder of his working career Sullivan continued his very personal union of structure and decoration whether it was for large business buildings, or for small banks like the Merchant's National Bank, Grinnell, Iowa (*Plate 102*) or the National Farmer's Bank, Owatonna, Minn.

After two decades of recovery from its great fire, Chicago was ready to present to the world a display of American progress centered in this burgeoning metropolis. A group of Chicago business men formed a committee in 1889 which proposed a "World's Columbian Exposition" to Congress and gained its approval. Congress in turn appointed a national commission to deal with foreign countries. D. H. Burnham, then in his early forties, became chief of construction heading a local Grounds and Buildings Committee. This last group was really responsible for setting the tone

*Plate 102.* MERCHANTS' NATIONAL BANK, GRINNELL, IOWA. 1914. Designed by Louis Sullivan. The shape is a solid block with but a few openings and a decorative cornice. Above the front door a large, almost overpowering mass of ornament is gathered around a circular window, the whole giving the impression of a box camera with a complicated lens. The material is brick of various shades of dark and light brown with a reddish cast. The circular window has stained glass, like the rose-window of some mediaeval French cathedral. PHOTOGRAPH BY WAYNE ANDREWS

of the Exposition (*Plate 103*). They worked with F. L. Olmsted as consulting landscape architect, they selected architects for each building, and they saw to it that each building met the overall requirements of the site and style of the whole exhibition. The names of the architectural firms engaged is a list of the very best architects in the country, but what

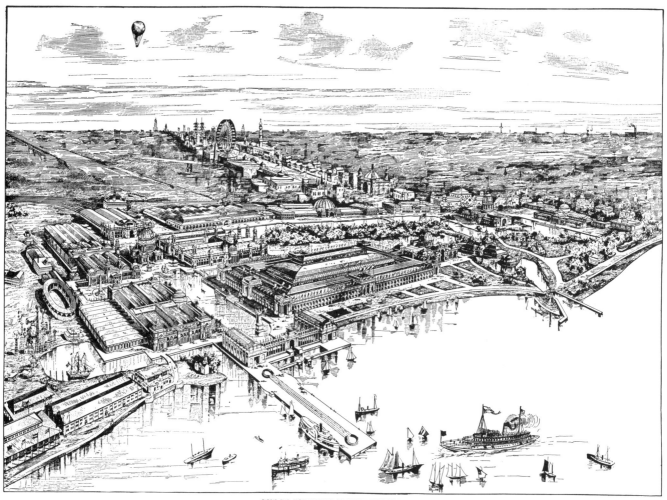

BIRD'S-EYE VIEW WORLD'S COLUMBIAN EXPOSITION

158

*Plate 103.* WORLD'S COLUMBIAN EXPOSITION OF 1893, CHICAGO, ILLINOIS. Frederick Law Olmsted, landscape architect, was the first consultant to the local corporation appointed to construct the Exposition. He worked with D. H. Burnham on ways to adapt the sandy, windswept shores of Lake Michigan to meet the requirements of an enormous enterprise. To make lagoons, wooded islands, and elaborately constructed exposition halls on such an ill-suited site was a task indeed. Shortly Burnham's partner, John Root, joined them with his talents for organization. As the moment came for actual construction, various other architects were invited to participate—R. M. Hunt; McKim, Mead and White; Van Brunt and Howe; Peabody and Stearns of Boston, and others. From *The Book of the Fair*, by H. H. Bancroft, Chicago and San Francisco, 1893. *Courtesy*, NEW YORK PUBLIC LIBRARY

they produced was simply a stupendous display of neo-Roman architecture. Their efforts seemed justified by the visits of vast crowds after the opening and by the plaudits of newspapers and critics. All but a very few saw the exposition as the greatest event of the century, a summing up of the power of the industrial revolution and a prediction of wonders to come. Among the few was Louis Sullivan, himself a rebel against the classical tradition and a visionary. "These crowds," he said, "were astonished. They beheld what was for them an amazing revelation of the architectural art. To them it was a veritable Apocalypse, a message inspired from on high. Upon it their

*Plate 104.* VIEW OVER THE LAGOON, WORLD'S COLUMBIAN EXPOSITION, CHICAGO, 1893.
PHOTOGRAPH BY THE CHICAGO ARCHITECTURAL PHOTOGRAPH COMPANY

imaginations shaped new ideals. They went away, spreading again over the land, returning to their homes, each of them permeated by the most subtle and slow-acting of poisons. A vast multitude, exposed, unprepared, they had not had time or occasion to become immune to forms of sophistication not their own, to a higher and more dexterously insidious plausibility. Thus they departed joyously, carriers of contagion, unaware that what they be-

160    *Plate 105.* Transportation Building, World's Columbian Exposition of 1893, Chicago. Designed by Adler and Sullivan. The exterior walls were polychrome with bright blues, orange, red, dark green and yellow. What a contrast to the barren whiteness of its classical consorts! Every other spandrel contained a white angel holding a scroll with an inventor's name inscribed. One should notice, however, that the architects, in spite of their radical use of color, did not depart entirely from the spirit of the Exposition's architecture. The arcades are Roman in origin and the great doorway arches Romanesque, if not Roman. photograph by the chicago architectural photograph company

held and believed to be truth was to prove, in historic fact, an appalling calamity. For what they saw was not at all what they believed they saw, but an imposition of the spurious upon their eyesight, a naked exhibitionism of charlatanry" (*The Autobiography of an Idea*). Sullivan's own contribution, the Transportation Building (*Plate 105*), was the only major

*Plate 106.* HENRY VILLARD RESIDENCES, NEW YORK, N. Y. 1883–1885. Designed by McKim, Mead and White, but the designer in the firm most closely associated with the project was Joseph Wells. He continued the work when Stanford White went travelling and argued until he was allowed to use the Palazzo Cancellaria, Rome, as his model, at least in part. Sometimes criticized for oversimplication of Italianate form, any restraint here is amply overcome by very sensitive spacing and proportioning of the windows. PHOTOGRAPH BY WAYNE ANDREWS

construction not dedicated to reviving past glories; it was the only building to interrupt Classical grandeur with the excitement and inventiveness of a new age. But the overwhelming acceptance of the grand classical manner across the nation for the next three decades was a tribute to the ingenuity and dedication to this end of Daniel Burnham and his associates in producing a spectacle of such high architectural quality. Yet the Exposition extinguished any interest kindled in the public mind for new designs until Frank Lloyd Wright appeared—and simultaneously a new wave of architectural fashion began arriving from Europe to replace the outmoded style of dressing buildings in classical clothing.

One of the firms tied most closely to the planning of the World's Columbian Exposition was that of McKim, Mead and White. The firm's earlier architectural triumphs had made it second to none in the East. For the Exposition they built the vast Agriculture Palace on the main lagoon. McKim and White, the designers of the firm (Mead was mainly the business executive), both had worked in the office of H. H. Richardson. Their opinions were his at first, but inevitably they turned away from their master to develop a style of their own. This was largely a reversion to the grand

*Plate 107.* W. G. Low Residence, Bristol, Rhode Island. 1887. Designed by McKim, Mead and White. This summer home, stripped of applied decoration, is almost an anachronism as it seems to herald the new simplicity and functionalism of the early twentieth century. The tradition of wood construction and shingle siding is from Richardson. The extension of this tradition reaches its climax in the work of F. L. Wright. photograph by wayne andrews

manner of the Renaissance and ultimately of ancient Rome. Whether building private residences or fulfilling public commissions, the firm always displayed a brand of design which expressed affluence without ostentation and won the approval of critics. The greatest care was given to arrive at good proportions, to select the finest materials, and above all to make the most of the site. Along Madison Avenue in New York they erected an Italian Renaissance palace for Henry Villard (*Plate 106*) resplendent with arcade, balconies, quoins decorating the corners, a base of regularly rusticated stone, and beautifully smooth masonry walls above. On the rugged seacoast at Bristol, R.I., they built a house for W. G. Low (*Plate 107*) of shingle siding soon weathered to a roughness consonant with its ability to withstand sea gales. Closely hugging the ground, asymmetrical as an enormous rock, without exterior polish, this house lingers stylistically in the Richardsonian

*Plate 108.* PUBLIC LIBRARY, BOSTON, MASSACHUSETTS. 1887–1892. Designed by McKim, Mead and White. The library, when founded in 1852, was said to be the world's first free municipal library. It cost $2,743,285. Many ranking artists collaborated in making this far more than a storage building and dispensary for books. Puvis de Chavannes decorated the stair hall, E. A. Abbey painted scenes from the legend of the Holy Grail, Saint-Gaudens was supposed to do the entrance sculpture, John Sargent was assigned one room, and so on. PHOTOGRAPH BY WAYNE ANDREWS

tradition. In the same year, however, the firm received the commission for the Boston Public Library (*Plate 108*), a far cry from country rustication, though as well situated in relation to its neighbors on Copley Square as the Low House was to the sea. The Library is reminiscent in several ways, without being a copy, of Labrouste's Bibliothèque Ste. Geneviève in Paris. The arched windows of the large reading room are glazed in the upper two-thirds but filled with stone inscriptions below; the ground story is mainly masonry surface with relatively small windows breaking up the slightly rusticated surface. Yet the whole effect is more Italianate than French, including the arcaded courtyard and the spacious interior rooms where no crude decorative forms in iron (Labrouste's reading room though advanced technically in the use of this material, fails utterly on aesthetic grounds) spoil the rich classical treatment. The Colosseum at Rome and the Tempio

*Plate 109.* ORIGINAL DRAWING FOR INTERIOR COURTYARD OF BOSTON PUBLIC LIBRARY, WEST ELEVATION. *Courtesy,* THE NEW-YORK HISTORICAL SOCIETY, NEW YORK CITY

Malatestiano at Rimini have more remotely made their mark on the Library's exterior.

Gone, but not forgotten by literally millions of Americans, is the great Pennsylvania Station in New York, yet there are many other New York buildings by McKim, Mead and White still standing. Each is different, even when intended for the same purpose, which shows the broad, imaginative approach the firm could take to designing. For instance, the Century Club, the University Club (1899), and the Harvard Club (1902–15; *Plate 110*)

165

*Plate 110.* HARVARD CLUB, WEST 44TH STREET, NEW YORK CITY. 1902–1915. Designed by McKim, Mead and White. The firm drew upon classicism wherever they found it—from ancient Greece to 18th-century England. This Georgian adaptation in brick with stone trim is (as always) an original design in that it copies no particular building, though without Adam, Chambers and others as antecedents, this design could not have been possible. PHOTOGRAPH BY BROWN BROTHERS, NEW YORK

have little in common decoratively, nor are any of the firm's vast number of city or country residences copies of one another. Compare the Oelrichs Residence, Newport (*Plate 111*) with any of the others and one begins to discover the remarkable range and fertility of these architect's minds. What they failed to see was that their approach was down a dead-end street. They were unable to understand Richardson's simplifications and love of materials for their own sake, they could not fathom Sullivan's separation of structure and ornament, and they could not bring themselves to exploit the possibilities of design inherent in the new materials available to them. But there was a man reaching his architectural maturity just at the time it became clear

*Plate 111.* MRS. HERMANN OELRICHS' RESIDENCE "ROSE CLIFF," NEWPORT, RHODE ISLAND. 1897–1902. Designed by McKim, Mead and White. Theresa Alice Fair married Hermann Oelrichs in 1890. Her father, James Graham Fair, developed gold and silver mining operations in Nevada in the 1870's, making himself very wealthy. He died in 1894 leaving millions to his children, but the money was not available because of estate litigations for seven years, whereupon the house was immediately built. In spite of such wealth, this little Versailles can hardly compare in size with its prototype. Nevertheless, it is well proportioned and decorated tastefully on the exterior and lavishly within. Original drawings, signed by William S. Richardson and dated 1898, are at the New-York Historical Society. Richardson was a member of the architectural firm from June 1895 to 1929. PHOTOGRAPH BY WAYNE ANDREWS

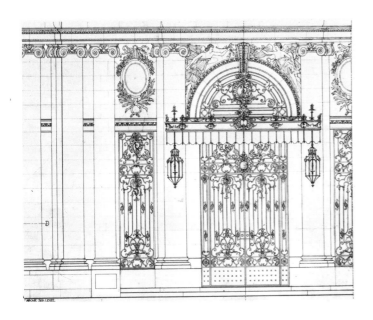

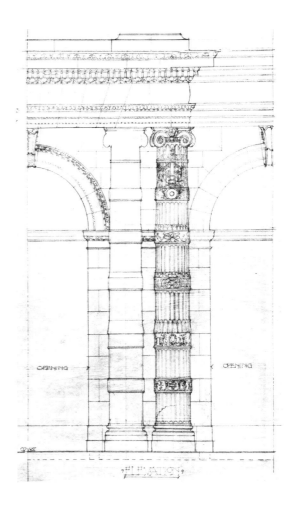

Plate 112.
DETAIL FOR IRONWORK AT PRINCIPAL ENTRANCE OF
OELRICHS' HOUSE, NEWPORT, RHODE ISLAND. Drawing
by W. S. Richardson. *Courtesy*, THE NEW-YORK
HISTORICAL SOCIETY, NEW YORK CITY

Plate 113.
DETAIL OF COLUMNS AND PORTICO ON GARDEN COURT OF
OELRICHS' HOUSE, NEWPORT, RHODE ISLAND. Drawing by
W. S. Richardson. *Courtesy*, THE NEW-YORK HISTORICAL
SOCIETY, NEW YORK CITY

Plate 114.
AN INTERIOR VIEW, OELRICHS' HOUSE, NEWPORT, RHODE
ISLAND. PHOTOGRAPH BY WAYNE ANDREWS

McKim, Mead and White had little more to offer than variations on their earlier successes. This was Frank Lloyd Wright.

Wright was born early enough to feed upon Richardson's genius, to work in the office of "Der lieber Meister" Louis Sullivan, and to feel the magnetic pull towards classic magnificence of McKim, Mead and White. Fortunately for him, and for American architecture in general, he was a genius able to shrug off injurious influences while appropriating the best. But much of his early work, before he divested himself of past architectural style, is not very satisfactory. He tried at first to revitalize old-fashioned house designs by inserting novel details and unusual proportions. Then he began to understand Sullivan's message, that "form follows function." Clearly, past styles had little relevance to an age in which so many new problems had arisen for the builder owing to the invention and wholesale manufacture of new materials, new industrial forms, new modes of trans-

168     *Plate 115.* WILLIAM H. WINSLOW HOUSE, RIVER FOREST, ILLINOIS. 1893. Designed by Frank Lloyd Wright. Winslow was the president of an ornamental iron works. The exterior of the first story is of long Roman bricks, the second story is lightly colored decorative tile, and the roof was originally terra cotta. The shape of the roof is unlike Wright's earlier houses in that it spreads amply like a turtle shell protecting all beneath it. From this developed the long cantilevered "Prairie house" roof of the next decade. In the stable at the rear, Winslow insisted on having a workshop and press room, to satisfy his typographic and printing hobby. *Courtesy,* HISTORIC AMERICAN BUILDINGS SURVEY, WASHINGTON, D. C.

portation, and consequent changes in the way of life. Wright was prepared
to meet the challenge of change, but to romanticize as well.

The first commission Wright had after resigning from the firm of
Adler and Sullivan in 1893 was the Winslow House (*Plate 115*). The
street view is one of geometric, abstract composure with a wide band of
colorful decoration below the eaves, all of which would have gained Sullivan's approval. In actuality the symmetry of the façade, the silence of its
form, is intentionally destroyed by masonry outcroppings on the other three
sides. It is as though Wright's pent-up feelings about design had exploded
with his new professional freedom. The Willitts House (*Plate 116*) drama-
tizes still further the possibilities of symmetry used asymmetrically. Certain parts, like the wings of the house, are in themselves symmetrically

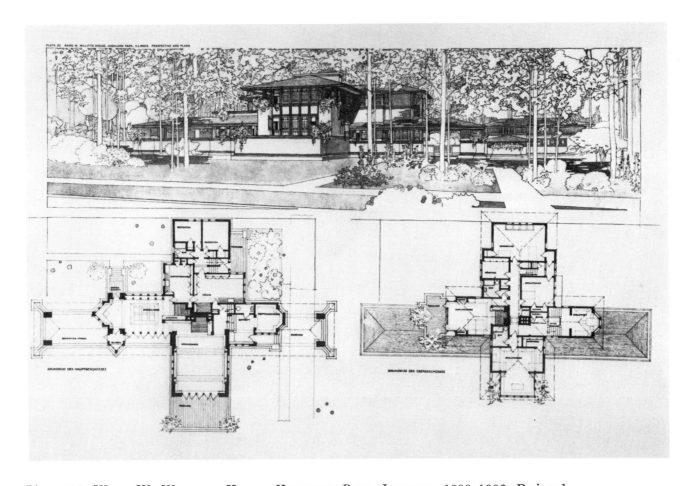

*Plate 116.* WARD W. WILLITTS HOUSE, HIGHLAND PARK, ILLINOIS. 1900–1902. Designed
by Frank Lloyd Wright. The plan is in the form of a cross with each arm satisfying a different
family need. Each room has its furniture, lights and window glass designed in harmony with
the particular space. (*Plates 116* through *119* are from *Ausgeführte Bauten und Entwärfe von
Frank Lloyd Wright, Wasmuth Verlag*, 1910)

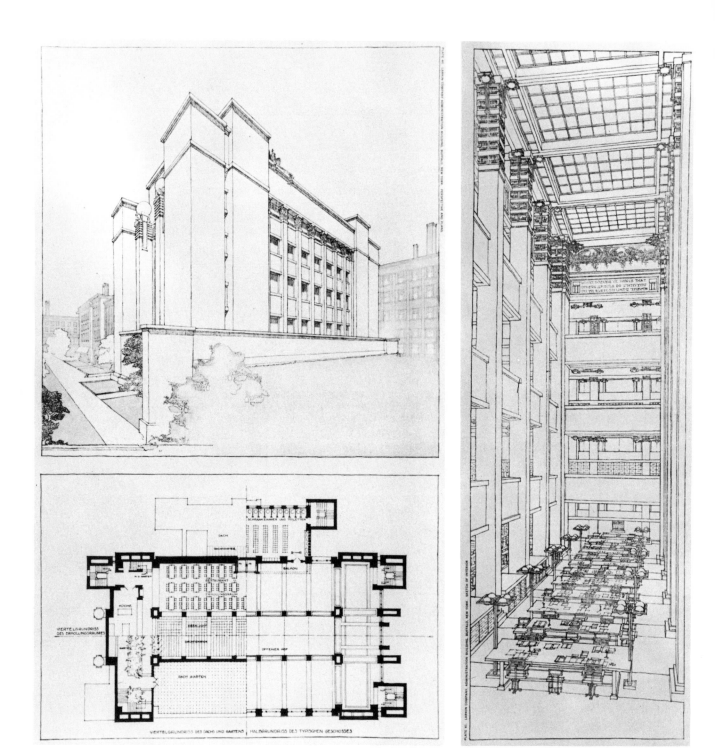

170     *Plates 117 and 118.* LARKIN BUILDING, BUFFALO, NEW YORK, 1904. Exterior, ground floor plan, and interior view. Designed by Frank Lloyd Wright. Destroyed 1950. This was the company's new administration building, so the interior is all office space. The ground floor contained most of the desks in one large open space lit by skylights. Balconies five stories high held company files and other services. Frankly industrial, yet humanly proportioned and not without decoration, this novel solution to administrative organization is a product of sheer genius. A later generation did not see it as such, but Europeans did and were inspired by its success both as architectural form and the expression of its use.

designed while the total combination is anything but symmetrical, no matter from which direction the house is seen. The dark rectilinear outlines surrounding large light areas, lacking in the Winslow House, are present here because of a new influence on Wright through his contact with Japanese art at the World's Columbian Exposition. This interest he maintained for many years, even to the extent of making a large collection of Japanese prints.

After 1900, fully in command of his architectural powers, Wright made great strides both structurally and expressively, and expanded his creative themes in new directions. Only mildly interested by Wright's new style in house designing, European architects who saw deviation from the usual in his concept of industrial design were most enthusiastic—and almost immediately began to emulate the young American master when they saw his works published. Wright's own countrymen, quite unimpressed, were very slow to accept his ideas. The Larkin Building (*Plate 117*) was admired by the Dutch architect H. P. Berlage. "Whatever concept one may have of an office building," said Berlage, "particularly here in Europe, there is no office building here with the monumental power of this American one. . . . I left convinced that I had seen a great modern work, and I am filled with respect for this master who has been able to create a building which has no equal in Europe." Americans, however, took so little interest in the building that it was allowed to be destroyed in 1950. Frankly industrial, the great corners towered up as though obliged to withstand the pressures of outside competition and to contain the centrifugal forces of machinery. In actuality it was an office building, but that it symbolizes the whole industrial process of which offices are only a small necessary part, lessened in no degree its expressive powers.

Outwardly less successful at expressing its function than the Larkin Building, Unity Temple (*Plate 119*) has an inner vitality and complexity equal to the variety and richness of thought espoused by Universalists. Like blocks in a Chinese puzzle the cubes of space are carefully interrelated so that all are necessary to the complete composition of both exterior and interior. Decoration occurs at several points, but never in such

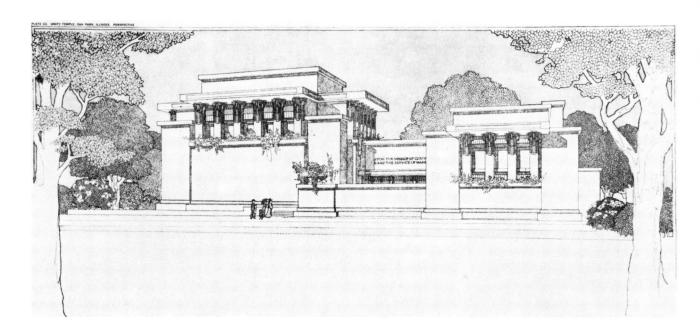

*Plate 119*. UNITY TEMPLE, OAK PARK, ILLINOIS. 1904–1907. Designed by Frank Lloyd Wright. Built of cast concrete, though at first it was to be of brick and stone. The change was probably made in the interest of economy. As a study in form, the building was greatly enhanced by the shift to a material producing large, flat unrelieved areas. By using this relatively new material some loss in time was incurred, and to judge from its exterior appearance a better combination of materials would have produced a more lasting surface.

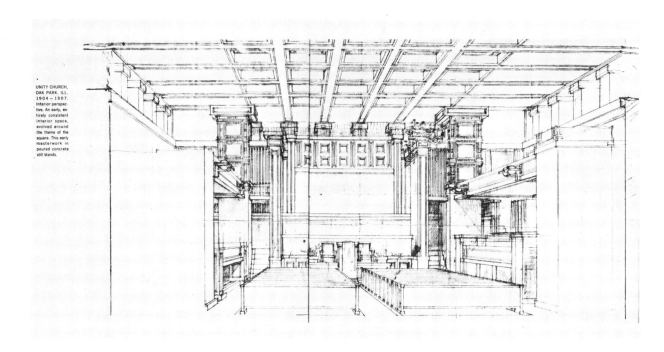

UNITY CHURCH, OAK PARK, ILL. 1904 – 1907. Interior perspective. An early, entirely consistent interior space, evolved around the theme of the square. This early masterwork in poured concrete still stands.

*Plate 120*. INTERIOR OF UNITY TEMPLE, OAK PARK, ILLINOIS. A drawing from Frank Lloyd Wright's *Drawings for a Living Architecture* (copyright 1959). REPRODUCED BY PERMISSION OF THE HORIZON PRESS, NEW YORK CITY

a way as to obscure the architectural forces required to establish a sense of firmness, composure and simple dignity. This is perhaps less true of the interior where Wright's sense of playfulness led him to hang his personally designed chandeliers from the high ceiling, give the walls zebra stripes, and put stairs, galleries and entries in such relationship to each other that the innocent visitor finds himself in a veritable maze.

The finest of Wright's "Prairie" houses is the Robie House (*Plate 121*). Corresponding as closely as any building could to the theories of its designer, this house is thoroughly successful. Its broad, asymmetrically hovering roof, cantilevered to a maximum degree for porches, clings (as Wright wished it) to the flat site. The horizontality harmonizing with prairie land, is further accentuated by the long, thin Roman bricks and framing bands of concrete. The interior, somewhat dark from the extended overhang and the low ceilings, displays Wright's dream of integrating

*Plate 121.* FREDERICK ROBIE HOUSE, CHICAGO, ILLINOIS. 1908–1909. Designed by Frank Lloyd Wright. The architect's basic principles of architectural design were never better satisfied than here. It fits the flat site by clinging to the ground with its long, spread-out roofline. A garage is part of the house, where previously the carriage house had been removed from the house. Inside Wright contrived to make space flow from one room to another by leaving out walls and doors where they had usually appeared, and by associating the inner spaces with the exterior yard by means of windows and interlocking walls. Most of the furniture and fixtures were produced to fit the exact spot needing them. There is a complete harmony of building, furnishings and site. *Courtesy,* HISTORIC AMERICAN BUILDINGS SURVEY, WASHINGTON, D. C. PHOTOGRAPH BY CERVIN ROBINSON

173

space by eliminating interior space separators wherever possible, calling it "flowing space," and romantically regarding it as his duty to relate the outer reaches of the house and yard to its interior. This he accomplished by mingling exterior with interior walls and by breaking the plane of the walls with protruding windows and overhanging ceilings. These extreme views on household organization have created major changes in house design ever since. Few houses are now built, with the exception of those mere replicas of past styles, which do not show the influence of Wright in one way or another. The high 19th-century ceiling has disappeared, larger windows give more light to interiors, and the dark, dank basement is no more. Wright should not perhaps be given entire credit for the revolution in house designing that has taken place, but he surely led the way.

During the 125 years preceding the First World War, American architecture went through various phases corresponding to changes in government, economy and society. Latrobe and Mills with their conscious emulation of Greek and Roman style paralleled the art of the statesmen leaning heavily on past republican forms of government to establish their own. Mid-century architecture reflects the pride and affluence of the industrial society seeking in less imaginative ways than one could wish a means of living with greater comfort amid the riches made available through exploitation of natural resources and inventive genius. While not really rising to the occasion as a whole, a few leaders appeared like Richardson and Sullivan who had vision beyond their days, and it was upon these that Wright built his own legendary career, a search for the way out of the 19th-century morass of revival styles, bad taste and material waste to a new way of life exemplified by his insistence on the freedom of the individual so ably expressed by the variety and beauty of his own architectural designs. As the 20th century unfolds we become increasingly aware, not only of the firm substructure of the best of the previous century's designs, but of the marvelous architectural development which has proceeded so fast, in spite of public doubt and disfavor in the early decades, to a point where it may be said that America is the center of modern architecture.

# PAINTING AND SCULPTURE

## by Alan Gowans

## THEME OF THE PERIOD

THROUGHOUT history, two forces have been at work to shape American culture—one, a native tendency towards isolated self-sufficiency; the other, influences from Europe making for change. Never was their interaction more obvious, however, than in the 19th-century development of painting and sculpture in the United States.

During this age, the native tendency toward self-sufficiency is represented in their several ways by native genre- and landscape-painters of many sorts; by the many portrait painters who carry on 18th-century if not limner traditions; by "primitives" of all shades, professional through amateur; by tombstone- and ship-carvers and their counterparts, sign- and coachpainters; by illustrators in books, magazines, and easel pictures; by popular artists from John Rogers and Currier & Ives' contributors to early comic-strip and motion-picture creators. Numerically, such artists comprise the great bulk of painting and sculpture done in the United States during the 19th century. In their persons and works, traditional attitudes toward the nature of the visual arts and the function of artists in society remained unquestioned. The other force working on 19th-century American art is represented by those comparatively few "advance-guard" or self-consciously "fine" artists who, if they have not been to or come from Europe, are at least aware to some degree of what is going on there, and follow at varying removes the tides of European taste and the great shift in thinking about what artists do in and for society that is going on abroad. Their influence is more leaven than overt, however. For to most 19th-century Americans the great cultural capitals of Europe—especially Paris, focus of the great revolution going on in art—seem very far away. Nineteenth-century American painting and sculpture reflected, more clearly than almost any other aspect

*177*

of life, the nation's traditional policy of non-entanglement in European affairs, enunciated by Washington and maintained essentially unbroken until Theodore Roosevelt's time. By 1900, advance-guard painting in Europe not merely looked very different, it had become a different kind of activity from what it was in 1800. Where once the accepted purpose of painting had been to please and edify by the discovery and perpetuation of objects or themes which possessed a quality called Beauty, and were capable of arousing "beautiful feelings" of pleasure, or awe or nostalgia, now it was to inspire and instruct through the creation and representation of a Reality of its own. Where once painting had been a medium through which experiences and ideas could be transmitted, now the act of painting was itself becoming the experience, the spectator's role being to share vicariously in it. But in America this basic change was hardly recognized, except by a few isolated individuals. John Singer Sargent or "the Ten" in New York represented in their different ways the general level of educated American taste by the end of the 19th century; and they were all much closer to Impressionism of the 1860's than to, say, Picasso in the early 1900's.

Yet the history of 19th-century painting and sculpture in the United States is like the motion of some planet being constantly affected by the subtle pull of another, unseen body. Only by keeping in mind that (besides the overt interaction of "native" with European influences) a major revolution in the concept of what art does in and for society is going on, and that American artists' thinking about themselves and their work is affected by it consciously or not, can we fully understand or properly appreciate what is happening in 19th-century American art and be prepared for the 20th-century development of the United States into a world center of "modern art."

## "A PERIOD OF ADJUSTMENT": FROM COLONIES TO NATION

THE first thirty-five years of the new Republic's cultural life were—perhaps inevitably—complicated, confused, experimental. All sorts of new possibilities presented themselves; all sorts of new ideas and old traditions were jostling for acceptance. At the time, it was difficult for many of the more thoughtful artists to find their bearings, and some of them went literally to pieces under the pressure of uncertainties and frustrations. In retrospect, however, the mainstream of development is clear enough. These thirty-five years were a time of transition from 18th-century classical to Victorian traditions, from concern with theoretical aesthetic values to an emphasis on literary and symbolic associations characteristic of the 19th century. And in retrospect, too, it is clear that there were two main lines of cultural development running throughout the period, both of them stemming from the implications of Independence. There was, first, a perpetuation and even a strengthening of colonial attitudes, on the part of those Americans—perhaps a majority—for whom Independence primarily meant isolation from Europe, a justification for withdrawal into self-sufficiency, an excuse for ignoring European culture and concentrating on simpler, native, utilitarian arts. Then, on the other hand, there was an unprecedented and conscious attempt to plant in America standards of taste comparable to or even more advanced than anything in Europe, by those painters and sculptors who considered Independence all the more reason to study and learn from European culture as never before. Now, they felt, Americans could study European models without fear of becoming docile imitators. They would prove what the Revolution had so dramatically implied, that institutions and creations based on republican liberty are inherently superior to the decadent manifestations of tyrannous absolutisms; they would take whatever the Old World had to offer in confident certainty of transforming it into something finer, nobler, more vital. And if all these contradictory currents made the period confusing, they also made it an exciting ferment.

### SURVIVAL OF COLONIAL ATTITUDES

IN pre-Revolutionary times the general cultural level of the bulk of the American population was low, and, among the lower classes especially, survivals of 17th-century and medieval traditions were common. Much of this was perpetuated into the 19th century. In the early Republic you could still find plenty of folk artists—professionals like tombstone-cutters and sign-painters, as well as amateurs from scrimshaw decorators to spinster watercolorists and needleworkers—working in timeless, styleless manners traceable back to the Middle Ages. Most are anonymous and long

180

*Plate 122.* THE PEACEABLE KINGDOM. By Edward Hicks (1780–1849). Beginning his career as a sign painter in 1799, Hicks later put his talent at the service of a schismatic movement among extreme Quakers led by his cousin Elias Hicks, aiming at reform of worldliness and intensification of Quaker spiritual life. To this end he painted dozens of versions of the Peaceable Kingdom—a theme which to his mind represented the spirit of original Quakerism, now so sadly degenerated. In them the spirit of Early Christian art lives again; these are good works conducive to salvation, icons in the old sense of "the substance of things hoped for"—the coming of that age described in *Isaiah* XI, 6–9, when "the wolf also shall dwell with the lamb, and the leopard shall lie down with the kid, and the calf and the young lion and the fatling together; and a little child shall lead them . . . They shall not hurt or destroy in all my holy mountain: for the earth shall be full of the knowledge of the Lord." In the background appears a naive rendering of Benjamin West's 1771 painting of Penn's Treaty with the Indians (now in the Pennsylvania Academy of Fine Arts) known to Hicks through a print. *Courtesy,* THE WORCESTER ART MUSEUM, WORCESTER, MASS.

*Plate 123.*

TAMANEND, figurehead of the U.S.S. Delaware,
launched at Norfolk, Virginia, 1820. Carved
by William Luke of Norfolk. (1790–1839).
Joiner, furniture-maker, shipcarver, a native of
Norfolk, William Luke was called in his
obituary an "untutored genius"; looking at this
accomplished piece of sculpture, we may well
agree. In such a work is the culmination of
two centuries of folk art in America. Here
survives the old tradition of colored sculpture
characteristic of the great ages of sculpture
from the Golden Age of Greece to medieval
cathedrals and T'ang China—now relegated to
children's toys. Here too survives the old tradition
of anonymous jack-of-all-trades craftsmanship
on the frontier, alternately turning skills to
parlor tables and wagon-tongues, summer-beams
and snowshoes. And finally, here survives the
old tradition of artistic endeavor involving
collaboration between the intellectual and the
artisan. In his humble way, Luke worked in the
same great tradition as the sculptors of the
Parthenon and Chartres, giving visual form to
ideas provided him by others—in this case,
the Delaware congressmen who suggested a bust
of this legendary chief of the Lenape Indians
as approximately emblematic of their State, citing
his description in the writing of Moravian
missionary John Heckewelder. Less erudite
generations of midshipmen at the Naval Academy
have long confused it with the better known
Indian hero Tecumseh. *Courtesy*, UNITED
STATES NAVAL ACADEMY, ANNAPOLIS,
MARYLAND. OFFICIAL U. S. NAVY PHOTOGRAPH

forgotten; only occasionally would the name of a *naive* painter like Edward
Hicks be preserved, and then only (in his own time at least) for reasons
extraneous to art (*Plate 122*). In the same general category, too, were
many of the itinerant and local portrait painters with which the country
still abounded. Among them were often men of considerable skill like
Jacob Eichholz of Lancaster in Pennsylvania or William Luke, the "untutored genius" of a ship-carver in Norfolk, Virginia (*Plate 123*); sometimes,

*181*

*Plate 124.*
COLONEL WILLIAM TAYLOR, by Ralph Earl (1751–1801). Colonial traditions survive almost unimpaired in this portrait of 1790. So close to the old art of the limners is it, so little resemblance does it have to Reynolds' or any other "grand manner," that you could hardly guess Earl had spent six or seven years studying in England. Vestiges of primitive additive composition are everywhere apparent—in the combination of side-view legs and frontal torso; in the left hand, so awkwardly foreshortened that it is obviously bigger than the right; in the landscape background, flat as if pasted onto the wall. Clearly this is a painted drawing, rather than a painting in the professional sense. *Courtesy*, ALBRIGHT-KNOX ART GALLERY, BUFFALO, NEW YORK. CHARLES CLIFTON FUND

too, like Ralph Earl of Litchfield, Connecticut (*Plate 124*), they even had some European study behind them. But whether by choice or by force of cultural circumstances in rural areas and isolated hinterland towns, their art seldom developed much past their 18th-century, or in some cases even 17th-century, face-painting precedents.

Somewhat more advanced was the art created for the urban middle class. In the small towns and cities of the new Republic a middle class, largely mercantile, had been developing for a century past and now, with the expulsion of the old British upper official class, it assumed new status and importance. Knowledgeable enough to disdain country and folk art, but still far from sophisticated in cultural matters, this class admired literal transcriptions of nature, technical dexterity, anecdotage—art that informed and entertained, or both, rather than more specifically aesthetic creations. Already in colonial times a considerable number of artisan-painters had appeared working in and for this middle-class taste, and they multiplied

*Plate 125.* FOURTH OF JULY CELEBRATION IN CENTER SQUARE, PHILADELPHIA, painted in 1819 by John Lewis Krimmel (1789–1821). As in 17th-century Holland, the triumph of republican institutions inspired individuals with new delight in familiar surroundings—a world which now seemed so satisfactorily under their control—so in the early American Republic, independence was followed by a burst of topographical and genre painting for bourgeois consumption. Besides Krimmel, one might cite Francis Guy (1760–1820), William Birch (1755–1834) and his son Thomas (1779–1851) and many more. This painting by Krimmel is of special interest because it also typifies so well bourgeois pride in civic progress. Behind the cross-section of Philadelphia citizenry rises the Pumping Station of the Philadelphia Water Works, designed by Benjamin Henry Latrobe in the most advance-guard manner of Parisian rationalist LeDoux, and near it is the "Nymph of the Schuylkill" by the city's leading sculptor, William Rush. And in Krimmel's case the pedigree of this kind of genre is particularly well demonstrated, too; according to Dunlap, his art was based on the fashionable anecdotal painting of David Wilkie, reigning favorite of Regency England, which in turn derived directly from the Dutch 17th-century genre. *Courtesy,* HISTORICAL SOCIETY OF PENNSYLVANIA, PHILADELPHIA

*183*

*Plate 126.* BALD EAGLE, Plate from *The Birds of America* (1827). Published 1827–1838 (folio edition) by John James Audubon (1785–1851). From the time of the first explorers, the distinctive flora and fauna of the New World were objects of wonder to European eyes, and subjects for some of the earliest art done in the hemisphere. Independence spurred a new pride in American distinctiveness on the part of Americans; in succeeding years Americans supported one book after another describing American nature, including William Bartram's (1739–1823) *Travels* of 1791, Alexander Wilson's (1766–1813) 9-volume *American Ornithology* of 1808–1814, and, most famous of all, Audubon's *Birds* and his *Viviparous Quadrupeds of North America* (plates published, 1842–1845; text, 1846–1854). *Courtesy,* THE NEW-YORK HISTORICAL SOCIETY, NEW YORK CITY

rapidly after the War. Their art represented a wide range of skills and interests. It included genre, of which John Lewis Krimmel's painting is so typical (*Plate 125*); the mechanical physiognotrace profile portraits of James Sharples (1751–1811) and Charles Saint-Memin (1770–1852); and the conversation portrait pieces of Matthew Pratt (1734–1805) and William Dunlap (1766–1839). It included quasi-scientific art like the topographical illustrations of W. R. Birch (1755–1834) and his son Thomas (1779–1851), the botanical and ornithological illustrations of William Bartram (1739–1823), Alexander Wilson (1766–1813) and J. J. Audubon (1785–1851). Also a typical middle-class expression was the development of political cartooning, inspired by the rise of a party system dependent on swaying the opinions of the multitude (*Plates 128 and 129*); and the rather naive attempts of cabinetmakers and woodworkers like Samuel McIntire to commemorate national ideals in sculpture (*Plate 130*). Most representative of all was the work of Charles Willson Peale and his family; in their self-consciously American egalitarianism, their common-sense refusal to attempt

*Plate 127.* BUFFALO DANCE, by George Catlin (1796–1872). Some 19th-century American artists chose Indian themes for their romantic associations with pristine virtue, American heritage, and the like. Catlin, Seth Eastman (1808–1875) and several other well-known painters of Indians belonged in the older tradition of objective reporting on the distinctive "wonders" of the New World, newly stimulated by pride in Independence, in the same manner as natural scientists Bartram, Wilson and Audubon. *Courtesy,* SMITHSONIAN INSTITUTION, WASHINGTON, D. C.

advance-guard styles, their scientific bent, the whole character of middle-class art is perfectly exemplified (*Plates 131–133*).

For any artists aspiring higher than lower- or middle-class taste, it had been as normal and necessary in colonial times to leave the American provinces and go to the political and cultural capital of the Empire as for

Plate 128.

A PEEP INTO THE ANTI-FEDERAL CLUB, anonymous cartoon, New York, 1793. It is no accident that the popular arts developed so remarkably in the United States, for they are essentially democratic, creations of and for public moods and opinions. In such a cartoon we see the main lines of American political history already beginning to appear—the division between conservatives and progressives, between the aristocratic principle of inequality and the egalitarian ideal, between those who see government as the defender of natural aristocratic rights, and those who see it as the preserver of egalitarian opportunity.

Here a Federalist supporter presents his case. Jefferson, standing to propose "whether it is better in the mind to knock down dry goods with this hammer or with his head to contrive some means of knocking down a Government" sets the pace for his shiftless band of intellectual parasites on the sound men of the market place—visionaries longing "for such a government as they have in Saturn," ne'er-do-wells, drunkards, sensualists, pirates, Negroes—all of them working under the Devil's approving eye. The work is still 18th-century in spirit, however—crowded in composition, complicated in meaning, more related to pamphleteering than journalism. Twenty years later and the technique will be very different, as we see in *Plate 129*.
*Courtesy*, FREE LIBRARY OF PHILADELPHIA, RIDGEWAY BRANCH

186

TERRAPIN'S ADDRESS.

Reflect, my friend, as you pass by ;
As you are, now, so, once, was I ;
As I am now, so you may be :—
Laid on your back to die like me !
I was, indeed, true Sailor born ;
To quit my friend, in death, I scorn.
Once Jemmy seem'd to be my friend,
But, basely, brought me to my end !
Of head bereft, and light, and breath,
I hold Fidelity, in death :—
For " Sailor's Rights" I still will tug :
And, Madison to death I'll hug,
For his perfidious zeal display'd,
For " Sailor's Rights and for Free Trade."
This small atonement I will have—
I'll hug down Jemmy to the grave.
Then Trade and Commerce shall be free
And Sailors have their liberty—
Of head bereft, and light, and breath,
The Terrapin, still true in death,
Will punish Jemmy's Perfidy :
Free Trade, and brave Sailors Free !

PASSENGERS REPLY.

Yes Terrapin, bereft of breath,
We see thee faithful still, in death :
Stick to't—" Free Trade and Sailor's Right :
Hug Jemmy—press him—hold him—bite—
Ne'er mind thy head—thou'lt live without it,
Spunk will preserve thy life—don't doubt it—
Down to the grave t'atone for sin,
Jemmy must go, with Terrapin.
Bear him but off, and we shall see
Commerce restor'd and Sailors Free !
Hug, Terrapin, with all thy might,
Now for " Free Trade and Sailor's Right :"
Stick to him, Terrapin, to thee the nation
Now eager looks :—then die for her salvation.
FLOREAT RESPUBLICA.
Banks of Goose Creek,
City of Washington,
15th April 1814.

FORD COLLECTION.

Plate 129. THE DEATH OF THE EMBARGO, newspaper cartoon drawn by John Wesley Jarvis (1780–1840) and engraved by Alexander Anderson, (1775–1870) in 1814. John Wesley Jarvis was a competent middle-class portrait painter, known as a bohemian and wit, and for his series of full-length portraits of military and naval heroes of the War of 1812 commissioned for the new New York City Hall. Here he applies his talents to satirizing the political fate of President James Madison, whose repeal of the Embargo Act (represented by the terrapin, in allusion to its being called a snapping turtle which destroyed American freedom on the seas) came too late to save him from the political effects of the resentment it aroused. Though the creature's head is severed, it clings to Madison's ear, dragging him down with it to destruction. In style Jarvis' cartoon already belongs to the 19th century; one of the first made to appear in a newspaper—the New York Evening Post—it concentrates on a single idea, using caricature, the grotesque, and humor to make its point. Popular arts like this helped educate a nation in the democratic process, and also set a precedent for an American "art of social consciousness" a century later. Courtesy, PRINTS DIVISION, THE NEW YORK PUBLIC LIBRARY, ASTOR, LENOX AND TILDEN FOUNDATIONS

187

artists from the rural shires of England. As Reynolds had come to London from Devon or Romney from Lancashire, so West (1738–1820) had come from Pennsylvania, Stuart (1755–1828) from Rhode Island, Copley (1738–1815) from Boston, Trumbull (1756–1843) from Connecticut, to make reputations and establish themselves in a place where patronage of advance-guard art was possible. Independence changed this situation. To remain in England meant becoming an expatriate, as it had not before. Loyal Americans felt it a duty to return home, if they could, and contribute their talents to the new nation; or if, as for West, returning was out of the

*Plate 130.*
GOVERNOR WINTHROP. Wooden bust by Samuel McIntire (1757–1811). In contrast to the mature professionalism of William Rush in cosmopolitan Philadelphia, Samuel McIntire in provincial Salem belonged almost entirely to the 18th-century artisan-craftsman tradition, as became painfully apparent in 1798 when his admirer and fellow-townsman, the Rev. William Bentley, commissioned him to make this bust from an old print, to be placed in the East Church. About the result, which in size and handling resembles nothing so much as a finial from some piece of Adamesque furniture, we can only agree with Bentley: "I cannot say that he has expressed in the bust anything which agrees with the Governour." McIntire's ship-carving, as compared to Rush's or William Luke's, showed the same stiff and primitively decorative character. *Courtesy*, AMERICAN ANTIQUARIAN SOCIETY, WORCESTER, MASSACHUSETTS

*Plate 131.* THE ARTIST IN HIS MUSEUM (1823). Self-portrait by Charles Willson Peale (1741–1827). Charles Willson Peale was an almost exact contemporary of Thomas Jefferson, and a kind of bourgeois version of him. He had many of the same qualities—versatility, insatiable curiosity of mind, dauntless Americanism. Peale had nothing of Jefferson's aristocratic sense for aesthetic tides of taste, however; though he had studied in London with West, he remained quite content to follow popular taste in America, and showed no inclination to lead it. In consequence, there was never for Peale any problem of a gulf between artists and society. In Peale's world, art, science, liberty and the pursuit of happiness were all part of the grand design of democratic living the new Republic had made possible—an attitude perfectly summed up in this self-portrait of Peale as an old man displaying the achievements of a lifetime assembled in his Independence Hall Museum: cases of stuffed American birds and animals, above them a row of his portraits of famous Americans, to the right his famous mastodon skeleton. *Courtesy,* THE PENNSYLVANIA ACADEMY OF THE FINE ARTS, PHILADELPHIA

189

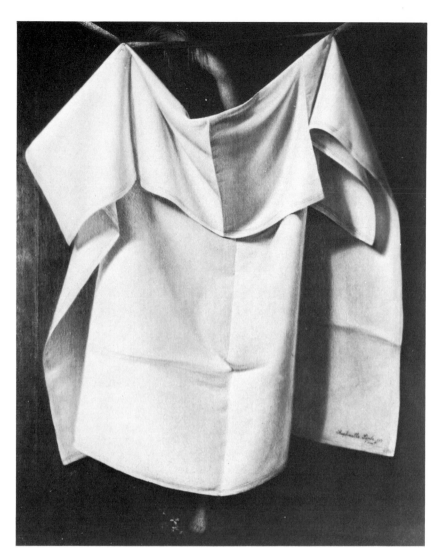

question, they could assist the cause by welcoming Americans in England and by sending pictures over (*Plate 134*). What success met American artists on their return from European training depended largely on how advanced an art they brought back, however.

Like so many other institutions in the new Republic, its upper-class structure was still fluid and tentative. For the first two decades, it was dominated by what came to be known as the Federalist party, essentially an old guard of wealthy merchants and landowners who had by luck or conviction chosen the patriot side in the Revolution and now considered themselves the country's rightful ruling class. Their hope was to minimize the

Revolution's implication for social democracy, limit its practical results to a replacement of British control by their own, and so carry on as an aristocratic oligarchy of the 18th-century sort. It followed that in matters artistic they favored a perpetuation of the 18th-century classical tradition in its last, Adamesque phase, which had already begun to appear in American architecture and furniture even before the Revolution; those painters and sculptors who could or would work in it enjoyed considerable success. Foremost among these were Gilbert Stuart, whose years in England and Ireland had made him master of the Gainsborough manner of portraiture (*Plate 135*), and exceeding wise in the whims of patrons; John Trumbull (*Plate 136*) well-connected champion of Reynolds' grand manner as practiced by Benjamin West; and William Rush, whose sculpture, though entirely a product of his local Philadelphia background, embodied comparable 18th-century classical principles (*Plate 137*). In short, for all its upper-class pretensions, this Federalist art remained essentially a perpetuation of colonial

*Plate 133.* THE COURT OF DEATH. By Rembrandt Peale (1778–1860). The secret of the Peale family's success was their entirely faithful and uncanny reflection of bourgeois taste. Though painted in 1820, this assemblage of figures in sculptural poses inviting "sublime" sentiments was thoroughly 18th-century "Gothick" in spirit, in form resembling West's neo-classicism of the 1770's—and a tremendous popular success. Partly the reason was that no matter how *retardataire* it was in fact, Peale presented it in good Early Victorian symbolic terms, sending it on tour as "The Great Moral Painting, a demonstration of the science of painting applied to its noblest purpose, the expression of moral sentiment." *Courtesy,* THE DETROIT INSTITUTE OF ARTS

191

attitudes and values rather than any basically new departure. Very different, however, was the attitude of the new party called, after its most representative figure, the Jeffersonians, which began to challenge Federalist political ascendancy with increasing success in the early years of the 19th century.

*JEFFERSONIAN ASPIRATIONS: ALLSTON, VANDERLYN, AND EARLY ADVANCE-GUARD PAINTING*

UNLIKE the Federalists, Jefferson and his followers saw in the Revolution potentialities for a fundamentally new kind of society, a distinctively

*Plate 134.* DEATH ON A PALE HORSE. By Benjamin West (1738–1820). This painting of 1817 is one of several versions going back to the turn of the century. It represents West's late "dread manner," the most determined attempt by the aging dean of American painters and President of the Royal Academy of Britain to accommodate himself to a shift in advance-guard taste that was inexorably leaving him behind. He described it as representing "the terrible sublime, and its various modifications . . . the opposite extremes of pity and terror," and thought of it as very up-to-date; but its tremendous popular success when exhibited in America only proved how *retardataire* American popular taste really was. For in retrospect the painting appears thoroughly 18th century in its artificiality of sentiment, far closer to the quaint "Gothick" of Walpole's *Castle of Otranto* than to the grandeurs of Turner or Delacroix, fully justifying Byron's jibe about "the dotard West, poor England's best." *Courtesy*, THE PENNSYLVANIA ACADEMY OF THE FINE ARTS, PHILADELPHIA

192

*Plate 135.* WASHINGTON AT DORCHESTER HEIGHTS. Painted in 1806 for Samuel Parkman of Boston by Gilbert Stuart (1755–1828). "There (in America) I expect to make a fortune by Washington alone. I calculate upon making a plurality of his portraits, whole lengths that will enable me to . . . repay my English and Irish creditors." So Stuart announced his intention of returning to the new United States after his years of study and practice abroad. He was fantastically successful; already in April 1795, there were 32 names on his list of subscribers, and ultimately the catalogue by Lawrence Park (*Gilbert Stuart*, New York, 1926) listed over a hundred Washington portraits by Stuart. Part of the reason for his success was a keen sense for stylistic tastes and trends. For culturally advanced Philadelphia, he devised the "Lansdowne" type of Washington, recondite with classical symbolism appealing to patrons who could understand the romantic classicism of the Early Victorian age; but for Boston and most other regions he perpetuated the more conservative 18th-century "grand manner" of portrait represented by this "Dorchester" type, which in theme and composition, if not in brushwork, could as well have come from the studio of Sir Joshua Reynolds. *Courtesy,* MUSEUM OF FINE ARTS, BOSTON (ON LOAN FROM THE BOSTON ATHENAEUM)

193

*Plate 136.* THE SURRENDER OF CORNWALLIS AT YORKTOWN, painted for the United States Capitol, 1817–1820, by John Trumbull (1756–1843). One of four paintings commissioned from Trumbull for the Rotunda under the dome of the Capitol. They were much criticized in their own time and since, ostensibly for historical inaccuracies, but more fundamentally, perhaps, because they belonged to an expiring 18th-century tradition of restraint, balance and decorum that was about to be displaced by the Victorian romantic point of view. And the fact may well be that Trumbull, who came from the same colonial social stratum as most of the Revolutionary leaders, and who had travelled up and down the coast sketching them soon after the War in preparation for just such a commission, captured the actual quality of this particular event far more accurately than the rising generation of romantic hero-worshipers wanted to admit.

*Washington . . . did strike even his contemporary associates as a reserved person. The war meant everything to him, but he did not—verbally speaking—rise to its major occasions. When the news of Saratoga reached him, he was having his portrait painted by Charles Willson Peale. 'Ah,' said Washington, reading the dispatch, 'Burgoyne is defeated'—and continued to sit. And when Cornwallis surrendered, Washington detailed one of his aides to notify Congress instead of composing the message himself. This goes beyond the laconic to a disappointing flatness.* (Marcus Cunliffe, *George Washington, Man and Monument*, Boston, 1958, Chapter 3.)

*Courtesy*, ARCHITECT OF THE CAPITOL, WASHINGTON, D. C. PHOTOGRAPH, LIBRARY OF CONGRESS

194

*Plate 137.*

WATER NYMPH AND BITTERN ("Nymph of
the Schuylkill"). Bronze replica made in 1854 of
the original life-size painted figure in pine made
in 1810 by William Rush (1756–1833) to
stand beside Latrobe's Center Square Water
Works in Philadelphia. Essentially belonging to
the last phase of 18th-century classical tradition,
its symbolism was drawn from Rush's copy of
the *Artist's Repository or Encyclopaedia of
the Fine Arts* (London, 1808)—the pose from a
classical Venus cast provided by Nicholas Biddle
for the Columbarium, "an association of the
Artists in America for the protection and
encouragement of the Fine Arts" founded in
1794, of which Rush was a charter member (it
was ancestor of the Pennsylvania Academy,
founded 1805). For the actual carving, however,
Rush insisted on working from a model, using
Nancy Vanuxem, daughter of a merchant who
served with Rush on the Watering Committee
of the Councils. (See *Plate 190*). Anticipating
in all these respects the social status and
prerequisites of a 19th-century professional
sculptor, Rush still perpetuated colonial traditions
in his regular utilitarian profession of ship-carver
and his predilection for painted sculpture; he
was thus a transitional figure, well justifying his
title of "first native American sculptor."
*Courtesy*, COMMISSIONERS OF FAIRMOUNT
PARK, PHILADELPHIA. PHOTOGRAPH,
PHILADELPHIA MUSEUM OF ART

*Plate 138.* MARIUS AMID THE RUINS OF CARTHAGE, painted by John Vanderlyn (1775–1852) during his second stay in Paris, 1805–1808. To us this picture, with its head copied from a marble bust in Rome, its body a pastiche of miscellaneous antique statuary, its background a model constructed in Vanderlyn's studio, now seems the quintessence of sententious artificiality. Not so when Vanderlyn was painting it. Then it was extravagantly admired as a perfect example of the neo-classical doctrine of Beauty. Beauty, so that doctrine went, is not absolute, but rather something determined by a consensus of the educated "generality of mankind." Since it was universally agreed—or so it seemed at that moment in history—that of all art Graeco-Roman is the most beautiful, it follows that the most beautiful painting is that which most perfectly imitates Graeco-Roman forms. So thought the Emperor Napoleon, when he awarded Vanderlyn a gold medal for this painting at the 1808 Salon; so thought advance-guard critics in Europe. And so fortified, Vanderlyn returned to America with high hopes that his kind of painting would in addition be recognized as the most appropriate for a Republic claiming to be the reincarnation of Ancient Rome. *Courtesy*, M. H. DE YOUNG MEMORIAL MUSEUM, SAN FRANCISCO

196

and independently American way of life, and they looked for a fundamentally new kind of art to express it. Architecture in particular they conceived less in aesthetic terms than as a means of communication, a visual language which would proclaim through conscious and deliberate symbolism the revolutionary ideals and aspirations they believed inherent in the idea of a Republic. And in architecture their new concepts were soon accepted. Such a building as Jefferson's Capitol at Richmond (*Plate 2*) in 1785 was not only advance-guard in American terms, but was one of the first conscious revivals of Roman architecture for systematically symbolic purposes anywhere; and by 1820 Roman or Greek Revival architecture was practically the official American way of building. But when a comparable departure from 18th-century principles was attempted in painting by Washington Allston and John Vanderlyn, it was a different story, unfortunately.

Allston and Vanderlyn went to Paris together in 1803; when they returned to settle in America a few years later, they brought back with them the most advanced painting of the day—the new ideals and attitude that would inform the Victorian age. Like Jeffersonian classical architecture, theirs was an art primarily concerned with symbolism of a more or less overt and literary sort. They were ready to put America in the van of European painting, as Jefferson had put her in the van of European architecture; but America was not ready for them. French-trained Vanderlyn's painting was a counterpart of the Empire style in furniture and the Roman Revival in architecture, recognized as such by Napoleon himself when he awarded the American painter a gold medal in 1808 for the moving associations of "Marius," brooding on the fate of men and nations amid the ruins of Carthage (*Plate 138*). But whereas there were a good many Americans architecturally sophisticated enough to accept the principle of reviving Roman building forms to symbolize modern republican ideals and aspirations, few were prepared to accept a revival of Roman forms in painting as comparably "American." When commissions were being awarded for murals to decorate the Capitol as restored after 1815, Vanderlyn was passed over in favor of the more conservative John Trumbull (*Plate 136*), and public taste never caught up with him until it was much too late to save his career.

*197*

Washington Allston represented basically the same kind of literary and symbolic mind; his was the kind of romantic impulse that motivated the Gothic Revival. He tried to bring to American painting the kind of advance-guard romantic attitude to Nature he had learned in England and France

*Plate 139.* THE RETURN OF COLUMBUS, mural in the Rotunda of the United States Capitol, Washington, by John Vanderlyn, 1842. As Vanderlyn's much-admired *Marius* was the auspicious beginning of his career, so this much-criticized *Columbus* was in effect its end. And ironically enough, it failed more than anything else because it appeared out of its time. Had it been painted in 1815 when Vanderlyn was at the height of his powers and the Classical Revival sweeping into popular favor, the story might have been different. But then official patronage had bypassed Vanderlyn in favor of John Trumbull's more conservative "grand manner," and in the intervening years Vanderlyn had been trying too long and too desperately to accommodate his ideals to American conditions. His command of classical principles remains firm, but it is compromised by now *retardataire* attempts to emulate the grand manner and intimations of fashionable romantic history painting. The result is a painting well short of Vanderlyn's best classical creations, but still classical enough in well-composed balance and dignity to bore an age increasingly infatuated with the idea of picturesqueness. *Courtesy,* ARCHITECT OF THE CAPITOL, WASHINGTON, D. C. PHOTOGRAPH, LIBRARY OF CONGRESS

198

(see *Plate 140*)—the sort of melodramatic feelings evoked by man's eternal struggle with Fate and the elements exemplified by Turner in England and Delacroix's painting of the 1820's in France, rather than the kind of 18-century Gothick implicit in West's much-admired *Death on a Pale Horse* (*Plate 134*), *Saul*, or *Lear*. But the sentiments Allston expressed in his famous letter to William Dunlap (author of the 1834 *History of the Rise and Progress of the Arts of Design in the United States*) about

*Plate 140.* RISING OF A THUNDERSTORM AT SEA, by Washington Allston (1779–1843). In contrast to the older generation of American painters who still clung to naively "Gothick" kinds of thrills and chills, the young Washington Allston as early as 1804 here shows himself master of mature Early Victorian romanticism. Through one of its most characteristic themes—the open boat on a stormy sea—he evokes its most characteristic feeling, the vicarious awe aroused by spectacles of puny men confronting the mighty and inexorable forces of Nature. *Courtesy*, MU-SEUM OF FINE ARTS, BOSTON

*Plate 141.* THE DEAD MAN RESTORED TO LIFE BY THE BONES OF ELISHA, by Washington Allston, 1811–1813. Returning from his European studies, Allston found little acceptance of the advance-guard romanticism he had mastered there; 18th-century traditions still dominated early 19th-century American taste. Attempting to adjust to the situation, Allston reverted to such Hogarthian genre as *The Poor Author and the Rich Bookseller*, and in works like this, to the older kind of "Gothick" romanticism—a contrived melodrama based on the short reference in II *Kings* xiii, 21, to a corpse by chance "cast into the sepulchre of Elisha: and when the man was let down, and touched the bones of Elisha, he revived, and stood on his feet." The attempted compromise provoked fatal inner tensions, made manifest in Allston's torturous switherings over what was to have been his masterpiece, *Belshazzar's Feast*; working on it first in the new manner, then in the old, then back to the new again, he finally destroyed his creativity altogether. *Courtesy*, THE PENNSYLVANIA ACADEMY OF THE FINE ARTS, PHILADELPHIA

200

"the poetry of color" in Venetian painting, "procreative in its nature, giving birth to a thousand things which the eye cannot see, and distinct from their cause," were even less intelligible in the early 19th-century America than Vanderlyn's neoclassicism; it would take another twenty years for the average educated American's understanding of picturesqueness and romantic Nature to reach the point where Allston's kind of romanticism could enter the mainstream of cultural life in the United States.

TOWARD AN AMERICAN ART: THE EARLY VICTORIAN PERIOD

(*circa* 1825—*circa* 1860)

THE deaths of Thomas Jefferson and John Adams in 1826, and the rise of Andrew Jackson to prominence in national politics, were symbolic of the end of an era. The experimental years of the Republic were over; the main outlines of its future development began to take firm shape. The new nation would be neither the Federalists' kind of oligarchy nor a thorough-going Jeffersonian democracy, but something in between. In the older Eastern States an oligarchy was beginning to form, though based less on land and heredity and more on commercial and industrial fortunes than the Federalists would have had it; but as yet the oligarchic ideal was quite overshadowed by the rapid development of the Midwest, which gave a basically Jeffersonian democratic character to the whole period. Problems persisted, as always, and some of them—sectionalism and slavery in partic-ular—were ominous; but by and large people in this age were basically motivated by an immense confidence in the future and a sense of security unprecedented in the world before. America was a big, rich, empty country where there was room for everybody and the crushing problems of inter-national war, unemployment, monopolistic capitalism and totalitarian social-ism were still over the horizon. Success of the American Experiment seemed assured. This is the mood we find overwhelmingly expressed in every aspect of painting and sculpture of the period.

By the mid-1820's literary associations and extraneous symbolism were being more and more taken for granted as primary values in painting and

sculpture. These are the distinguishing qualities of the Victorian attitude to
art; their general acceptance marks the beginning of the Victorian era
proper, which lasts well into the 20th century and indeed in some enclaves
still lives on. Since arts concerned with storytelling and visual description—
the most obvious kinds of extraneous symbolism—are inherently easier to
comprehend than arts concerned with more purely pictorial and aesthetic
values, and given the nation's great self-satisfaction with the prevailing
state of American affairs, it is not surprising that in this first phase of the

202

*Plate 142.* CONGRESS HALL, painted 1821, by Samuel F. B. Morse (1791–1872). Studying
this meticulous record of the old House of Representatives as it looked when Latrobe rebuilt it
after 1814 (it is the present Statuary Hall), we are not surprised at Morse's later photographic
interests—he was one of the first Americans to study Daguerre's process. Yet this is more than
pre-photography. Morse classicizes the scene; in contrast to contemporary descriptions of what
was all too often a brawling and disorderly legislative body, he presents an image of *gravitas*,
*pietas*, *simplicitas*—all those Roman qualities of seriousness, self-discipline, and clarity requisite
and proper in a reincarnation of the *senatus populusque Romanus*. *Courtesy*, THE COLLECTION
OF THE CORCORAN GALLERY OF ART, WASHINGTON, D. C.

Victorian era, until the Civil War, American painting and sculpture enjoyed public support and sympathetic understanding as never (relatively speaking) before or since.

In the course of these thirty-five years, three phases of taste may be identified—by no means mutually exclusive, but still more or less definable in terms of the type of symbolism and extraneous association predominantly

*Plate 143.* EXHIBITION GALLERY OF THE LOUVRE, painted 1832, by Samuel F. B. Morse. When Morse, sculptor Horatio Greenough, and writer James Fenimore Cooper were all together in Paris in 1832, they represented the cream of American advance-guard culture; this picture, painted at that time, epitomizes their Early Victorian concept of artistic creation. Art is above all for them a matter of eclectic erudition. Here the student sits, surrounded by the whole history of painting—or at least, for the Early Victorian painter, all that mattered: Titian and Claude, Van Dyck and Poussin, Murillo and Coreggio; Venetian, Florentine, Flemish, French painting in the Renaissance tradition. His training consists of studying them, so that when the time comes, he will unerringly know how to select the most appropriate historical forms to express given ideas; it is thus the counterpart to Cole's *Architect's Dream* (see *Plate 153*). *Courtesy,* SYRACUSE UNIVERSITY COLLECTION, SYRACUSE, NEW YORK

203

favored. In the decade 1825–1835, classical themes and the large, crisply outlined forms associated with the Greek Revival had most appeal to educated American taste. 1835–1845 were years when the romantic natural-

*Plate 144.*
PORTRAIT OF THOMAS HANDASYD PERKINS, painted by Thomas Sully (1783–1872) in 1831–1832. Though the sitter is not in Roman costume, and a setting of Roman arches is only vaguely suggested, this is nonetheless a truly classical portrait; Sully's presentation of patrician bearing and power is such that a toga would be superfluous. Looking at his portrait of this first king of Boston's merchant princes, it is no surprise to learn that Perkins refused to be George Washington's Secretary of the Navy, on grounds that his personal fleet was more numerous, and he would do the country better service by looking after his own property.
PHOTOGRAPH, *courtesy* MUSEUM OF FINE ARTS, BOSTON. PAINTING ON DEPOSIT FROM THE BOSTON ATHENAEUM, BOSTON, MASSACHUSETTS

ism we associate with the Greek Revival was particularly favored. It in turn generated a persuasive vogue for picturesqueness which characterized the years 1845–1860, affecting the treatment of every style and subject.

*Plate 145.*
PORTRAIT OF AMOS LAWRENCE, by Chester Harding (1792–1866). Harding, famed as the "frontier painter," is perhaps more interesting as a symbol of the egalitarian opportunity of the early Republic than as a painter *per se*. It is extraordinary to consider that, beginning as a man who at the age of twenty barely knew how to read, let alone paint, he could "improve himself" to the point where he mixed freely with the great of Eastern society—like this famous Boston philanthropist—and painted portraits instinct with basic classical principles. *Courtesy*, NATIONAL GALLERY OF ART, WASHINGTON, D. C. GIVEN IN MEMORY OF THE RT. REV. WILLIAM LAWRENCE BY HIS CHILDREN, 1944

*Plate 146.* PAT LYON AT THE FORGE, by John Neagle (1796–1865). A conspicuous example of the sturdy self-reliance and prosperity fostered by the young American Republic is this portrait, commissioned in 1826 and completed 1827. Though at the time Lyon was a rich man, he specified "I want you to paint me at work at my anvil, with my sleeves rolled up and a leather apron on," in the smithy where he got his start in life. Most significant is the cupola seen through the window in the background; it represents the Walnut Street Jail, where as a young man Lyon was incarcerated for several months on an entirely groundless charge of robbing the Bank of Pennsylvania. That he could rise above what he considered upper-class persecution to become a successful hydraulic engineer and prominent citizen, Lyon attributed to the virtues of American democratic processes; this picture was specifically commissioned as a monument to them. *Courtesy*, MUSEUM OF FINE ARTS, BOSTON. PAINTING ON DEPOSIT FROM THE BOSTON ATHENAEUM, BOSTON, MASSACHUSETTS

*EARLY VICTORIAN ROMANTIC CLASSICISM*

THE decade from 1825 to 1835 marked the height of the Greek Revival in American architecture, when Grecian forms were adapted to everything from banks to privies, by every kind of builder, from professional architects capable of the most erudite accuracy to local carpenters interpreting guide-book plates in their own idiom. Painting and sculpture in this decade manifested a comparable preoccupation with classical themes and forms, and a comparable diversity in handling them. The range of classical expression in painting is well illustrated by a comparison of such representative figures as Thomas Sully, Samuel F. B. Morse, Chester Harding and John Neagle, all at their peak in these years. Morse is entirely a man of the new Victorian period; he understands completely the Victorian principle of using the art of the past for symbolic and allusive purposes, and he knows the art of the past well; when he paints the legislators of the Republic assembled (*Plate 142*), or the hero Lafayette, or his own daughter, he needs no specifically Grecian paraphernalia to achieve an expression of classical man reincarnate, in sure command of a measured, ordered, precisely defined American classical world. The same spirit animates Sully's work, though in form it is more reminiscent of 18-century classicism, deriving from Stuart (*Plate 144*). Neagle and Harding represent counterparts in painting to those local classical revival builders who flourished all over America in these years; their classicism is an indigenous vernacular, spontaneously nourished by a confidence, security, and self-sufficiency in American life, so inherent as to foster instinctive understanding of the basic principles of classical art—definition, precision, commensuration, self-containment (*Plates 145* and *146*).

Since it was through statuary that Graeco-Roman art was chiefly known to the 19th century, the classical enthusiasms of Early Victorian America supported a remarkable efflorescence of sculptors, comparable to the painters' diversity of range and deep native roots. Morse's counterpart in sculpture was Horatio Greenough—erudite, theoretically minded, far enough ahead of popular taste to suffer for it, as the reception of his great *Washington* so dramatically revealed (*Plate 147*). Hiram Powers' sculpture, like Sully's painting, was thoroughly classical in feeling but retained lingering overtones of 18th-century rococo (*Plate 148*). John Frazee's career parallels Chester Harding's; beginning life as a poor tombstone-cutter in New Jersey, the spirit of the times encouraged his spontaneous evolution toward a remarkable classical vernacular expression (*Plate 149*).

*Plate 147.*
GEORGE WASHINGTON. Heroic statue, by Horatio Greenough (1805–1852). When the 1832 Congress commissioned a $5000 statue of Washington from Horatio Greenough to be placed in the Capitol Rotunda, he was twenty-seven years old, and the naive enthusiasm of Early Victorian America for classical allusion was at its height. There was universal approval for Greenough's idea of combining a body of the famous Olympian Zeus with a head derived from Houdon's statue of Washington, and unifying the whole with the cold neo-classical stylization of Antonio Canova. Nine years later, when Greenough shipped the finished work from his Florence studio to Washington, that enthusiasm was beginning to wane; hard things were said about the artificiality of his concept. And when in 1843 the statue was moved out of doors, because of the sculptor's failure to take its architectural setting into account, disenchantment was complete. Its nakedness, painfully apparent on the mall, provoked first scandalized resentment, then ridicule. Finally, in the 1890's the statue came to rest in an obscure corner of the Smithsonian Institution where now it can be admired, if not on aesthetic grounds, at least as the largest of monuments to the dream of Rome renascent on the Potomac. *Courtesy*, SMITHSONIAN INSTITUTION, WASHINGTON, D. C.

*Plate 148*. THE GREEK SLAVE, by Hiram Powers (1805–1873). Born in Vermont, growing up in a family that moved successively to western New York and Ohio, graduating to portrait sculpture from clockmaking and waxworks, Hiram Powers in both his early life and his art was the perfect embodiment of the culture of Greater New England in Early Victorian America. After a few years' working at portraiture in Washington, Powers settled permanently in Italy (1837). *The Greek Slave* was first exhibited in 1843, with such great success that Powers made five more copies and acquired national stature; but as Montgomery C. Meigs, superintendent of construction at the Capitol put it when Powers demanded what Meigs considered undue freedom on the basis of proven genius, "The immense popularity of the Greek Slave is probably due to its meaning being within the comprehension of all. Its eminent beauty alone would not have gained it such success." Precisely. It was just far enough behind advance-guard taste for the general public to appreciate it (the theme refers to the Greek-Turkish war celebrated by Byron and Delacroix in the 1820's); the average man understood it as a symbol of liberty in the same obvious and uncomplicated way he "understood" the "meaning" of the classical columns on a Greek Revival temple-house. *Courtesy*, COLLECTION OF THE CORCORAN GALLERY OF ART, WASHINGTON, D. C.

*Plate 149*. BUST OF THOMAS HANDASYD PERKINS, executed *circa* 1830 by John Frazee (1790–1852). This is one of a series of busts commissioned from Frazee for the Boston Athenaeum following the great success of his memorial portrait of John Wells in St. Paul's Church, New York (1824)—which was hailed as the first marble bust carved in America by a native American. Raised in the poorest circumstances on a New Jersey farm, beginning his career as an itinerant cutter of milestones, sills, and tombstones, Frazee had none of Thomas Sully's cosmopolitan sophistication, and the contrast is apparent in their respective portraits of Perkins (see *Plate 144*.) Frazee's depiction of Perkins as literally a "noble Roman" expresses his sitter's patrician aspirations with the same naive directness as the tidy temple-houses being built for prominent citizens in the small towns and cities of the Republic everywhere at this same time. *Courtesy*, THE BOSTON ATHENAEUM, G. M. CUSHING PHOTOGRAPH

*EARLY VICTORIAN ROMANTIC NATURALISM*

ONE of the reasons Washington Allston's romanticism had found such relatively small response in the early years of the 19th century was that the frontier was still much too close for many Americans to take much pleasure contemplating spectacles of man confronting vastnesses of Nature

*Plate 150.* LANDSCAPE WITH A HOUSE, by Thomas Doughty (1793–1856). Here a leader of the "Hudson River School" gives pictorial form to the picturesque ideal expounded by Andrew Jackson Downing in his famous *Treatise . . . on Landscape Gardening*, published about the same year (1841):

210

*A romantic valley, half shut in on two or more sides by steep rocky banks, partially concealed and overhung by clustering vines and tangled thickets of deep foliage. Against the sky outline breaks the wild and irregular form of some old, half-decayed tree . . . (This is) an illustration of the picturesque. (p. 64)*

Vines clamber over the house, breaking any classical precision of outline, while below, huntsmen pursue what was once universally (and on the frontier still) a necessary way of life in America, now an aristocratic recreation. *Courtesy*, THE PENNSYLVANIA ACADEMY OF THE FINE ARTS, PHILADELPHIA. PHOTOGRAPH BY PHILLIPS STUDIO

*Plate 151.* KINDRED SPIRITS, by Asher Brown Durand (1796–1886). Long and justly famous as the perfect example of the full-blown romantic mood in America is this painting of 1849, representing poet William Cullen Bryant and painter Thomas Cole lost in contemplation of the wild grandeurs of Nature. Philosophically it represents an attitude to Nature midway between the classical 18th-century and the organic 20th. They are *in* Nature, in a way the classical mind, with its concept of a sharp division between reasoned human order and natural chaos, could not approve; but they are not yet *of* it. They remain detached from and superior to Nature; there is nothing here of the 20th-century sense of Nature being an integral extension of human powers. *Courtesy*, ART AND ARCHITECTURE DIVISION, THE NEW YORK PUBLIC LIBRARY, ASTOR, LENOX AND TILDEN FOUNDATIONS

and Time. By the mid-1830's, however, the frontier was rapidly receding to the West, and a generation appeared confident enough of its command over Nature to enjoy the wilderness vicariously. It is no accident that one of the most popular books on art in this period was Andrew Jackson Downing's *Treatise . . . on Landscape Gardening* (1841), which deplored the old classical concept of a sharp division between the measured works

*Plate 152.* THE RETURN, painted for William Van Rensselaer of Albany, by Thomas Cole, 1837. This work, and its companion *The Departure*, form one of several series treating the theme of inexorable cosmic decay painted by Cole for advance-guard patrons (another was the famous *Course of Empire* commissioned by Luman Reed). Their specific inspirations was Volney's *Méditations sur les révolutions des Empires* (1791); their general inspiration, that romantic enjoyment of awesome feelings aroused by the vicarious contemplation of men facing mighty forces of Time and Nature. Turner's painting in England is probably the best known expression of this, and Cole probably knew it well, for he had come to America from England in 1818; he was abroad again in 1829–1832. In such pictures we see particularly well the characteristic Early Victorian use of architectural forms symbolically—whereas in *The Departure* the architecture is vaguely Romanesque-Italianate to symbolize "civic enterprise," "secular life," and the like, here it is Gothic, evoking ideals of religious consolation, "old, forgotten, far-off things and battles long ago." *Courtesy,* THE CORCORAN GALLERY OF ART, THE W. W. CORCORAN COLLECTION, WASHINGTON, D. C.

212

of man's reason and the untamed chaos of Nature's wilderness, advocating instead of classical self-containment the integration of architecture into "naturally" landscaped grounds. The same wealthy and leisured class that could afford the luxury of a Downing-landscaped estate also was willing and able to support a "Hudson River School" of painting on similar principles. Such a man as Luman Reed—erudite, humane, a successful businessman who patronized American art not because it was the socially acceptable or chauvinistic thing to do but because he genuinely respected what American artists were doing—was representative of the best state of American

*Plate 153*. THE ARCHITECT'S DREAM, inscribed "Painted by T. Cole for I. Town, Archt., 1840." Unintentionally providing a counterpart to Morse's *Louvre*, Thomas Cole (1801–1848) here presents a similar concept of the art of architecture—as a matter of picking and choosing from the vast reservoir of historical knowledge (embodied in the folios on which the architect reclines) those forms most suitably symbolic for given occasions. It is said that Town disliked the picture, and possibly the concept is more Cole's than his—though in fact nothing could better express the rationale of Town & Davis, first really professional architectural firm in the United States, than this. Be that as it may, the picture certainly expresses Cole's use of architectural backgrounds for emotional and symbolic associations in his own paintings. *Courtesy*, TOLEDO MUSEUM OF ART, TOLEDO, OHIO. GIFT OF FLORENCE SCOTT LIBBEY, 1949

213

214

*Plate 154.* Picnic in the Catskill Mountains, by Henry Inman (1801–1846). A counterpart of A. B. Durand's famous *Kindred Spirits* on the practical level of everyday tastes and habits is this painting of *circa* 1840. Very far indeed from the 18th-century classical concept of gracious living amid polished mahogany under elegant chandeliers is this idea of eating in the open air; equally far from classical ideals of balance and symmetry, the picturesquely blasted tree so prominent in the foreground. *Courtesy,* THE BROOKLYN MUSEUM, BROOKLYN, NEW YORK

culture in this period, and a fine culture it was. And the work of painters like Thomas Doughty, Asher B. Durand and Thomas Cole (*Plates 150–154*) was equally impressive evidence of the extent to which American painters were already realizing the Jeffersonian dream of democratic cultural potentialities. While their concept of landscape painting obviously owes a good deal to study of European prototypes like Turner, John Martin, Salvator Rosa, or Ruysdael, the kind of landscape they paint is recognizably American; for the first time since settlers faced the unknown wilderness, Americans were able to look at their land with real objectivity, as something to enjoy, free alike of compulsion to boast or niggling self-deprecations. In their persons and in their paintings the romantic naturalists and their patrons of the 1830's and 40's represent a new stage of national maturity. The same is true of the theories of romantic naturalism preached by sculptor Horatio Greenough; that he did not carry them into practice was regretted then and ever since.

## PERVASIVE PICTURESQUENESS

By the mid-1840's, the new cultural maturity and aesthetic attitudes promoted by the Hudson River painters and their patrons were being manifested on an ever-broader scale. Not only did the number of serious artists and knowledgeable patrons increase rapidly, but even the popular arts showed more and more evidence of civilized sophistication and a rising level of taste. Now the full tide of Victorian aesthetic attitudes had set in, "picturesqueness" was the quality sought above all in every aspect of cultural life. In architecture it was apparent in the Italianate manner, dominant by the 1850's, which melted down the old classical forms, transformed them into a vehicle for expressing a romantic integration of man and Nature. In literature, it was apparent in the style of a writer like Nathaniel Hawthorne, whose themes were wrapped in long wreaths of words like the vines climbing over an Italianate villa. Even in oratory the old precision of 18th-century classical phrasing, which had survived as persistently as classical idioms in sculpture, was dissolved; writing on *Living Orators in America* in 1849, E. L. Magoon declared that Henry Clay's eloquence represented "style of a new order, conceived and executed in a very bold and difficult manner, the aggregated beauty and magnificence of Grecian symmetry, Gothic picturesqueness, and the irregular firmness of a feudal castle"—we might call it the Italianate manner of speaking. The same thing happened in painting. Pervasive picturesqueness completed the

*Plate 155.* WATCHING THE CARGO, painted in 1849 by George Caleb Bingham (1811–1879). Bingham was the Great Master of American illustrative painting. Combining studies in Düsseldorf, Philadelphia, and New York with solid roots in his native Missouri, Bingham moulded great symbolic images of the American ideal in its heyday. He gave monumental form to themes which in the hands of lesser men like Richard Caton Woodville (1820–1855) or James H. Cafferty (1819–1869) remained simple genre, making scenes like these three figures guarding cargo removed from a grounded steamboat images of a new kind of life—unprecedented in security and scope for individual self-realization—which American democracy had made possible. A new Eden inhabited by new Adams! *Courtesy,* STATE HISTORICAL SOCIETY OF MISSOURI, COLUMBIA, MISSOURI

216

dissolution of any surviving vestiges of the 18th-century's rigid categor-
izations of subject matter into hierarchies of "beautiful subjects" and
"noble feelings"; all were swept away in a flood of "picturesqueness"
that bathed every kind of subject indiscriminately.

Perhaps the most striking result of this development was the thorough

*Plate 156.* STUMP SPEAKING, by George Caleb Bingham. All too often artists in 20th-century
America were men isolated from society at large by misunderstanding and prejudice on both sides.
Not so in the 1840's and 1850's. Then, art. could be and was "by, of, and for the people" without vulgarity or inverted snobbishness. Of this, Bingham is a great example. He can paint the
kind of open-air frontier democracy that spawned Lincoln, Webster and Douglas, with no super-
ciliousness or condescension, because he was part of it. To the end of his life he was active in
politics; his two great post-War canvases, *Order Number 11* and *Major Dean in Jail* were
frankly political in intent, high-minded protests against the corruption of the Reconstruction era.
*Courtesy,* THE BOATMEN'S NATIONAL BANK OF ST. LOUIS. COLLECTION OF THE ST. LOUIS MER-
CANTILE LIBRARY ASSOCIATION, ST. LOUIS, MISSOURI

217

domestication of the concept of picturesqueness. The lingering reminiscences of Claude and Turner, or West or Lawrence, still perceptible in the heyday of Cole and Sully, now largely disappear. Painting and sculpture alike exhibit a brand of picturesqueness which, like their subject matter, is recognizably and pre-eminently American. A school of genre-painters and illustrators appears, represented at its best by William Sidney Mount, George Caleb Bingham, and John Quidor, capable of depicting the American social scene without either vulgarity, or primitivism, or quaintness;

218    *Plate 157.* Long Island Farmhouses, by William Sidney Mount (1807–1868). Long before architects McKim and White made their famous pilgrimage to discover and reproduce as fashionably patriotic symbols the old shingled farmhouses of New England, painters like Mount saw in them unpretentious statements of the good life. Mount's pictures are Eastern counterparts to the American Eden Bingham painted in the West. This scene on eastern Long Island, where 17th-century New England settlers had left their characteristic architectural mark, was painted *circa* 1855. *Courtesy,* THE METROPOLITAN MUSEUM OF ART, NEW YORK. GIFT OF LOUISE F. WICKHAM, 1928, IN MEMORY OF HER FATHER, WILLIAM H. WICKHAM

theirs are no longer Americanized variants of Steen's or Ostade's brawling peasants, nor yet the idealized and sentimentalized "common folk" of later generations, but honest records of people enjoying life, liberty, and the pur-

*Plate 158.* WOLFERT'S WILL, by John Quidor (1801–1881). In his own time, Quidor was not particularly well regarded; to *au courant* critics of the 1850's, his sort of illustration of literary anecdotes seemed impossibly old-fashioned, a middle-class perpetuation of the early 19th-century fondness for David Wilkie, Allston, or West. Yet to us today Quidor typifies the more homely and unpretentious kind of mid-19th-century Americanism; his art has the same sturdy un-selfconsciousness, humorous imagination and slight naivete, and the same peculiar attraction, as vernacular country Gothic or Italianate building. This painting of 1856 is characteristic. The broad theme has a contrived quaintness that is dated; it is taken from *Tales of a Traveller* by Washington Irving, whose fancified tales of "picturesque" Dutch New York particularly appealed to Quidor, himself a native of Tappan on the Hudson. But nothing could be more universally American than the immediate subject—Wolfert Webber, in the act of drawing up a will to dispose of his farm, learns from his lawyer that it will soon be "laid out into streets, and cut up into snug building-lots," so that "whoever owns it need not pull off his hat to the patroon!" whereupon he sits up on his deathbed and announces that now he has something to live for, he intends to postpone dying indefinitely. *Courtesy,* THE BROOKLYN MUSEUM, BROOKLYN, NEW YORK

219

suit of happiness in their own ways (*Plates 155–158*). The same straight-forwardness characterizes the landscapes and portraits of John Kensett and William Page, George Inness and Frederick Church; these men set down coolly selective reports on what they see, whether in Rome or Rhode Island or Quito, free of bombast, pretension or apology (*Plates 159–162*). The picturesque spirit even influences sculpture where, for obvious reasons, the spell of classical symbolism was so much harder to escape than in painting. Erastus Dow Palmer's *White Captive* (*Plate 163*) was picturesquely conceived and honestly observed in a way Powers' *Greek Slave*-cum-Venus-de-Medici had not been. Thomas Crawford, like Greenough, acted all too feebly on his own dictum that "the darkness of allegory must give way to

*Plate 159.* SHREWSBURY RIVER, by John F. Kensett (1818–1872). Classical discipline and serenity are combined with a picturesquely romantic concept of nature in this painting of 1859, just as they are in the fashionable Italianate villas of the period, or as they were in Kensett's own years of study in London, Paris, and Rome from 1840 to 1848. *Courtesy*, THE NEW-YORK HISTORICAL SOCIETY, NEW YORK CITY. FROM THE ROBERT L. STUART COLLECTION

*Plate 160.* PORTRAIT OF SOPHIE CANDACE STEVENS PAGE, painted in 1860 in Rome by William Page (1811–1885). An interesting counterpart to the reigning Italianate architectural style is this portrait of the artist's third wife. He softens the lines of the Colosseum, giving it the typical Italianate vagueness of form; the same simplification is apparent in the treatment of the figure. Though living in Rome from 1849 to 1860, Page was not an expatriate in the later sense; the predilection for architectonic form and classical themes (*Cupid and Psyche, Infant Bacchus, Venus,* etc.) which earned him the title of "American Titian" during the 1850's was much more in keeping with American than European tastes. *Courtesy,* THE DETROIT INSTITUTE OF ARTS

221

common sense"; his Indians looked like Greek warriors (*Plate 164*) and his Roman figure of *Armed Freedom* atop the Capitol dome looked, as Professor Larkin has said, like "a pregnant squaw." Possibly the horse on which Clark Mills' *General Jackson* sat was far from the most distinguished in its long line of antecedents, which went back through Bernini to Leonardo—but still these sculptors had at least the merit of a native originality and inventiveness their predecessors lacked, and what is more,

222     *Plate 161*. THE DELAWARE WATER GAP, by George Inness (1825–1894). In many ways, Inness' three great pictures of the 1860's—this one of 1861, the *Delaware Valley* and *Peace and Plenty* of 1865—mark a culmination of the Golden Day in American culture. Here are some of the most monumentally mature statements of that combination of classical order and romantic grandeur which so distinctively characterized American art and life in the 1840's and 50's, still free of any suggestion of the vapidity and formlessness which developed in years to come, alike in Inness' work and the nation's cultural life. *Courtesy*, THE METROPOLITAN MUSEUM OF ART, NEW YORK. MORRIS K. JESUP FUND, 1932

they practiced their craft at home, with American materials and under American patronage. Indeed, one of the most telling features of this last phase of the Early Victorian period is the official recognition and preference given American sculptors over foreigners, in contrast to practices in earlier years of the Republic.

It was undeniable, however, that by mid-century the level of advance-guard art in America was farther behind Europe than it had been earlier; possibly this was to be expected in this most self-sufficient of all periods in American history, when the Mexican War and the annexation of California pushed the boundaries of the nation all the way to the Pacific, when "54–40

*Plate 162.* SMALL COVE IN GRAND MANAN ISLAND, CANADA, by Frederick Edwin Church (1826–1900). This painting of 1851 admirably illustrates the combination of classical structure and picturesque theme so characteristic of its time, but already presages something of the literalness of Church's later work. *Courtesy,* COOPER UNION MUSEUM, NEW YORK, N. Y.

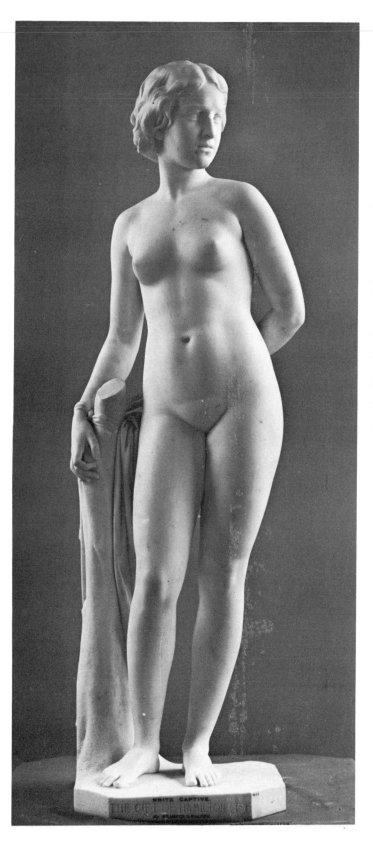

*Plate 163.*

THE WHITE CAPTIVE, by Erastus Dow Palmer (1817–1904). Palmer began his career as an upper New York State carpenter, took up cameo-cutting by accident, graduated to clay and marble when fine cameo-detail gave him eye trouble. Americans were proud of this completely self-trained sculptor, and showered commissions on him; he in turn was proudly American. In this statue of 1858, and his *Indian Maid* two years earlier (Metropolitan Museum, New York), he set himself to create a more American work to rival Hiram Powers' popular *Greek Slave* (see *Plate 148*). His contemporaries believed that he had succeeded, and posterity has generally agreed. The head is modelled on his own daughter; the body is that of a real woman rather than a pastiche of classical Venuses; the subject—a victim of Indian warfare on the frontier—evokes a picturesque past related to American ideals and concerns. *Courtesy*, THE METROPOLITAN MUSEUM OF ART, NEW YORK. GIFT OF HAMILTON FISH, 1894

or fight" was an election slogan, and American eyes generally were turned westward rather than east. In compensation, however, the level of popular taste rose steadily higher, as if to fulfill the democratic promise. Mathew B. Brady's photographic studio, Currier & Ives' prints, *Harper's* and *Leslie's* illustrated magazines, all maintained remarkably high standards, employed

*Plate 164.* THE DYING CHIEF CONTEMPLATING THE PROGRESS OF CIVILIZATION by Thomas Crawford (1813–1857). Designed by Crawford for a pediment on the Senate wing of the United States Capitol, this was part of a large commission executed by him in connection with Thomas U. Walter's enlargement of the Capitol in the 1850's; Crawford also designed *Armed Freedom* atop the dome, cast in bronze by Clark Mills in 1860. Though Crawford thought of himself as a "realist" and wrote that "the darkness of allegory must give way to common sense," his concept in fact illustrates, like Palmer's work in the same period, how thoroughly Eastern intellectuals romanticized the Indian, once the horrors of Indian warfare had receded to the West. *Courtesy,* THE NEW-YORK HISTORICAL SOCIETY, NEW YORK CITY

*Plate 165.* PORTRAIT OF SAMUEL F. B. MORSE, photograph by Mathew B. Brady (1823–1896). Brady studied painting with Morse at the National Academy of Design in New York (1841), and learned photography from him. His photographic portrait of Morse still belongs to the first age of photography, when it was thought of more as a device to assist painters than an art in its own right. Except for the monochrome and flat literalism of detail, it shows no essential difference from a studio portrait of the period. With telegraphic apparatus before him and suggestion of a furled curtain behind, this sitter is presented much as he might have been by any fashionable painter from the sixteenth century on. *Courtesy,* LIBRARY OF CONGRESS, WASHINGTON, D. C.

consistently able and occasionally outstanding artists; seldom if ever in American history have the levels of fine and popular art been so near (*Plates 165–168*). To many critics looking back on the 1840's and 1850's, they seemed a "Golden Day" in American civilization, a time when

Plate 166. DEAD BOY IN THE ROAD AT FREDERICKSBURG, photographed by Mathew B. Brady with a stereoscopic camera, May 3, 1863. Very different from Brady's earlier work are the photographs made by him and his staff—most notably Alexander Gardner—for what he hoped would be a national photographic archive of the Civil War. In works like this, Brady's original training as a painter is evident in his keen eye for pictorial elements—horizontal and vertical compositional lines establishing the plane of his subject; but the stark drama is something only a camera could capture. Where once painting mothered photography, now photography begins to teach painters, becomes a major influence on the development of "realism" as the goal of later-19th century painting. *Courtesy*, LIBRARY OF CONGRESS, WASHINGTON, D. C.

227

there was no particular gulf between artists and their public, when Americans of means were proud to buy American art as the expression and creation of a democratic culture they believed superior to any in the world. The Civil War, shaking this superb self-confidence and bringing in its train a host of major upheavals in American life, decisively marked the end of an era.

HOME TO THANKSGIVING.

*Plate 167.* HOME TO THANKSGIVING, colored lithograph published by Nathanial Currier (1813–1888) and J. M. Ives (1824–1895) in 1867, from the painting by George Durrie (1820–1863). Like Durrie's other work published by Currier & Ives in the 1860's (e.g., the "Winter in the Country" series), this was originally painted a decade or so before, and expressed the characteristic delight of those times in the simple dignity of American life. In the 1860's and 70's its popularity had other overtones, however. As more and more Americans moved into cities to face the complex social and industrial problems of speedy post-war industrialization, they became nostalgic for the lost simplicities of country life. Furthermore, Durrie's landscapes represented New England, which as the center of Abolitionist agitation and champion of the Union in the War was acquiring a legendary aura as the "cradle of early American virtues." *Courtesy,* MUSEUM OF THE CITY OF NEW YORK. HARRY T. PETERS COLLECTION

228

ARTS IN CRISIS: HIGH VICTORIAN AMERICA (*circa* 1860—*circa* 1885)

THE United States emerged from the Civil War a different sort of country. All the old values had been called into question, and while apparently vindicated, somehow remained doubtful as they had not been before. The confident and self-sufficient spirit of the pre-war period did not exactly disappear afterwards; indeed, it was loudly reasserted. Rather too loudly to carry conviction, however; it was as if people were trying to re-establish the old pristine faith by sheer force of noise in the face of tremendous social, political and economic changes that were making the old formulas ever more meaningless. Realizing the situation, more sensitive spirits began to seek new formulas, but so suddenly had it developed, and the old certainties dis-

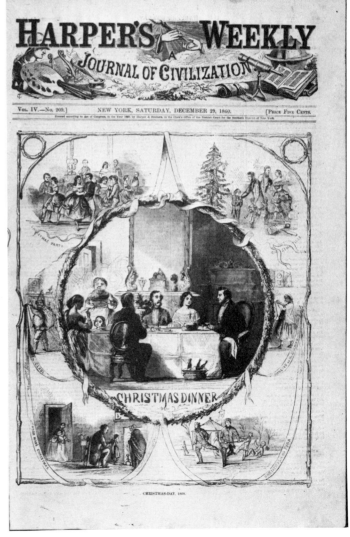

*Plate 168.* CHRISTMAS DINNER, a full-page cut from the Saturday, December 29, 1860 issue of *Harper's Weekly: A Journal of Civilization.* Founded in 1857, *Harper's Weekly* commanded a circulation of 120,000 within four years. Its early issues abundantly reflect the immense security and self-confidence felt by Americans in the 1850's; its articles contrast American strength and stability with the vice, corruption and folly rampant elsewhere in the world, and its illustrations characteristically proclaim the certain reward of industry and intelligence in this land of opportunity for all. But already in this issue there appear ominous drawings of Charleston harbor, showing Forts Sumter and Moultrie; by the end of the 1860's *Harper's* will be finding plenty of crime, corruption and misery at home in a nation transformed by civil war. *Courtesy,* THE NEW-YORK HISTORICAL SOCIETY, NEW YORK CITY

solved, that new ones to replace them could not immediately be found. The result was that art in this period, even more than in the early years of the century, was characterized by confusion of purpose, searchings for nobody-was-quite-sure-what, with nowhere a clear sense of direction. Only in retro-

*Plate 169.* MEN OF PROGRESS, by Christian Schussele (1824 or 1826–1879). Schussele, a native of Alsace who came to the United States in 1848, and was head of the Pennsylvania Academy of Fine Arts at his death (Eakins succeeded him), is now largely forgotten; and so, but for a few, are the nineteen men Jordan Mott commissioned him to paint in 1857 as responsible for "the triumphs of present civilization." Nevertheless, the picture remains a great monument to the spirit of mid-19th-century America, its confidence in the future, its pride in American accomplishment. All those depicted are Americans whose discoveries furthered technological advancement, in fields from dentistry (Dr. Morton, first to use ether anesthesia) and architecture (James Bogardus, cast-iron prefabrication) to agriculture (Cyrus Hall McCormick), physics (Joseph Henry) and firearms (Samuel Colt). Schussele's composition effectively furthers the theme—though each figure exists (and was painted) independently, all contribute significantly to the whole. *Courtesy*, NATIONAL PORTRAIT GALLERY, SMITHSONIAN INSTITUTION, WASHINGTON, D. C.

spect is it evident that the course of development was away from the insular and simple culture appropriate to a small and isolated nation, toward a more cosmopolitan and international culture expressing the emergence of the United States as a major world power. And once again American culture was polarized around two opposite forces—the lure of Europe, with its new ideas and its old sophistications; and a longing for the "American ideal," however inexorably receding under the pressure of events.

*Plate 170.* PAINTING OF THE 4TH PENNSYLVANIA CAVALRY, 1861, by an anonymous naive painter. Naive paintings of primitive meticulousness like this were still reasonably common up to the Civil War. Essentially products of a rurally based society, manifesting primitive principles common to folk art at all times and places, they were soon made rare by post-war industrialization, urbanization and mass media. *Courtesy,* NATIONAL GALLERY OF ART, WASHINGTON, D. C. COLLECTION OF EDGAR WILLIAM AND BERNICE CHRYSLER GARBISCH

### THE AMERICAN IDEAL

"AMERICANISM" of the pre-war sort remains strong well into the 1870's, but its characteristic qualities were steadily exaggerated to the point of distortion and sometimes unwitting parody.

Romanticism all too often became sentimentality. You could see this particularly well in sculpture, where the reigning favorites of public taste in

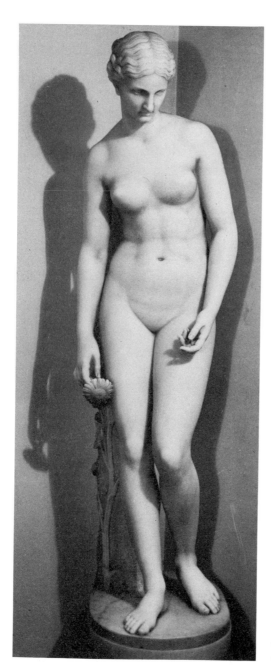

*Plate 171.*
CLYTIE, by William Henry Rinehart (1825–1874). A well-known and characteristic work of a sculptor famous for what High Victorian America called "ideal" subjects—*Love Reconciled with Death*, *Sleeping Children*, funerary monuments like those in Greenmount Cemetery, Baltimore; and many more. Avant-garde critics nowadays scorn their "sentimentality" and condemn the "bourgeois escape" they provided from "social realities," forgetting how in those times it was still far from generally conceded that the business of art was to expose social injustice, most people assuming that the arts ought to make their audiences feel somehow better about the world, not worse. *Courtesy*, TRUSTEES OF THE PEABODY INSTITUTE OF THE CITY OF BALTIMORE

232

the later 1860's and 1870's were works like Harriet Hosmer's *Zenobia*, the "high heroic ode" Hawthorne first saw in 1862; the *Clytie* William Henry Rinehart brought back from Italy in 1872 (*Plate 171*); or Randolph Rogers' *Nydia* (*Plate 172*)—

"... *the blind girl of Pompeii, which had a great popular success, particularly among Americans, who ordered many replicas for their houses. She was depicted as listening intently, groping her way with a staff. I once went to his studio, and saw seven Nydias, all in a row, all listening, all groping, and seven marble-cutters at work, cutting them out. It was a gruesome sight.*" (D. M. Armstrong, Day before Yesterday, *New York, 1920, p. 194*)

*Plate 172.*
Nydia (The Blind Girl), by Randolph Rogers (1825–1892). A minor sensation at the 1876 Centennial in Philadelphia, this was the most popular work of a versatile sculptor who, among his other claims to fame, designed the "Columbus" doors of the Capitol in Washington. He reputedly modeled the log cabin emblem which won the 1840 campaign for William Henry Harrison, in the process launching one of the most persistent myths in American architectural history. *Courtesy*, THE ART INSTITUTE OF CHICAGO. GIFT OF MRS. URI BALCOM

233

Individuality all too often became eccentricity. We think of Elihu Vedder (*Plate 173*); of Harriet Hosmer, perennial tomboy, infatuated with perpetual motion; or of William Rimmer, claiming to be a son of the lost French Dauphin, self-trained physician, sculptor, anatomist, and painter who, as Dr. Richardson has put it, "exhausted himself struggling with granite or clay without knowing the simplest procedures that a month in a workshop would have taught him" (*Painting in America*, New York, 1956, p. 261); or of Albert Pinkham Ryder pursuing his visions in defiance of all conventions—social, economic, technical, aesthetic alike (*Plate 174*).

*Plate 173.* THE PHILOSOPHER, painted in 1867 by Elihu Vedder (1836–1923). Vedder's works of the 1860's and 1870's, like their author, are perfect manifestations of the drifting, searching, erratic spirit of American culture in those decades. The *Lair of the Sea Serpent* (1864, Museum of Fine Arts, Boston), or this *Philosopher* make the starkest of contrasts with the solid, gregarious, self-satisfied characteristic of art in the 1840's and 1850's and dramatically symbolize the sense of alienation, disillusionment, and despair that gripped sensitive minds in the aftermath of the Civil War. *Courtesy,* COLLECTION OF THE NEWARK MUSEUM, NEWARK, NEW JERSEY

All too often the old penetrating empiricism disintegrates into feats of technical virtuosity. To be sure, there are things to admire in the *trompe l'oeil* performances of William Michael Harnett, John Peto, or John Haberle (*Plate 175*), but theirs are hardly accomplishments of the same order as Mount's or Bingham's or even Raphaelle Peale's. And where once "Americanism" in art meant a naively honest kind of recording, now it increasingly implied something exaggerated, artificially chauvinistic—sometimes bombastic and theatrical, like Albert Bierstadt's gigantic canvases of the Western country (*Plate 176*), or Emanuel Leutze's stagy historical melo-

*Plate 174.* JONAH, by Albert Pinkham Ryder (1847–1917). Living alone in small rooms, picking his way through heaps of trash, working and reworking personal visions in heavy massed pigment of his own manufacture, Ryder was a living symbol of the dilemma of creative art in the American culture of his time. The reclusion of his life and the eccentricities of his technique were matched by his predilection for themes of alienation like this. *Courtesy,* SMITHSONIAN INSTITUTION, WASHINGTON, D. C.

236

*Plate 175.* GRANDMA'S HEARTHSTONE, by John Haberle (1856–1933). Despite the wide-spread use of photography, "magic realism" continued to be practiced by a number of painters in the later 19th century—Haberle, W. M. Harnett (1848–1892) and John F. Peto (1854–1907) are among the best-known of them. This is the largest and possibly the masterpiece of their works; its theme is the now customary nostalgia for earlier, simpler times. *Courtesy,* THE DETROIT INSTITUTE OF ARTS, DETROIT, MICHIGAN

dramas (*Plate 177*), Brumidi's decorations on the national Capitol (*Plate 178*), or Alexander Calder's on Philadelphia's new City Hall (*Plate 179*)—more often the kind of cute and folksy anecdotage represented on their several planes of appeal by academicians like Thomas Hovenden, by illustrators of all sorts, and by that prolific purveyor of sculptural culture in plaster to the middle-class masses, John Rogers (*Plates 180–183*).

Only occasionally, as in the early graphic work and painting of Winslow Homer (*Plates 184* and *185*) did "Americanism" rise above this banality to the level of great art. In the arts as in political life, the older American spirit was largely limited to such negative and intrinsically sterile expressions of the "best people's" demands for reform as the political cartooning of Thomas Nast (*Plate 186*).

*EUROPEAN IMPORTATIONS*

EVEN had it not seemed to so many creative minds that the "Americanism" vein, so rewarding in the 1840's and 1850's, was now largely worked out, a turning toward Europe would probably have been inevitable in the 1860's and 1870's; in any event, the Civil War assured it. Gone was the old characteristic certainty of the "Golden Day" that America had all the answers, domestic and foreign; possibly the New World had something to learn from the Old after all. Improved communications made it ever easier for Americans to visit Europe, and for European ideas to penetrate here; while more and more Americans found it possible and even mandatory to study in Europe. Museums displaying European art began to appear one after the other in this period—in the course of the 1870's museums along modern lines appeared in New York, Philadelphia, Washington, and Boston, followed in the 1880's by Chicago, Cincinnati, Detroit, and others. Old art schools were revamped, and new ones founded. But the same European ideas that inspired such innovations also drew more and more ambitious artists away from them to their source across the Atlantic.

In earlier times, Emerson had declared, "Nature being the same on the banks of the Kennebec as on the banks of the Tiber—why go to Europe"? Now he was answered by young Elihu Vedder, who told the sage:

237

*Nature is the same everywhere, but literature and art are Nature seen through other eyes, and a literary man in Patagonia would be at a great disadvantage. Here he has all that is essential in the way of books; but to the artist, whose books are pictures, this land is Patagonia. (E. Vedder,* The Digressions of V.*)*

*Plate 176.* Mount Corcoran (now Mount Langley), by Albert Bierstadt (1830–1902). At first sight, Bierstadt's Western landscapes look like bigger versions of Hudson River painting in the 1830's—the same picturesquely blasted trees, the same delight in unspoiled scenic grandeur, the same invitation to poetic reverie. But there are salient differences. It is not only that the scale is so much bigger, the emphasis on wildness so much more blatant—as if now that railroad tracks line the Hudson and factories foul the Merrimac, Americans almost hysterically need assurance that theirs is still the open unspoiled land it used to be. Even more, the difference is in the quality of human presence. In Durand's *Kindred Spirits*, for instance (*Plate 151*), man is in intimate personal contact with Nature. Here no human being is to be seen. Instead, man is present in the abstract—in the designation of the mountain, named for a remote Eastern merchant and banker, W. W. Corcoran (1798–1888)—patron of Bierstadt and founder of the Corcoran Gallery (1872)—who had never seen it. It is as if this picture were an allegory of the post-Civil War change from an America of small businesses and one-family farms based on intimate human contacts, into a nation dominated by corporate organizations whose mines and farms and factories were increasingly controlled by financiers as unknown to those who worked for them as they were ignorant of the actual operations involved. COLLECTION OF THE CORCO-RAN GALLERY OF ART, WASHINGTON, D. C.

238

Or again, in the words of Henry James's Mr. Theobald, the American dilettante painter languishing in self-imposed Florentine exile:

*Our crude and garish climate, our silent past, our deafening present, the constant pressure about us of unlovely conditions, are as void of all that nourishes and prompts and inspires the artist as my sad heart is void of bitterness in saying so. ("The Madonna of the Future" in the* Atlantic Monthly, *1873.)*

Vedder's attitude was typical of the post-war generation of American artists, pilgrimaging to Europe in subservience to a concept of art as

*Plate 177.* WASHINGTON CROSSING THE DELAWARE, by Emanuel Leutze (1816–1868). Although most of Leutze's adult life was spent in Germany, his series of famous scenes from American history (of which this is one) made him famous in the 1850's, earned him a commission to paint a mural of "Westward the Course of Empire Takes Its Way" for the United States Capitol in 1860, and by the 1870's an enormous reputation in America. This picture, popular from the moment it was first exhibited in 1852, must still be one of the best-known American paintings. Leutze's meticulous anecdotes, grotesquely enlarged, appealed particularly and irresistibly to the post-War compulsive need for bombastic psychological reassurances of American greatness. *Courtesy,* THE METROPOLITAN MUSEUM OF ART, NEW YORK. GIFT OF JOHN S. KENNEDY, 1897

239

something divorced from social functions, serving no need beyond its own existence, degraded by contact with everyday life, fit only to hang in galleries and be admired on special occasions by a select few. Some sought their revelation in Munich, others in England, Holland, and Italy; but most went to Paris, which in the 1860's and 1870's was decisively emerging as the unchallenged center of European artistic life.

240     *Plate 178.* APOTHEOSIS OF WASHINGTON, fresco in the United States Capitol, by Constantine Brumidi (1805–1880). Native artists received many large commissions in connection with the program of enlarging the national Capitol in the 1850's, but it is significant of trends to come that the largest single painting commission went to an Italian who had emigrated after the political troubles of 1849, and of the temper of the post-War period that his frenetically patriotic and old-fashionedly grandiose performance received enormous acclaim after its completion in 1863. *Courtesy,* ARCHITECT OF THE CAPITOL, WASHINGTON, D. C. PHOTOGRAPH, LIBRARY OF CONGRESS

*Plate 179.* COLOSSAL BRONZE STATUE OF WILLIAM PENN, executed by Alexander Milne Calder (1846–1923) for the Philadelphia City Hall. Larger than the United States Capitol, Philadelphia City Hall was largely built during the 1870's, though not entirely completed until 1907. It is perhaps the finest single monument of High Victorian architecture in America, and it was entirely in keeping with the spirit of the building and of the times that its tower, for long the highest in the country, should be crowned with what to a later age would seem the enormous malapropism of this bombastic monument to the great exemplar of Quaker modesty and unworldliness. Calder, who was trained in Britain and had worked on the Albert Memorial in London, came to the United States in 1868 and was employed by architect John McArthur in 1872 to design and model the whole lavish sculptural program of the City Hall, on which he worked for more than twenty years. He was father of A. Stirling Calder (1890–1945) and grandfather of the mobilist, Alexander Calder. *Courtesy*, CITY OF PHILADELPHIA, OFFICE OF THE CITY REPRESENTATIVE

241

Paris offered them no new certainties to replace the ones they had lost, however. Instead, they found the unsettling effects of industrialism, nationalism, and expanding scientific knowledge on cultural life even more advanced. Paris was in the midst of a fundamental revolution in painting. New technical advances—paint in tubes, chemical pigments—were undermining established conventions of composition and formal picture-structure. The principles of photography, widely disseminated in France during the 1840's, were beginning to force a revision of accepted principles of sight.

*Plate 180.* BREAKING HOME TIES, by Thomas Hovenden (1840–1895). That this was one of the most popular pictures exhibited at the 1893 Fair in Chicago is no accident. The young "nobody" who leaves his humble home to find fame and fortune is one of the most enduring themes in American folklore, celebrated in American arts from the 18th to the 20th century, and never entirely without foundation, even though it came true much oftener in the mid-19th century than in earlier or later times. *Courtesy,* PHILADELPHIA MUSEUM OF ART, PHILADELPHIA, PENNSYLVANIA

These and other historical factors were encouraging radical new concepts of the whole theory and function of painting. Already in the 1850's Gustave Courbet had formally published his manifesto on Realism, declaring that painters' concern should no longer be with Beauty of form or nobility of sentiment; rather, Reality should be their goal—they should be teachers, seers, leaders of men.

*Plate 181.* THE VILLAGE POST OFFICE, by Thomas Waterman Wood (1823–1903). The same age that gloried in such enormous Second Empire piles of picturesqueness as Mullett's New York Post Office of 1870 also—and not incongruously—looked back with nostalgia on the earlier, younger, simpler America that had been left behind. So began a tradition of ostentatiously "folksy" painting—of rural simplicities sugared for city consumption—that survived well into the 20th century. Wood enjoyed the same success with his Vermontiana in the 19th century (the main collection of his works is in the Wood Art Gallery, named for and bequeathed by him, in Montpelier, Vermont) as Norman Rockwell with his in the 20th. *Courtesy,* NEW YORK STATE HISTORICAL ASSOCIATION, COOPERSTOWN, NEW YORK

243

*Plate 182.* THE BOYHOOD OF LINCOLN, by Eastman Johnson (1824–1906). Eastman Johnson might well have been a painter like William Sidney Mount or George Caleb Bingham, but his six years of study abroad—in Düsseldorf where he was a friend of Leutze, and in Holland— killed the simplicity and universality of his vision, replaced it with a knack for dramatizing the folksy particular. This aptitude—in material terms a very profitable one—was already matured in 1859 when he painted his immense popular success, *Negro Life in the South* ("My Old Kentucky Home"). After the war, it became an obsessive cliché, encouraged by the national temper of nostalgia for the old rural America of genuinely free opportunity. *The Nantucket School of Philosophy* is one example, whose title speaks for itself. This picture of 1868, which shows how the Lincoln legend was already flourishing only three years after the President's death, derived its great appeal from essentially the same roots. *Courtesy,* MUSEUM OF ART, UNIVERSITY OF MICHIGAN, ANN ARBOR

Against such radicals were ranged the Academies, defenders of old traditions, carrying on classical categories of "Beautiful" subject-matter from the 18th century, appropriately modified to suit Victorian predilections for anecdotage and extraneous ideology. Through the 1860's and 1870's and into the 1880's, these Academies overwhelmingly dominated the New

*Plate 183.*

CHECKERS UP AT THE FARM, by John Rogers (1829–1904). *Checker Players* was John Rogers' first venture into sculpture. Exhibited at Chicago in 1859 while Rogers, a machinist by trade, was working as a clerk in the office of the City Surveyor, it made him locally famous and initiated his career. This is the fourth version of the subject, made in 1877 when Rogers was at the height of his popularity. Rogers' idea of "democratic" sculpture, available to the general public at low prices through mass production of plaster replicas (this item, for instance, sold for $15), had enormous appeal to a generation more and more inclined to measure ideas in dollars and cents. Even more appealing was Rogers' instinct for themes recalling an idyllic America of rural virtues, far removed from the problems of post-War American living. That few American artists have been as extraordinarily admired as Rogers is an apt commentary on the taste of those times. James Jackson Jarves and Ralph Waldo Emerson vied in extolling "The Laureate of Home," and in 1874 a writer in *Farm and Fireside* declared that:

*what Hogarth was in pencil, Canova and Michaelangelo in marble, Reynolds and Landseer on canvas—all the excellencies of these masters in art have their illustration in the plaster of John Rogers.*

—Quoted in Chetwood Smith, *Rogers Groups*, Boston, 1934, p. 2.

*Courtesy,* THE NEW-YORK HISTORICAL SOCIETY, NEW YORK CITY

Realists; and most Americans, with nothing in their backgrounds to prepare them for such radically new concepts of painting, gravitated naturally to the Academic point of view, to the fashionable and famous studios of Gérôme and Fortuny, Bouguereau, and the Académie Julian.

In the French Academies, American students learned a disciplined theory of picture-making which made pre-war American art seem painfully naive and gauche. Comparing American painting of the 1830's and 1840's

*Plate 184.* Prisoners from the Front, by Winslow Homer (1836–1910). Though worked up in 1866 from sketches made by Homer in his capacity as war-artist correspondent for *Harper's Weekly*, this is a work thoroughly in the broad classical spirit of the 1840's and 1850's. In its plainer way, it belongs in the great Renaissance-Baroque tradition of self-explanatory and immediately intelligible pictures like Valasquez's "Breda," Raphael's "Disputa" and Masaccio's Brancacci frescoes. As E. P. Richardson has so neatly said:

*In its contrast between the pale, earnest civilian-in-uniform on the one side (Col. Francis Barlow of the 61st N. Y. Volunteers) and on the other the haughty, graceful cavalier-officer, elegant even in his rags, it tells us all one needs to know about the two temperaments which were at war in that conflict.*—From *Painting in America*, New York, 1956, pp. 314–315.

*Courtesy,* the metropolitan museum of art, new york. gift of mrs. frank b. porter, 1922.

*Plate 185.* Gathering Autumn Leaves, by Winslow Homer, *c.* 1873. Superficially, Homer's painting around the 1870's seems not unlike much other work of
that time. At first sight, a subject like this reminds us of something Currier & Ives
might have printed, or of such popular favorites as the assorted news- and berry-boys
of John George Brown (1831–1913). But the basic quality is quite different.
Homer is painting a vanishing age, and he knows it. His figures—of which this
one is typical—have a lonely sadness about them that inevitably recalls Rembrandt
and the sad clowns of Watteau, and Picasso's early work to come. Like theirs, his are
evocations of a dying world, through which they move but to which they do not
belong. Like his predecessors, Homer secures his effects both by formal picture-
structure—here, the dark foreground shadows, for instance, which isolate the figure
in its own plane—and by subtle symbolism, such as the broken branch of withering
leaves. *Courtesy,* the cooper union museum, new york, n. y.

247

# TWO GREAT QUESTIONS.

"WHO STOLE THE PEOPLE'S MONEY ?" — DO TELL . N.Y. TIMES.          'TWAS HIM.

*Plate 186.* WHO STOLE THE PEOPLE'S MONEY? Cartoon in *Harper's Weekly* Aug. 19, 1871, by Thomas Nast (1840–1902), one of a series attacking the political machine of William Marcy (Boss) Tweed over the years 1870–1872. During the Civil War Lincoln is supposed to have called Nast "our best recruiting sergeant," and during the first dozen post-War years his fame, as crusading "reformer" in *Harper's*, inventor of the images of Santa Claus, of the Democratic donkey and the Republican elephant, rose steadily higher. Thereafter his popularity quite as rapidly declined, until in the end he was saved from destitution only by an appointment to the consulate in Ecuador in recognition of his long services to the Republican party. Nast's decline in the 1880's and 90's is directly attributable to the climate of the times; his work did not change, but public ideas on reform did. Nast belonged to what Eric Goldman in *Rendezvous with Destiny* (New York, 1952, Chapter II) called the "patrician reformers," who believed that "reform, especially reform that would get rid of rum-soaked Irish political machines, was the function of the Grand Old Party, the party of the respectables," and who would be satisfied with "honest government," otherwise leaving employers and public officials entirely uncontrolled. By the 1880's such thinking was manifestly inadequate and hopelessly old-fashioned, and Nast's cartoons, with their quadrennial fulminations against Democratic slavery and corruption found less and less audience. *Courtesy,* PRINTS DIVISION, NEW YORK PUBLIC LIBRARY, ASTOR, LENOX AND TILDEN FOUNDATIONS

248

with the work of W. M. Chase or Elihu Vedder, William Morris Hunt's murals for the State House in Albany or those of his pupil John LaFarge for Trinity Church in Boston, Americans felt the same sense of shame at having once been so provincially naive, the same satisfaction in their newly acquired sophistication, as when they compared the simple temple-like structures that had once served them for banks and mansions with the grandly picturesque piles of columns and balconies, and brackets and mansard roofs of a "General Grant" villa, or the new State War & Navy Building in Washington, the New York Post Office, or the grandiose City Hall in Philadelphia, built to commemorate the Centennial of 1876 (*Plate 70*). New York, in closest communication with Europe of all American cities, increasingly became the center of American artistic life, and here the results of the new sophisticated attitudes were most apparent. Just as the 1860's and 1870's saw New York architecture dominated by a wave of foreign-born or foreign-trained architects, so the more thoroughly academically trained a painter made himself, the smaller market he found for his work at home. Already many Americans were finding their home atmosphere so intolerable as to become permanent expatriates. Already the more pretentious and nouveau-riche American patrons were openly preferring European art to American. Increasingly used to European travel, they could see little point in buying French Academic paintings by their own compatriots; why acquire American imitations of Gérôme or Bouguereau, they were asking, when for just a little more you could get the real thing? It is no accident that a "colonial revival" in architecture and furniture began in the 1870's, gained impetus in the 1880's, and became widespread in the 1890's; it was an outward symptom of a relapse into cultural colonialism which was manifested in painting by the fact that whereas competent painters could make good livings in Early Victorian America, by the 1870's it was only the rare eccentric who tried to make a living solely by selling his paintings—the arts seemed to be fast retrogressing to their status of a hundred years before. Adulation of European culture did not mean receptivity to the newer European ideas, unfortunately; quite the opposite. Those relatively few Americans attracted to the advance-guard point of view of the New Realists found life even harder, recognition even more elusive, than their Academic counterparts. Yet there were some who essayed it, among them men later recognized as the "Old Masters" of American art.

Earliest of these was Thomas Eakins of Philadelphia. Though his official mentor was the academician Gérôme, Eakins' concept of painting was in fact far closer to the kind of Realism preached and practiced by Gustave Courbet. He made the same choice of socially realistic rather than beautiful subjects *per se*; put the same emphasis on "scientifically" photographic literalness of form (*Plates 190* and *191*). And though Eakins, in a typically American way, was less class-conscious and more

*Plate 187.* THE PARTHENON, ATHENS, by Frederick Edwin Church, 1871. Restlessly travelling all over the world in search of subjects—to Palestine and Ecuador, to Labrador and the West Indies—and painting what he saw with increasingly photographic literalness, Church's later career symbolizes the post-War loss of American self-confidence, the country's frantic searching for some new inspiration to replace the old certainties. *Courtesy*, THE METROPOLITAN MUSEUM OF ART, NEW YORK. BEQUEST OF MARIA DE WITT JESUP, 1915.

*Plate 188.* THE ARCH OF TITUS, painted by George Peter Alexander Healy (1813–1894), Frederick Edwin Church, and Jarvis McEntee (1828–1891) in Rome, 1869. In the history of American painting, the precocious and long-lived G. P. A. Healy is one of the bridges between pre- and post-War eras, between Early and High Victorian. In form, a painting like this is still in the "Italianate manner" of the 1850's—compare it, for instance, with William Page's portrait of his wife (*Plate 160*). But there are ominous differences in concept. Involving the collaborative effort of Church and Church's erstwhile pupil McEntee—a fashionable landscape painter in the 1870's—it was worked up from photographs of the artists (to be seen at the right of the painting) and a photograph of the poet Longfellow with his daughter. It is an ostentatious tour-de-force, a statement to the world that Americans are now "grown up" and as much at home in the Old World as in the New. And Healy himself was particularly symbolic of a new age. An American painter before the war, he established himself abroad immediately afterwards (Rome 1867–1872, and Paris 1872–1892) and for a quarter-century competed successfully with Beaux-Artsmen for portrait commissions from wealthy Americans travelling abroad, as well as from European notables. *Courtesy,* COLLECTION OF THE NEWARK MUSEUM, NEW JERSEY. BEQUEST OF DR. J. ACKERMAN COLES, 1926

251

influenced by vestigial romanticism than Courbet, he had the same impulse to shock the bourgeoisie when he could—ultimately this trait, in particular his insisting on nude models whether essential or not, forced him out of his position at the Pennsylvania Academy. Given the native American taste for literalness, it is not surprising that Eakins and his successor at the Academy—Thomas Anshutz (1851–1912), who shared most of his views —were able to make a living at painting; but the same provincialism

*Plate 189.* THE FLIGHT OF NIGHT, by William Morris Hunt (1824–1879). A preliminary study for one of two large murals Hunt executed for the new State Capitol of New York at Albany in 1878, this is a fine example of Parisian Beaux-Arts training of the sort Hunt received in Paris with Couture (1847–1853). In his day Hunt was regarded as the leading "advance guard" painter in America, and as son-in-law of Thomas Handasyd Perkins, he was able to impress Boston society with his liking for the Barbizon School and French painting generally. And when in the decade or two after 1865 Boston, acclaimed as capital of the "State that saved the Union," became the cultural center of the United States, Hunt was indirectly responsible for a quarter-century and more of strong French influence on American arts. Hunt might well have been the Henry Hobson Richardson of American painting—in many ways their careers and attitudes were similar. But whereas Richardson's Trinity Church was an outstanding success, Hunt's murals designed during these same years exhausted him physically and mentally to the point of suicide. To crown the irony, the murals soon disintegrated from damp. *Courtesy*, THE PENNSYLVANIA ACADEMY OF THE FINE ARTS, PHILADELPHIA. PHOTOGRAPH BY PHILLIPS STUDIO

252

militated against their gaining much public prestige. Younger painters thought so highly of Eakins and Anshutz as to make them one of the great inspirations for social realism in 20th-century American art, but when on occasion famous painters came to Philadelphia and inquired after Eakins as the outstanding artist of the place, Philadelphians were

*Plate 190.* WILLIAM RUSH CARVING HIS ALLEGORICAL FIGURE OF THE SCHUYLKILL RIVER, by Thomas Eakins (1844–1916). Though the immediate inspiration for Eakins painting this subject in 1877 was probably the general enthusiasm for a "colonial revival" engendered by the Centennial of 1876 in Philadelphia, such a choice was typical of Eakins' determined Americanism in the face of increasing cultural subservience to Europe, manifest throughout his career. It also illustrates his admiration for "Realism"; as a painter who had studied anatomy in medical school to perfect his art, Eakins identifies with the sculptor who insisted on working from Nature no matter how unnecessary the idealized subject made it. And it also illustrates Eakins' penchant for "shocking the bourgeoisie," like the French "Realists" of the 1860's, Courbet and Manet; citing Rush's precedent, he asked Philadelphia society women to pose nude for him and enjoyed the sensation thus caused, even though it eventually cost him his position at the Pennsylvania Academy. *Courtesy,* PHILADELPHIA MUSEUM OF ART, PHOTOGRAPH BY A. J. WYATT, STAFF PHOTOGRAPHER

253

astonished. Fashionable opinion had never considered him a "top man," and after leaving the Academy in 1886 he was largely forgotten. Almost a century later there was the same reaction when Mrs. John F. Kennedy bought two paintings by Thomas Anshutz—who in the world was he?

*Plate 191.*
THE THINKER, by Thomas Eakins. By 1900, when Eakins painted this work, he was an aging man long since dismissed from his teaching post at the Pennsylvania Academy and generally forgotten; painting largely alone, for his own satisfaction, he perpetuates the spirit of earlier times. In form this picture recalls Manet's manner of the 1860's, which Eakins had known during his student days in Paris. Its theme evokes the typical loneliness of creative individuals of the post-Civil War decades. And like so many of Eakins' works, it ultimately recalls that lost America of individual independence and self-sufficiency in the 1840's and 1850's, to which Eakins always spiritually belonged. *Courtesy,* THE METROPOLITAN MUSEUM OF ART, NEW YORK. KENNEDY FUND, 1917

*Plate 192.*

HEAD OF AN OLD MAN, by Frank
Duveneck (1848–1919). A fine example
of the inherent contradictions of
Duveneck's painting. He never forgot
what he had seen in Europe as a student
at Munich—here are intimations not
only of Leibl, but of Manet's brushwork
and even Cezanne-like structure—but
Duveneck never seemed to grasp the
rationale behind the "New Realism" of
Europe. What were means to an end
for the European innovators remained for
him only means—stylistic clichés which,
once admired, were soon forgotten.
*Courtesy,* SMITHSONIAN INSTITUTION,
WASHINGTON, D. C. GIFT OF
JOHN GELLATLY

Representative of a second stage in the evolution of the New Realism
in painting was Frank Duveneck of Cincinnati. From Wilhelm Leibl, in
Munich, Duveneck had learned a kind of broad brushwork (ultimately
derived from Hals and Rubens), whose startling immediacy made much the
same sensation in the American art world when first seen in Boston during
the 1870's (*Plate 192*), as Edouard Manet's brush-stroke impressionism

255

in Paris a decade or so before. Duveneck proved no Manet, however. Like Sargent later, he had seized on superficial mannerisms of the "new painting" without understanding or accepting its rationale—i.e., that insistence on honesty of vision which motivated and justified brush-stroke impressionism proper. Basically, Duveneck was far more concerned with High Victorian picturesqueness than with Reality as such; precisely for

*Plate 193.* Nocturne, Blue and Silver, Battersea Reach, painted before 1877 by James McNeill Whistler (1834–1903). Writing for *Art News Annual*, 1946, on "Mrs. Gardner and the Treasures of Fenway Court," Morris Carter described this as a "calm, mysterious picture of a London twilight along the Thames, a dark symphony in smoky blues and shadowy oranges . . . characteristic of his art in which everything is subservient to the sensitivity of his feeling." It aptly summarizes the fundamental difference between Whistler and the Impressionists whom he studied among and superficially resembled. A "sensitivity of feeling" so close to idealization, plus Whistler's exotic dash of Japanese delicacy and art for art's sake, was a combination with irresistible appeal for American upper-class collectors like Mrs. Jack Gardner of Boston; but it was something else again from the disciplined visual investigation which motivated true Impressionist reality in painting. *Courtesy,* ISABELLA STEWART GARDNER MUSEUM, BOSTON, MASSACHUSETTS

256

this reason, his career in the United States was a sound success, but did little or nothing to counteract the prevailing provincialism of American culture in his time.

Of all Americans in the 1860's and 70's, James McNeill Whistler unquestionably came closest to understanding and acting on the full implications of the new painting being a basically different kind of activity, of pictures no longer conceived as window-like means of presenting some Beauty or Reality outside themselves, but constituting Beauty or Reality on their own (*Plate 193*). Passages in his later pictures especially seem almost to anticipate abstract expressionism. More dramatically than any other American painter Whistler exemplified, too, the artist's new claims as a seer and leader of men; more than any other single event his famous lawsuit with John Ruskin made the Anglo-American art world aware of what a revolution was going on in the concept of the role of painting and painters in society. But Whistler's example ultimately hurt the cause of advance-guard painting in his time far more than it helped. That Ruskin happened to be his adversary was peculiarly unfortunate, because Ruskin's social writings had near-Biblical inspiration for precisely those early Progressives who might otherwise have been expected to provide the most receptive American ground for the new art. In consequence they, like the public at large, sympathized with Ruskin's position in the argument, gave Whistler no support, and condemned him to remain a querulous voice complaining in the wilderness of cosmopolitan expatriation, without any significant influence on American art in his generation. The net effect of Whistler's career was in fact to demonstrate that the more personal and subjective art becomes, the more uncertain is the place of artists in society. Everybody understood what industrial designers and "popular artists" like illustrators and political cartoonists were and did, as they steadily took over one after another of what had been the traditional functions of artists—communication, entertainment, edification, and so on; but the place of fine art in community life became ever more vague and indefinable. Yet in proportion as the advance-guard artist's accepted role in society disintegrated, his claims to leadership of society expanded. Where once painting and sculpture had been means of giving fame, now for the advance-guard they were means of getting it. In large part because of Whistler's example, however, this new attitude was late being established in America; the third and last phase of Victorian art began with conservative and traditional attitudes dominant everywhere.

SOME MORE EQUAL THAN OTHERS: THE ARTS IN LATE VICTORIAN AMERICA (*circa* 1885–1913)

By the mid-1880's the upheaval of the Civil War was beginning to subside. A new generation was coming to maturity which had been too young to experience it, or to remember what pre-war America had been like. Its representative artists were prepared to come to terms with the new America whose shape was now becoming clear—with a nation and a culture predominantly determined by the rise of great industrial and commercial corporations whose power (already in the 1870's the astonishment of even as advanced an industrial country as Britain) by the 1880's was influencing every aspect of life.

Back in the days of the American Revolution, Dr. Johnson in England had scornfully demanded "How is it that we hear the loudest yelps for liberty among the drivers of Negroes?" The Civil War, which had purported to silence that kind of criticism, in fact raised it in a virulent new form. Now, replacing slave-owners yelping for liberty, a new breed of corporation industrialists and financiers appeared, preening themselves on inalienable rights and privileges they would never have dreamt of conceding to men in their mills and mines and yards. The political liberty and national sovereignty for which the War had been fought had once been living realities for the great majority of Americans, living as they had on their own land or engaged in small businesses, able to make or take a hand in all decisions affecting their personal lives and destinies. Now more and more Americans found themselves in their daily work living under a system absolute as the Pharoahs'—their lives governed by decisions in which it was taken for granted they should have no part, given no more voice in the conduct of affairs directly concerning them than Louis XIV's peasants. And the attitudes and assumptions governing corporation administration quickly spread far beyond industrial or commercial life proper. Hospitals, public school systems, and particularly the new American universities founded in the post-Civil War period, were all increasingly governed on the corporation model, with decisions on all matters, professional or not, reserved to specifically administrative officers and trustees rather than those directly concerned.

*Plate 194.* EL JALEO, painted in 1882 by John Singer Sargent (1856–1925). One of Sargent's most dazzling technical performances, this was (and is) the focal point of the "Spanish Room" at Fenway Court, designed by Mrs. Jack Gardner especially for it. The Spanish subject and the broad brushwork show Manet's influence; and at first sight it would seem that Sargent has surpassed his mentor. But appearances are deceptive. What attracted Manet in Spanish art was its atavistic tradition of "Realism," and he recognized Velasquez's brushwork and optical effects as means to that end. Sargent, on the other hand, with unerring instinct for what would please his upper-class American patrons, chose to depict the superficial and picturesque froth of Spanish culture—the gaiety, the color, the Latin rhythms; he produced a piece of decoration, not a work of Realism. In other words, Sargent's work was advance-guard in every respect but the one that counted. *Courtesy*, ISABELLA STEWART GARDNER MUSEUM, BOSTON, MASSACHUSETTS

259

The broad cultural consequences of all this may be summed up as the rise of a new aristocracy based on corporate wealth, the appearance for the first time in America of a genuine proletariat, and a steady suppression of individualistic expression in favor of organized corporate patterns of behavior. And as always, painting and sculpture mirrored life. Though increasing numbers of American artists were affected by the idea of Realism as the goal and standard of art, it was more an unconscious assumption than anything explicitly formulated, as in Europe; they tended to interpret it according to their patrons' prejudices—for the new aristocracy, as an eruditely literary idealism, and for the new proletariat, as earthy and vulgar literalism.

### ART FOR THE NEW ARISTOCRACY

Now as never before, American cultural life fell under the dictation of wealthy families. Most of these having been established or confirmed by the Civil War's undiscriminating stimulus to large-scale industrialization, their cosmopolitan pretensions rarely rested on much pedigree; of the successful businessmen listed in the *Dictionary of American Biography* as born between 1820 and 1849, C. Wright Mills found in his study of "The American Business Elite" that 43% had begun life in the "lower" or "lower middle" class, as compared with 37.2% for the 1790–1819 generation and only 29.3% for the generation 1850–79. Only a small fraction had any kind of hereditary background for playing the role of a cultural élite. Consequently, in contrast to the European landed gentry who for generation after generation had patronized art from the Middle Ages through the 18th century and so were sure enough of their social position to dare support advance-guard movements, the new American patrons were basically timid, conventional, *retardataire* in taste. To ensure themselves against exposure to ridicule, they collected "names" recognized by "the best authorities," which most commonly meant the conservative element in the art world of London and Paris, and the works of the Barbizon School, late Corot, Rosa Bonheur and the like. A few of the more venturesome or perceptive, like Martin Ryerson and the Havemeyers, began to acquire Impressionists and Old

*Plate 195.* DAUGHTERS OF THE HONORABLE PERCY WYNDHAM, painted by John Singer Sargent, 1899. No doubt about it, Sargent was born in the wrong time and place. Though he used the techniques of his chronological contemporaries Manet and Renoir, he was the spiritual contemporary of Reynolds and Gainsborough. Reynolds would have thoroughly approved the subtle idealization of a portrait like this which equated three upper-class women with the Three Fates on the classic Parthenon; he would have regarded it as a fine example of his "grand manner," a fulfillment of the artist's duty to make the world a nobler place than it is. Reynolds, however, would never have tried or wanted to think of it as "realistic," as Sargent and his contemporaries were wont to do. *Courtesy,* THE METROPOLITAN MUSEUM OF ART, NEW YORK. WOLFE FUND, 1927

261

*Plate 196.* Virgin Enthroned, by Abbott Thayer (1849–1921). In Thayer's art, even more than in Sargent's which it technically so much resembles, is the perfect expression of the moral dichotomy splitting Late Victorian America. The land of the free, of opportunity for all, has become the land of privilege; the American dream of a basically new kind of life has sunk into prosy boasting about a life merely wealthier and more secure than other nations'. Where once Americans proclaimed that they were leaders of mankind towards new ideals, now they proclaim themselves of all nations the most materially prosperous. It is the kind of dichotomy Europeans noted as characteristic of Americans in this generation—of Woodrow Wilson, Churchill declared that he was two men, one an idealist nobler than any the world had ever seen, the other a petty party politician. Thayer's art is the one side of this coin—ideal, pure, virtuous, quasi-Greek, entirely aloof from any political or social realities. For the other side of the coin, we need to consider the concept of mankind embodied in, say, "The Yellow Kid" (*Plate 201*). *Courtesy,* THE FREER GALLERY OF ART, SMITHSONIAN INSTITUTION, WASHINGTON, D. C.

Masters—Rembrandt, Hals, Titian, Murillo; Mrs. Jack Gardner of Boston, who followed the advice of that persuasive young Harvard aesthete, Bernard Berenson, was regarded as a maverick indeed for buying in the Quattrocento. And at the Chicago Exposition of 1893, Mrs. Potter Palmer struck a rich vein by moving to bring the vogue for "colonial American," already popular in architecture, indoors, with a collection of "early American" furniture and decorative arts. Having boxed up the American dream of equality and put it away on a shelf suitably wrapped for display on state occasions, the new aristocracy began to compensate by idealizing the heritage of an America even more colonial and oligarchic than their own.

Insofar as the new aristocracy patronized American artists at all, idealization was what it wanted, demanded, and got. Typifying the kind of art they favored was the painting of John Singer Sargent (*Plates 194 and 195*) and Abbott Thayer (*Plate 196*); the sculpture of Augustus St. Gaudens, John Quincy Adams Ward, and Daniel Chester French (*Plates 197–200*); and the "popular art" of C. D. Gibson. Significantly, all these men displayed a certain "modernism" of technique. Sargent's brush-stroke impressionism was undeniably masterly, and Thayer's competent enough; Gibson's drawing style was a brilliant graphic counterpart to it. St. Gaudens, Ward, and French, all paid nominal service to Realism of concept and texture. But in every case, this modernism was specious and superficial; all these men were incorrigible idealizers. Quite as much as Reynolds or Gainsborough, they held to and acted on the principle that the artist's job was to ennoble his themes; they heartily agreed with Reynolds when he discoursed that "Historians tell us Alexander the Great was low and mean in appearance; the painter ought not so to represent him." Any financier or nouveau-riche or tarnished public servant could entrust their commemoration in oil or bronze to artists like these, certain that posterity would be shown only their best. In politics or finance or social life disgrace might abound, but that is of no concern to them. Theirs is a world of noble men and elegant women; of classical nymphs personifying fortitude and honor, innocent virtue and devoted motherhood; their themes are pure patriotism, un-

264    *Plate 197.* MONUMENT TO GENERAL WILLIAM TECUMSEH SHERMAN, designed by Augustus St. Gaudens (1848–1907). The portrait bust was modelled as early as 1877; the monument was unveiled in Central Park, New York City, 1903. Sherman said that war was hell, but St. Gaudens made it glorious, creating an idealized general led by a goddess of peace and victory, the whole made believable by discreet touches of literalism. His famous "Puritan" (1887) was another example of literal details and "modernistic" play of textures superimposed on a basically and thoroughly idealized concept—an exact counterpart in sculpture to John Singer Sargent's approach to painting. PHOTOGRAPH FROM CITY ART COMMISSION, NEW YORK CITY

selfish public service, highminded emotions unsullied by crass or petty cares. In terms of the broad movement throughout the 19th century away from Beauty and towards Realism, this art of the new American aristocracy represented as distinct a retrogression as their huge and correct Mediterranean villas and Louis Seize palaces, their 13th-century Gothic cathedrals and Imperial Roman railroad stations. And just as this was an age when class

*Plate 198.*
MEMORIAL AT GRAVE OF MRS. HENRY ADAMS, Rock Creek Cemetery, Washington, D. C., executed by Augustus St. Gaudens, 1887. On the few occasions when St. Gaudens found a patron like Henry Adams, free of nouveau-riche cultural colonialism, he could rise to poignant personal expression; this work is the supreme example. Befitting as pure a work of art as was ever done in 19th-century America, St. Gaudens gave it no name. PHOTOGRAPH FROM NATIONAL PARK SERVICE, U.S. DEPARTMENT OF THE INTERIOR

distinctions were more invidious and obvious than ever before, when limit-
less wealth and bottomless misery presented their most extreme contrasts,
when the new palaces and public monuments stood in all their unheard-of
grandiosity and erudition next to slums of unparalleled wretchedness, so
while extravagantly highflown idealism flourished in its "fine" arts, its
"popular" arts sank lower and lower into trivial vulgarity.

*Plate 199.*
STATUE OF HENRY WARD BEECHER,
by John Quincy Adams Ward
(1830–1910). In the post-Civil War
decades, Ward was famous for
incorruptible "realism" but it was
surface, not fundamental. Despite the
literalism of details of this statue, executed
in 1891 to honor a famous, flamboyant,
controversial public figure (born in
1813, Beecher died in 1887), Ward
made of it an idealized type rather than
the portrait of an individual—the fearless
and spotless spiritual leader,
representative of Pilgrim heritage—
an evocation, like the apple-cheeked
rustics and unspoiled landscapes of the
same era, of what America could or
ought to have been, rather than what
it was. PHOTOGRAPH FROM CITY ART
COMMISSION, NEW YORK CITY

*ART FOR THE NEW PROLETARIAT*

EXCEPT for Southern slavery—which was feudal rather than industrial in rationale—there was in America before the Civil War nothing like a permanently submerged proletariat in the European sense. As George Orwell noted, "There were social distinctions, and there was poverty . . . but there

*Plate 200.*
THE REPUBLIC, by Daniel Chester French (1850–1931). Along with the grandiose Imperial Roman Administration building by Richard M. Hunt, this sixty-five-foot high statue set the tone of the World's Columbian Exposition of 1893 in Chicago, in the contrast of its frigidly correct stylization (it was one of the first examples of deliberate archaization in academic sculpture) with the spontaneous inventiveness of that earlier Jeffersonian classicism which the Fair purported to evoke. The classical forms which once had been vital symbols of the great dream of a new society of freedom and equality have now become a façade behind whose authority class privilege is sheltered from the criticism of reformers. For a quarter-century more the "Imperial Façade" perfected at the Chicago Fair performed that function so admirably that Frank Lloyd Wright, speaking in retrospect for the old "progressive" movement generally, could write of men like Hunt and French that "they killed Sullivan and they nearly killed me." *Courtesy,* MRS. PENN CRESSON, AND THE CHESTERWOOD STUDIO MUSEUM, STOCKBRIDGE, MASSACHUSETTS

was not then . . . an all-pervading sense of helplessness. There was room for everybody, and if you worked hard, you could be certain of a living—could even be certain of growing rich; this was generally believed, and for the greater part of the population it was even broadly true." ("Riding Down from Bangor," in *Shooting an Elephant*, New York, 1957.) With the immense and sudden post-War industrialization of the United States this happy state of affairs came to an end, unfortunately. Now a genuine proletariat was created, partly by depressing the native working-class, partly by indiscriminate recruiting of cheap labor in Europe and uncontrolled immigration generally. By the 1890's, the cultural result was evident in a steady degradation of American popular arts, which half a century earlier had achieved such a remarkably high level. Now instead of Currier & Ives (*Plate 167*) the characteristic art of the masses was the comics and advertisements of the "yellow press." In them ideas were reduced to primitive stereotypes—the dumb Swede; the comic darkey, so faithful and so content in his "place"; the villain with twirling moustachios and the hero, clean of jaw, clear of eye, empty of brain; above all, crude evocations of the great goddess Chance. No Lincolns or Clays or Washingtons—self-made men through the democratic process—in this art, but newsboys rescued from their slummy destiny by the happy accident of finding a rich banker's wallet to return, clerks emancipated from drudgery because they happened to be standing by when the boss's child wandered into the path of some speeding train. Inverted snobbery ran rampant, the counterpart of aristocratic idealism—the "Yellow Kid" (*Plate 201*), and "Happy Hooligan," are typical examples of the proud cult of poverty, stupidity and vulgarity.

### THE SUPPRESSION OF INDIVIDUALITY

AMONG the great middle classes at the end of the century the theory of individual integrity and freedom of action remained strong; its practice, however, became increasingly difficult. Mass production, giant organizations of industry, the decline of self-sufficient farming and small trades, all worked to encourage standardization of values and behavior. In art the spirit of

A FEW THINGS THE VERSATILE YELLOW KID MIGHT DO FOR A LIVING

Plate 201. THE YELLOW KID, by Richard Felton Outcault (1863–1928). The comic strip in concept goes back at least to sequences of pictures by Rudolf Toepffer of Geneva in the 1830's, developed and refined by Gustave Doré in France and Wilhelm Busch in Germany, among others. Outcault was one of several American pioneers of the form in the new mass media of the 1890's; others included Rudolf Dirks ("Katzenjammer Kids"), James Swinnerton ("Little Jimmy") and F. B. Opper ("Alphonse and Gaston"). Outcault's "The Yellow Kid," owed its popularity primarily to inverted snobbery. After Hearst bought Outcault's services (he was, among other later accomplishments, creator of "Buster Brown"), "Hogan's Alley" was continued by no less a master than George Luks. This was far from the only such marriage of fine and popular arts à la Hogarth—Feininger, of Bauhaus fame, also drew the "Katzenjammer Kids" for a time. Admirers of early comics have attempted to relate the "Yellow Kid" to the Josh Billings-Artemus Ward-Finley Peter Dunne tradition in American humor; if so, it is in an infinitely debased form. But it was from such roots that H. C. ("Bud") Fisher (1884–1954) created the first mature comic classic, "Mutt and Jeff," in 1907. The examples given are reproduced with permission from Thomas Craven's *Cartoon Cavalcade* (New York, Simon and Schuster, Inc., copyright 1943).

269

270

*Plate 202.* WASHDAY TROUBLES. A still from the 1895 motion picture. *Washday Troubles* was a significant cultural, social, and technological document. Running only a minute or two, it was characteristic of the very first moving pictures primarily made as marvels to bemuse yokels at country fairs and idlers at amusement arcades in the cities. As such, it set the tone of American movie-making for the next forty years—commercial ventures, aimed at the lowest common denominator of taste. And that level of taste is revealing—crude stereotypes of the "stage darkey," to be laughed at for comical incompetence, a variant of the "village idiot" school of humor. It belongs in the same category of artistic convention that saw tramps (e.g., "Happy Hooligan") and slum children as figures of fun, of vicarious escape from respectability and responsibility. As such, it is the cousin of, say, Alfred in Shaw's *Pygmalion*, and the ancestor of the "hillbilly" and "Western" genres of later popular arts. *Courtesy,* FILM STILLS ARCHIVE, THE MUSEUM OF MODERN ART, NEW YORK CITY

*Plate 203.*

THE CHINESE MUST GO. Lithographed card by the J. Worth Manufacturing Company, advertising the "Missouri Steam Washer" (*circa* 1895). The vulgar mixture of patriotism, racial prejudice and commercial interest inherent in this representation of a washing machine, trousered like Uncle Sam, chasing the canny pigtailed Chinaman (note the moneybag) back to Asia is typical of the crassness of sentiment and crudely stereotyped imagery of popular arts at the turn of the century.

*Courtesy*, COLLECTION OF ALAN GOWANS

the times was manifest in the appearance of collective "styles," schools of painting in which it was hard to distinguish one individual's work from another's. Here and there a few determined men stood out against the trend, but the cost was high. Ralph A. Blakelock (*Plate 204*) is a sad example; pursuing his subtle pictorial visions regardless of the dictates of schools, he was persecuted, exploited, finally driven out of his mind.

For all practical purposes, the exercise of individuality involved expatriation. So Winslow Homer could successfully defy convention only by retreating from the centers of American culture to the isolated fastness of Prout's Neck in Maine, with occasional trips to the West Indies; to realize her "unwomanly" ambition to be a painter, Mary Cassatt had to live permanently in Paris.

### VARIETIES OF REALISTIC EXPERIENCE

BY the late 1880's and 1890's, Realism was in the artistic air; willing and consciously or not, artists of all shades, from aristocratic flatterers to the crudest comic-strip creators, were affected by it to some degree. Its expression varied widely, however, according to the audience addressed.

271

272    *Plate 204.* BROOK BY MOONLIGHT, by Ralph Albert Blakelock (1848–1919). One of the few American painters in his time who thought of pictures in anything like terms of textural patterns and "significant form" independent of whatever was represented, Blakelock intuitively grasped one of the central concepts of the New Realism in painting. Such advance-guard brilliance went totally unappreciated, however. This picture of *circa* 1890, climaxing a long story of cheating and insult, sold for so little that it precipitated Blakelock's mental breakdown, which progressed until in 1899 he was permanently confined in an asylum. *Courtesy*, THE TOLEDO MUSEUM OF ART, TOLEDO, OHIO, GIFT OF MR. AND MRS. EDWARD DRUMMOND LIBBEY, 1916

*Plate 205.* AFTER THE HURRICANE, BAHAMAS. Watercolor by Winslow Homer, *circa* 1899. Winslow Homer went to Paris for a few months in 1867, but he was one American painter Paris had nothing to teach. The premises of the New Realism—that pictures can have lives of their own independent of subject-matter—he intuitively knew; its conclusion—that picture-making should be an end in itself—he rejected. He had to find his mature self in isolation; the magnificent result appears in paintings of his last twenty years like this. The play of geometric against free form creates a powerful design in itself, its abstract qualities reinforced by the water-color medium which Homer began to take up as early as 1873. But it is more than mere visual pattern— in the contrast of geometric forms like the ruins of the boat and the Negro's head with the surrounding chaos is an evocation of the old classical concept of the individual's struggle with Nature. Such a painting at once recalls the traditions of Jeffersonian America and anticipates the "human comedy" of 20th-century writers like Saroyan, Dos Passos, and Hemingway (this work, and even more Homer's "Gulf Stream" of 1898, could be illustrations for *The Old Man and the Sea*). Homer's interest in manual labor stems from the same inspiration; in the "forgotten men" of the Gilded Age he believed was a repository of the old, uncorrupted American virtues. Famous as the painter of lonely fisherfolk, Homer also deserves to be even more famous as the greatest— perhaps the only great—painter of Negro life. *Courtesy,* THE ART INSTITUTE OF CHICAGO, MR. AND MRS. MARTIN A. RYERSON COLLECTION

273

274

*Plate 206.* CARESSE ENFANTINE, by Mary Cassatt (1855–1926). Some critics have maintained that Mary Cassatt, so thorough and so permanent an expatriate, was hardly an American at all; and certainly her fundamental technique is that of French advance-guard Social Impressionists like Degas and Renoir. But her idealized themes—the glories of Motherhood—are quite as fundamentally typical of the taste of the upper-class American society whence she came. (Confer, for example, Thayer's theme in *Plate 196*). *Courtesy*, SMITHSONIAN INSTITUTION, WASHINGTON, D. C.

Realism had always been endemic in the popular arts, of course; to communicate, to amuse by pointing up contrasts between facts and fancy had been the stock in trade of cartoonists since the genre first appeared. However sadly decorous Opper or Davenport might be, compared to Thomas Nast or the free-wheeling satirists of the early Republic, they did continue developing their art, shaping a weapon for the progressives and muckrakers of the early 20th century. But now Realism began to appear among the "fine" artists too. They interpreted it quite differently, however. For them Realism meant fidelity to historic models. Thus, if you belonged

*Plate 207.*
THE SCRAPER, by Charles Henry Niehaus (1855–1935). A typical example of the "academic" concept of Late Victorian Realism in America—an escape from the uncertainties and confusions of the post-War decades through coldly studied imitations of impeccable standards "certified" by the approval of the ages. Such art is, of course, much more a matter of scholarly reproduction than of spontaneous creativity; it is a counterpart to the archaeological architecture or "period" furnishings of mansions by Hunt, Carrère and Hastings, and like figures at the turn of the century. *Courtesy,*
BROOKGREEN GARDENS, MURRELLS INLET, SOUTH CAROLINA

*Plate 208.* ATHENS, by John LaFarge (1835–1910). Beaux-Arts "Realism." Three figures, one copied from the statuary, one from the wall-painting, and one from the architectural sculpture of Antiquity comprise this model of classical "correctness," executed in the years 1893–1894. *Courtesy*, BOWDOIN COLLEGE MUSEUM OF FINE ARTS, BRUNSWICK, MAINE

to a "classical" school, it would no longer do to make mere allusions to classical themes, pay lip-service to classical proportions and principles, as in the benighted times of the old Classical Revival; now Reality demanded you be thoroughly classical. Men like Frederick MacMonnies or F. D. Millet knew Greek and Roman drapery, furniture, gestures; no archaeologist could have reason to complain of inaccuracies in any classical work of theirs. Or if you specialized in "medieval" themes, like Edwin Austin Abbey, you were expected to be truly and accurately medieval in every detail (*Plate 209*). One consequence of such emphasis on erudition was to make this a great period for historical illustration—the "Delaware" school led by N. C. Wyeth and Howard Pyle (*Plate 210*), and the "Western" school of which Frederic Remington (*Plate 211*) was the best-known figure, being outstanding. Looking back on it, we generally think today of this kind of scholarly eclectic realism as cold, lifeless, leading nowhere; in its day, however, it seemed very different. Then it appeared as a means of bringing order out of High Victorian chaos, and those who opposed it appeared as perpetuators of post-war confusions.

Chief of these recalcitrants were Mary Cassatt and Winslow Homer. By French standards, they were hardly "rebels" at all. Though her technique was the Impressionism of Manet and Degas, and her settling in Paris for a painting career in itself an act of defiance against conventional American mores of her time, her subject-matter could hardly have been more decorous—mothers and children, her chief stock in trade, held an even more hallowed place than Lincoln or Washington in the American hierarchy of

*Plate 209.* THE QUEST OF THE HOLY GRAIL. Mural commissioned in 1890 for the Boston Public Library. Completed 1902 by Edwin Austin Abbey (1852–1911). This panel is entitled "The Departure." In its own time, considered the masterpiece of an instinctive antiquarian, famed for its antiquarian accuracy, now generally considered of purely antiquarian interest—a specimen of Beaux-Arts academic "Realism" in the medieval vein. *Courtesy,* THE TRUSTEES OF THE BOSTON PUBLIC LIBRARY

*Plate 210.* "TWO KNIGHTS DO BATTLE." An illustration from *The Story of King Arthur and His Knights*, by Howard Pyle, New York, 1903. By his admirers, Howard Pyle (1853–1911) was regarded not only as a great illustrator, but a significant painter in his own right—and with some justification, for no one embodied the spirit of Late Victorian art in America better than he. His art had all the characteristic erudition of Beaux-Arts architecture or sculpture. Whether it were King Arthur or Robin Hood or buccaneers on the Spanish Main or scenes from Early American history, his subjects were always as "scientifically" and archaeologically "correct" as possible (though of course, like all artists, he was stamped by his times—his "Thomas Jefferson," for example, composes the Declaration for all the world in the manner of a late 19th-century writer in his study). He had the characteristic tendency of his age to idealization—even Pyle's pirates look noble, somehow. And all his art, by the very literalness of his depictions of bygone times, so free from the problems of respectable, responsible, Late Victorian America, shares the typical "escapism" of Late Victorian academic art. Whether one likes it or not depends on one's concept of what art is and ought to do, of course. His illustrations are counterparts in their way of Sargent and Ward on the one hand, of "Washday Troubles" and "Happy Hooligan" on the other. *Courtesy,* THE NEW YORK PUBLIC LIBRARY, ASTOR, LENOX AND TILDEN FOUNDATIONS

278

acceptable themes for painters (*Plate 206*). Homer, too, was very far from being a Seurat, a Van Gogh, or a Picasso. His experiments in technique revealed a concept of pictorial color as Realities in themselves far more advanced than any other painter of his day in America; but through it all he never entirely forgot his beginnings as an illustrator,

*Plate 211.*

THE BRONCO BUSTER, by Frederic Remington (1861–1909). "When you Europeans get your eyes on my bronze you will say 'Ah, there! America has got a winner.' It's the biggest thing I ever did, and if some of these rich sinners over here will cough up and buy a couple of dozen, I will go into the mud business."[1] So Remington wrote after casting this work in 1895; and he was right. He had taken up sculpture in 1892 after the paintings based on his 1880–1886 stay in Montana had not proved as popular as he had hoped. After some revision, 240 copies of the "Bronco Buster" were cast. One of them was given to Theodore Rosevelt as a parting gift from his Rough Riders in 1898— an entirely appropriate choice, for the idealization of masculinity and activity for its own sake perfectly suited Roosevelt's temperament.
PHOTOGRAPH FROM BROOKGREEN GARDENS, MURRELLS INLET, SOUTH CAROLINA

[1] Quoted from P. Bigelow, "Frederic Remington," *Quarterly Journal* of the New York Historical Association, X, 1929, p. 48, in B. G. Proske, *Brookgreen Gardens*, Brookgreen, 1943, p. 63

never would agree that "a picture is not a window" (*Plate 205*). Abstract expressionism would not number Homer among its antecedents.

Only in the last decade of the century were a few feeble tremors from the convulsive advance-guard movements in European art felt in the United States. In 1895 Homer Martin made a great sensation with his *Harp of the Winds* (*Plate 212*) a work which, while basically conceived in terms of High Victorian picturesqueness of theme and mood, showed some recognizably Impressionistic qualities; in that year, too, a group of

*Plate 212.* THE HARP OF THE WINDS, by Homer Martin (1836–1897). A great popular favorite in its own time (1895), this timidly sensitive combination of Impressionistic vision with Barbizon sentiment and color represented the highest flight of American taste in the 1890's. *Courtesy*, THE METROPOLITAN MUSEUM OF ART, NEW YORK. GIFT OF SEVERAL GENTLEMEN, 1897

281

*Plate 213.* STREET SCENE IN WINTER, painted in 1901 by Childe Hassam (1859–1935). New York at the turn of the century—or is it Paris in the 1870's? Chronologically it is the one; technically and spiritually the other. Never since the 17th century had the cultural lag between the New and the Old World seemed so long, or so painfully obvious, as at this moment; this advance-guard art was truly provincial, as "Mutt and Jeff" (say) was not. *Courtesy*, THE METROPOLITAN MUSEUM OF ART, NEW YORK. BEQUEST OF GEORGE D. PRATT, 1935

timid followers of European pointillistic Impressionism in New York and Boston was organized under the name "Ten American Painters." Among the more representative figures of "The Ten" were Theodore Robinson (*Plate*

*Plate 214.* WILLOWS, by Theodore Robinson (1852–1896). Theodore Robinson had studied with Monet and might, perhaps, have wished to emulate the great pointillistic Impressionist. But New York was not Paris; Monet might make a living with studies of light, but Robinson could not. As a result, pictures like this are best described as retrogressive hybrids—Monet interpreted in terms of the late Corot, still a reigning favorite thanks to William Morris Hunt's efforts two decades before. *Courtesy,* THE BROOKLYN MUSEUM COLLECTION, BROOKLYN, NEW YORK

*214*) who had actually studied with Monet, Childe Hassam (*Plate 213*), and John W. Twachtman (1852–1902). That even as restrained an emphasis on pictorial surface and decorative qualities *per se* as theirs could arouse controversy in the mid-1890's was a telling commentary on the cultural colonialism of the era; for they represented not advance-guard art of the 1890's, of course, but rather of the 1870's. Not until the early 1900's would reaction against this cultural colonialism begin to appear, manifest in Theodore Roosevelt's foreign policy, in the Progressive movement and the "Ash Can School" at home; not until 1913 would the New Realism of Europe make any significant impression in the United States. And that is beyond the scope of this chapter.

## BIBLIOGRAPHICAL NOTE

SINCE this chapter was first written, I have had several books published which amplify and further develop a good many of the points made in it. The division of 19th-century American culture into Early, High, and Late Victorian eras is worked out in detail in *Images of American Living: Four Centuries of Architecture and Furniture in the United States.* (Philadelphia and New York, Lippincott, 1964.) The first of a two-volume study on what the activity called "Art" does in society was published in 1966 as *The Restless Art: A History of Painting and Painters 1750–1950* (Philadelphia and New York, Lippincott); besides extended discussions of Eakins and Homer, the section on "The American Experience" (pp. 380–398) is especially relevant here. *The Unchanging Arts*, appearing in 1969 (Lippincott), considers the history and development of those arts which now perform the functions in society which Painting successively abandoned over the last two hundred years—illustration (popular illustration such as Currier & Ives and John Rogers' groups, narrative paintings, Bingham and Mount and their followers in book illustration and related arts, comics, movies, animated cartoons); persuasion and conviction (political and social cartoons with special attention to American examples); intrinsic and extrinsic symbolism in architecture, tombstones, etc.; substitute imagery (photography, with much pertinent American material); and decoration. A book of major significance for understanding the development of American painting in the early 19th century is Lillian B. Marshall, *Patrons and Patriotism, the Encouragement of Fine Arts in the United States—1790–1860* (University of Chicago Press, 1966); in a review in the *Pennsylvania Magazine of History and Biography* (July 1967, pp. 365–66), I discussed how it documents the controversy between those who thought of painting as an activity directed towards social usefulness and those who considered it as Fine Art, an end in itself. Though it might be criticized for too slanted a selection of examples, John McCoubrey's *American Tradition in Painting* (New York, 1963), analyzing what he considers a peculiarly American formal mode of vision, deserves serious attention by anyone interested in the field. The best general presentation of American painting remains, I believe, Edgar P. Richardson's *Painting in America* (revised edition, New York, 1965) which contains a detailed bibliography on individual painters of the 19th century.

# THE DECORATIVE ARTS

## by Joseph T. Butler

Today the decorative arts from Washington to McKinley remain largely unexplored by serious scholars. While it was once the year 1800 at which scholarly interest waned, of late 1830 has become the date; the reason given is that quality declined with the Industrial Revolution and the resultant cessation of the handcraft system. The enormous mass of material which has come down from the period 1830–1900 has been another stumbling block, for the machine made possible the production of a vastly greater quantity of things than earlier hand methods. Even a preliminary sifting of this material reveals that much of real worth was produced and that the machine could be harnessed to create new materials and further manage to produce highly innovative objects. Many of the origins of the design revolution of the 20th century lie in the 19th. Is it not worthwhile to consider what was there?

The period 1789–1900 was one of rapid and constant change in the American decorative arts. Immediately following the Revolution, the English decorative arts were still carefully imitated by American craftsmen. It was the great era of classicism and all decorative objects fell under its design influence.

Classicism persisted in one form or another until the mid-19th century and Europe remained a dominant factor in determining taste. The time lag in transplanting style from Europe to America was now greatly shortened, however, because of improvements in communication.

Along with transplanted European styles came improvements in science and technology, and during the first half of the century the United States began to take her place beside Europe through inventions and improvements of the Industrial Revolution. The shop method, in which a craftsman with the aid of assistants conceived and fashioned a single

287

object, began to be overridden by the factory method, where a group of machinists was able to mass-produce the integral parts of an object and later assemble it.

With the waning of the late forms of classicism toward the end of the first half of the century, another series of historical revivals began. The 19th-century decorative arts were strongly and constantly under the influence of this revivalism and eventually borrowings were made from virtually every known design vocabulary—from the courts of the Bourbon kings to the harems of the Ottoman Empire. Toward the end of the century these revival styles were often so mixed and confused in a single object that it was impossible to determine the idiom which its creator had in mind. Indeed, the dominant mainstream of design throughout the century was historical revivalism.

While severe critics of the century maintain that after the 1830's, with the disappearance of the handcraft system, no distinguished decorative objects were produced, they are generally thinking in terms of confused historical revivalism. These critics do not look closely enough, for throughout the period there were proficient craftsmen and gifted designers who produced objects which were outside the vocabulary of revivalism. In retrospect, these products might be thought of as the progressive or innovative design influences of the period, for they set the background for the design revolution which was to take place in the 20th century. Instead of concentrating on imitating the past, these men developed new materials, new methods, and new design forms. It was in this area that Americans began to evolve a truly original inventive style which was not derivative from European influences.

Both historical revivalism and progressive trends will be treated in this essay. Since style is generally best seen in furniture, this subject will be treated first and in greater detail than the other decorative arts categories. The succession of historical revivals will be carefully developed under this topic but it is to be remembered that the design of glass, silver, ceramics and so forth was influenced as strongly as that of furniture. Under these other topics, innovations and progressive developments will be stressed with some information on historical revivalism included.

FURNITURE

*MAINSTREAMS OF STYLE DEVELOPMENT: HISTORICAL REVIVALISM*

*The Federal Period.* During the 1780's European classicism first began to influence furniture style in America. This first phase of classicism, which began *circa* 1790 and was to last until *circa* 1810, was based on the style which had been developed in England by Robert Adam. Its chief inspiration was Pompeian ornament; delicacy, overall symmetry and straight lines were its characteristics. Publications of furniture designs in England by George Hepplewhite and Thomas Sheraton were imported by Americans and became instrumental in setting what was called the Federal style.

Principal characteristics of this style were the square tapering leg, the round reeded leg, and the shield-shaped chair back. Inlay became as popular as carving as a decorative device; it often assumed such forms as the bellflower, eagle, urn, and feather. Many inlays were executed in exotic tropical woods while glass panels with *églomisé* (painting in white and gold in reverse on glass) were also set into furniture. Painting and japanning were popular methods of decorating furniture surfaces. Tambour construction (a round movable frame which can be opened and closed) was an innovation of the period and the sideboard and work table were probably the two most important new forms which evolved. The principal woods in use were satinwood, mahogany and bird's-eye maple.

The chief areas where cabinetmakers were producing this type of furniture were Boston, Salem, New York, Philadelphia and Baltimore. John Seymour (*circa* 1738–1818) and his son Thomas (1771–1848) were important Boston cabinetmakers of the time. The excellent design and careful construction of their furniture gives it a superior position among Federal pieces. They often painted interior compartments on cabinet pieces a greenish blue and this survives as one of the trademarks of their work (*Plate 215*). The architect Samuel McIntire (1757–1811) is most closely associated with the furniture of Salem. While he was not actually a cabinet-maker, his elaborate carvings of sheaves of wheat, baskets of fruit, and

Plate 215.
TAMBOUR DESK, HEPPLEWHITE STYLE, attributed to John and Thomas Seymour, Boston, 1795–1810. Case of piece mahogany inlaid with holly and satinwood. Tambour construction is to be observed in the doors which are delicately inlaid with bellflower swags. The pulls are enamel. *Courtesy*, BAYOU BEND COLLECTION, HOUSTON, TEXAS

Plate 216.
SQUARE WORK TABLE, HEPPLEWHITE STYLE, with figured birch and mahogany, and canted corners. Attributed to John and/or Thomas Seymour, Boston, *circa* 1800. One of the most beautiful American work tables. *Courtesy*, HENRY FRANCIS DU PONT WINTERTHUR MUSEUM, WINTERTHUR, DELAWARE

cornucopias on pieces of furniture made by others, are works of minor sculpture (*Plate 217*).

In Philadelphia, Henry Connelly (1770–1826) and Ephraim Haines (1775–1820) produced furniture of great delicacy and quality in a personal interpretation of the Sheraton style (*Plate 220*). Much still remains to be learned about the Baltimore cabinetmakers of the time. However, a large body of painted furniture survives with documented Baltimore histories. Thomas Renshaw, listed in the Baltimore directory for 1814–1815, was the maker of a labeled settee of the painted "fancy" Sheraton type which is preserved in the Baltimore Museum of Art (*Plate 222*).

New York, which was beginning its career as the style and taste center of America, also became an important cabinetmaking center during the Federal period. Slover and Taylor, who worked in partnership between 1802 and 1804, produced furniture in the Sheraton style which is character-

291

*Plate 217.* SOFA, SHERATON STYLE, MAHOGANY, carving attributed to Samuel McIntire, Salem, Massachusetts, *circa* 1800. The carving of the basket of fruit, swags, roses and sprays of laurel are all indicative of the work of Samuel McIntire. *Courtesy,* BAYOU BEND COLLECTION, HOUSTON, TEXAS

Plate 218.
POLE SCREEN, SHERATON STYLE, MAHOGANY.
Salem, Massachusetts, *circa* 1800. For sheer
virtuosity of carving, this pole screen is probably
the most elaborate example dating from the
early 19th century. *Courtesy*, HENRY FRANCIS
DU PONT WINTERTHUR MUSEUM,
WINTERTHUR, DELAWARE

Plate 219.
LOOKING GLASS, GOLD LEAF AND GESSO
OVER WHITE PINE FRAME. Albany or New
York City, *circa* 1805. Elaborate looking glasses
of this type have long been associated with the
great houses of the Hudson River Valley.
*Courtesy*, HENRY FRANCIS DU PONT WINTERTHUR
MUSEUM, WINTERTHUR, DELAWARE

ized by a half-daisy carved on the cresting rail of chairs and settees (*Plate 223*).

It was also in New York that one of America's most famous names in cabinetmaking, Duncan Phyfe (1768–1854), began his career working in the Federal style. Phyfe came to America from Scotland in 1783, settled briefly in Albany, and was working in New York in 1792. After 1795 he maintained the city's most fashionable cabinetmaking shop. His earliest works are in the Sheraton manner with square backs containing interlaced motifs and round reeded legs. The cresting rails of chairs and settees were carved with bowknots and floral motifs (*Plate 225*).

*Plate 220.*
SIDE CHAIR, SHERATON STYLE, MAHOGANY.
Attributed to Henry Connelly, Philadelphia, *circa* 1810. The carving of the foot is typical of the work of Connelly. *Courtesy*, PHILADELPHIA MUSEUM OF ART

By the Federal period, marked regional characteristics in furniture gradually began to disappear. There was now a faster and more efficient communication system between the various parts of the nation and cabinetmakers became more aware of urban styles and their proper execution. In New England a light stretcher was generally retained to support the legs of a chair; Rhode Island chairs used the *kylix* or tazza in their splats rather than the usual urn form; the quarter fan is often found as an inlay in New York furniture; Baltimore cabinetmakers used a bellflower row

294

*Plate 221.* TRIPOD OR PILLAR-AND-CLAW CARD TABLE, MAHOGANY, New York City, *circa* 1810. Several variants of this model of table were made in New York City and, as here, the reeding frequently extends from the end of a leaf to the iron paw foot. *Courtesy,* HENRY FRANCIS DU PONT WINTERTHUR MUSEUM, WINTERTHUR, DELAWARE

with a dot separating each separate husk. These are some of the minor regional differences which were carried over into Federal furniture.

*The Empire Style.* One of the most interesting things to note about Duncan Phyfe was that his work evolved from the Federal style through the Empire style and actually into an early version of the Rococo revival for he did not retire until 1847. He was probably the most dominant factor in creating the Empire style in the United States. This style was the second stage in the development of classicism and it was popular in the United States from *circa* 1810 until *circa* 1825. The Empire style was largely based on designs which Charles Percier and François Fontaine executed for Napoleon. It was a more literal or archaeological interpretation of classicism which proposed to actually reproduce antique furniture forms, especially those of Rome. Such Greco-Roman motifs as swans, dolphins, acanthus leaves, and monopodium were used on furniture which was heavy, massive and cubical. Napoleon's Egyptian campaign reintroduced the art of that country into the design vocabulary. In England, Thomas Hope combined all of these antique elements into the furniture which he designed; it was he who was instrumental in originating the Regency style.

Phyfe was using saber legs on *klismos* or Grecian chairs as early as 1807. He made the curule or Roman base popular for chairs and settees as well as the lyre and harp splat for chair backs (*Plate 226*). Another New York cabinetmaker important in establishing the American Empire style was Charles-Honoré Lannuier (1779–1819). His French background gave him an intimate knowledge of the Directoire and Empire styles and his work is often more ornate than that of Phyfe. He used elaborate French ormolu mounts on his furniture and his naturalistic carving has a fine sculpturesque quality (*Plate 227*).

By 1820, the column with ornate capital began to appear on cabinet furniture and the winged lion's paw was to be seen on sofas; furniture became increasingly heavy. Elaborate stenciled decorations, often in gold, were used on pieces of this type (*Plate 229*).

The production of "fancy" Sheraton chairs continued with great mo-

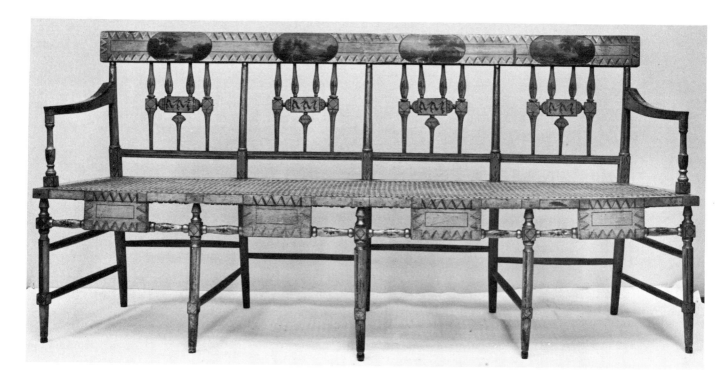

*Plate 222.* SETTEE, HEPPLEWHITE STYLE, PAINTED LIGHT WOOD. Labeled "Thomas Renshaw, Baltimore," *circa* 1815. This type of furniture was closely based on English prototypes which had their origins in the works of Adam and Hepplewhite. The great body of existing American painted furniture was made in Baltimore. *Courtesy*, THE BALTIMORE MUSEUM OF ART

mentum during the Empire period. These chairs had light frames which were painted and sometimes stenciled and had rush or caned seats. The most famous maker of these chairs was Lambert Hitchcock (1795–1852); he founded a factory in Hitchcocksville, Connecticut in 1825 where these chairs were mass-produced (*Plate 231*). They were innovative for their time because they were shipped disassembled and were put together by the purchaser. Another cabinetmaker who was ahead of his time was S. Gragg of Boston. He is known to have been working about 1815 and produced chairs and settees of oak and hickory which are remarkable because they were of bent-wood construction. The Shakers also began to produce a remarkable

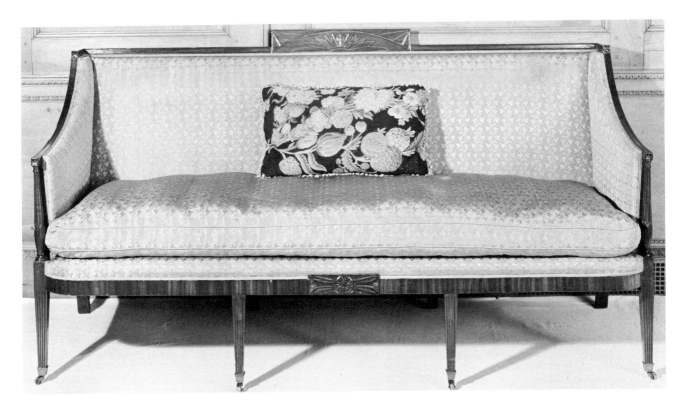

*Plate 223.* SOFA, SHERATON STYLE, MAHOGANY, *circa* 1805. Attributed to Slover and Taylor. The half-daisy carving on the cresting rail is typical of the work of Slover and Taylor. This sofa has a rare additional feature—the carving on the skirt. *Courtesy,* MRS. GILES WHITING

type of furniture. It was a simplification of classical lines resulting in a style which was almost ascetic. Shaker chairs were mass-produced and continued to be made in much the same form into the 20th century.

*Late Classicism*. The last phase of classicism began in the 1830's and lasted until the early 1850's. This phase was greatly influenced by the style of the French Restoration. While the massiveness still survived, furniture surfaces were stripped clean of ornament and the "C" and "S" scroll supports began to dominate (*Plate 232*). The plain classical style was widely disseminated through John Hall's *The Cabinet Maker's Assistant* (Baltimore, 1840),

298

*Plate 224.*
TALL CLOCK, MAHOGANY AND MAHOGANY VENEER ON CHERRY WITH SATINWOOD INLAYS. "George Jones, Wilmington, Del." is painted on dial. *Circa* 1810–1820. It is probable that each of the 20 inlaid stars represents a state, which would then place the clock 1817–1818, a date considerably later than its cabinetwork would indicate. *Courtesy*, HENRY FRANCIS DU PONT WINTERTHUR MUSEUM, WINTERTHUR, DELAWARE

*Plate 225.*
ARM CHAIR, SHERATON STYLE, MAHOGANY. Made by Duncan Phyfe, *circa* 1800–1810, for William Bayard, New York. This type of chair, with carved bow knot and darts on the cresting rail, represents Phyfe's earliest style. *Courtesy*, MUSEUM OF THE CITY OF NEW YORK

which also had the distinction of being America's first natively produced furniture design book. Hall includes 198 plates in this work which show infinite uses of scrolls in elliptical curves.

The late classical style found enthusiastic support in the cabinetmaking firm of Joseph Meeks and Sons (1797–1868) of New York. The Meeks company produced large quantities of this type of furniture; it often had a soft wood base which was overlaid with thin strips of mahogany veneer (*Plate 235*). Andrew Jackson Downing (1815–1852), writing in 1850, includes illustrations of this type of furniture in his *Architecture of Country Houses* (New York). He called the style Grecian and said that it was the most popular at the time for private residences.

*Plate 226.*
SIDE CHAIR, EARLY EMPIRE STYLE, MAHOGANY.
Made by Duncan Phyfe, 1810–1820, for the
Pearsall family, New York. Another piece from
Phyfe's early period, this example is especially
interesting because of the Roman *curule* or
"X" base. *Courtesy*, MUSEUM OF THE
CITY OF NEW YORK

*Plate 227.*
CARD TABLE, EMPIRE STYLE,
MAHOGANY. Made by Charles-Honoré
Lannuier, New York City, *circa* 1815,
for a Baltimore merchant James Bosley.
The carving of the winged caryatid
represents the best work of the Empire
carver. While this piece has only two
applied metal mounts, Lannuier often
used more. *Courtesy*, MARYLAND
HISTORICAL SOCIETY

*Plate 228.*
DRESSING TABLE, EMPIRE STYLE,
MAHOGANY VENEER AND GILT
DECORATION ON PINE AND POPLAR.
Probably New York City, *circa* 1825.
The gilt acanthus painting on the mirror
supports and the gilt capitals and feet
contrast elegantly with the mahogany
and black paint. The piece is put
together with wooden pins so that it
can be disassembled. *Courtesy*, NEILL P.
ANDREWS, HASTINGS-ON-HUDSON,
NEW YORK

300

*The Gothic Revival.* The Gothic revival was not as popular in the United States as it was in England, where its roots lay. Downing, who advocated Gothic for use in libraries, admits that it was not as popular as the other styles and the small number of pieces which survive today probably testify to that fact. The style was based on the design vocabulary of Gothic archi-

*Plate 229.*
WARDROBE, EMPIRE STYLE, MAHOGANY. In the manner of Joseph Meeks and Sons, *circa* 1830–1835, New York City. One of the interesting features of this piece is the use of Gothic pointed arches in the door of a classical body. The stenciled decoration is of the highest order. *Courtesy*, MUSEUM OF THE CITY OF NEW YORK

tecture and the pointed and lancet arch, crocket, rosette and tracery were its chief ingredients (*Plate 239*). The earliest type of Gothic furniture combined one or more of these elements into a basically classical structure.

Gothic was more popular as an architectural style and architects working in the idiom sometimes designed furniture to be used *en suite* with a house. Alexander J. Davis (1803–1892), an important exponent of the

*Plate 230.*
SIDE CHAIR, FANCY SHERATON STYLE. New York, 1815–1825. This chair, one of a pair, has a painted scene which is said to be a Hudson River view. The landscape is in natural colors and the original color of the chair dark green with gilt decoration. *Courtesy*, SLEEPY HOLLOW RESTORATIONS, TARRYTOWN, NEW YORK

style, designed furniture which was executed by Richard Byrnes of White Plains, New York. John Jelliff (1813–1893) of Newark, New Jersey, also worked in the Gothic style and produced furniture of great delicacy and beauty. Robert Conner published his *Cabinet Maker's Assistant* in New York in 1842; this was the first book of Gothic furniture designs to be published in the United States.

*Plate 231.*
SIDE CHAIR, FANCY SHERATON STYLE, MAPLE AND HICKORY. Painted and stenciled, 1825–1830. Marked on seat rail "L. Hitchcock, Hitchcocksville, Conn. Warranted." Chairs of this type were in common use in America. *Courtesy,* THE HENRY FORD MUSEUM, DEARBORN, MICHIGAN

303

*The Elizabethan Revival Style.* The Elizabethan style actually took its inspiration from the design vocabulary of the era of Charles I and II rather than that of Elizabeth I. Its chief characteristic was ball and spiral-twist turning and it was popular simultaneously with the classical and Gothic (*Plate 240*). Chairs were the most popular form produced in this style; they often had elaborate needlework backs and seats and resembled the *prie-Dieu* (*Plate 241*).

*Plate 232.* SOFA, FRENCH RESTAURATION STYLE, MAHOGANY, *circa* 1835–1840. The use of "S" and "C" scrolls is clearly demonstrated in this piece in which the mahogany veneers have been handsomely matched. *Courtesy*, LYMAN ALLYN MUSEUM, NEW LONDON, CONNECTICUT

Plate 233.
ARMCHAIR, FRENCH RESTAURATION
STYLE, MAHOGANY, *circa* 1840.
Probably New York. Chairs of this type
were often called "Sleepy Hollow" after
the popular story written by Washington
Irving. Furniture of this type offered the
ultimate in comfort. *Courtesy*, NEILL P.
ANDREWS, HASTINGS-ON-HUDSON,
NEW YORK

A popularization of the style produced great quantities of cottage
furniture in which the spiral-twist was simplified to a ball or spool turning.
Baroque split-spindles were also sometimes applied to the surface. This
furniture was made of soft wood and was painted with elaborate floral and
scroll decorations. It was generally produced in matching sets—bedroom sets
being the most common—and was favored by Downing for country houses
because of its practicality, attractiveness and inexpensiveness.

305

*The Rococo Revival Style.* The most popular of all furniture styles in the 19th century was the Rococo; it enjoyed a great vogue from the late 1840's until the end of the 1880's. Its inspiration was the curvilinear and graceful furniture of the court of Louis XV and its chief design elements were a delicate use of the "C" and "S" scroll and the cabriole leg. The naturalistic carving of flowers, birds, fruit, and sometimes human figures, was very popular on furniture of this type (*Plate 242*). Elaborate and intricate carving could be produced through newly developed mechanized techniques and Rococo furniture, probably more than any other of the century, was mass-produced in enormous quantities from walnut in a cheap and debased manner.

John Henry Belter (1804–1863) was probably America's chief exponent of quality production of furniture in this style. Belter was German by birth and served his apprenticeship in Württemburg. He migrated to New

*Plate 234.* SOFA, FRENCH RESTAURATION STYLE, MAHOGANY, *circa* 1840. Probably New York. The winged ends are very French in their treatment and the "S" scrolls anticipate the Rococo revival. *Courtesy,* NEILL P. ANDREWS, HASTINGS-ON-HUDSON, NEW YORK

*Plate 235.*
PIER TABLE, FRENCH RESTAURATION
STYLE, MAHOGANY VENEER ON POPLAR,
*circa* 1840–1845, New York. Pier tables
were usually placed between two
windows, generally in a parlor, with a
looking glass hanging above; an object
was generally displayed on the bottom
shelf against the mirrored background.
*Courtesy,* THE NEWARK MUSEUM
COLLECTION, NEWARK, NEW JERSEY

York and is first listed in the directory of that city in 1844. His shop on
Third Avenue near 76th Street, which was run by the factory method, became as fashionable as had Phyfe's before him. In addition to the excellence
of the design and detail of his furniture, Belter was of great importance because of technical innovations in furniture construction which he perfected.

*Plate 236.*
ARMCHAIR, FRENCH RESTAURATION
STYLE, MAHOGANY. *Circa* 1845, New
York. Comfortable chairs of this general
type were often referred to in
contemporary sources as "Voltaire"
chairs although the reason for this
remains obscure today. *Courtesy*,
SLEEPY HOLLOW RESTORATIONS,
TARRYTOWN, NEW YORK

The carving on Belter's furniture was so intricate that it would have
been difficult to carve from a solid board because of the configuration of
the grain; therefore, lamination was used to give strength and substance.
This process consisted of gluing together layers of wood (rosewood, oak,
ebonized hard wood) which were about 1/16-inch thick, the grain of one

*Plate 237.*
SIDE CHAIR, RESTAURATION-GOTHIC
STYLE, MAHOGANY. *Circa* 1848, New
York. A chair identical to this stamped
"A. & F. Roux" exists. The partnership
had a shop on Broadway in the years
1848–1849. *Courtesy,* NEILL P.
ANDREWS, HASTINGS-ON-HUDSON,
NEW YORK

*Plate 238.*
SIDE CHAIR, RESTAURATION-GOTHIC
STYLE, MAHOGANY. *Circa* 1848, New
York. A drawing shows chairs of this
type in use in the Lincoln cabinet room
of the White House. Bills survive to
prove that these chairs were made by
Joseph Meeks and Sons. This chair does
not have the exaggerated profile found
in the Roux chair. *Courtesy,* NEILL P.
ANDREWS, HASTINGS-ON-HUDSON,
NEW YORK

309

Plate 239.
CORNER WHATNOT, GOTHIC REVIVAL STYLE,
MAHOGANY, *circa* 1850–1860. One of the
original furnishings of the Robert Milligan house,
Saratoga, New York. The pointed arch and
tracery characteristic of Gothic design are clearly
discernible in this piece. *Courtesy,* THE
BROOKLYN MUSEUM, BROOKLYN, NEW YORK

Plate 240.
WHATNOT CABINET, ELIZABETHAN REVIVAL
STYLE, ROSEWOOD, *circa* 1850, probably New
York. The spiral or baroque twist of the supports
is the distinguishing feature of the Elizabethan
revival style. *Courtesy,* THE BROOKLYN MUSEUM,
BROOKLYN, NEW YORK

310

piece running against the grain of the two on either side. The layers could vary from three to sixteen although the average number was from six to eight. The laminated panels were then steamed in molds so that undulating curves and shaped surfaces were achieved and a single panel formed the back of a piece of seat furniture. Extra carved pieces were sometimes glued to the frame if the building-up of an area were desired (*Plates 243, 244, 245*).

*Plate 241.*
SIDE CHAIR, ELIZABETHAN REVIVAL STYLE, ROSEWOOD, *circa* 1845. Made for the Van Wyck family of New York. Such low or slipper chairs had their origins in 18th century design and were used in the bedroom or hall. *Courtesy,* MUSEUM OF THE CITY OF NEW YORK

*311*

*Plate 242.*
SIDE CHAIR, (BALLOON-BACK) ROCOCO
REVIVAL STYLE, MAHOGANY PAINTED WHITE
AND GILDED, New York, *circa* 1845. The
balloon-back was one of the 19th century's most
original contributions to design. It evolved from
modifications of the *klismos* shape. *Courtesy,*
FOUNTAIN ELMS, MUNSON-WILLIAMS-PROCTOR
INSTITUTE, UTICA, NEW YORK

*Plate 243.*
SLIPPER CHAIR, ROCOCO REVIVAL STYLE,
LAMINATED ROSEWOOD. Attributed to John
Henry Belter, New York City, 1850–1860.
The intricate pierced back is made up completely
of elements taken from nature. The delicacy
of the cabriole legs is typical of Belter's hand.
*Courtesy,* JOSEPH T. BUTLER

312

*Plate 244.* TABLE, ROCOCO REVIVAL STYLE, LAMINATED ROSEWOOD. Made for Mr. and Mrs. Carl Vietor, 1856–1861. Label reads "J. H. Belter & Co. Factory Warehouse, 552 Broadway, Manufacturers of all kinds of fine furniture, New York." The label on this table is one of several which are present on Belter's works. Such a table generally stood in the center of a parlor with a grouping of chairs around it. *Courtesy*, MUSEUM OF THE CITY OF NEW YORK

Although Belter applied for several patents on his laminating and steaming processes, there were other cabinetmakers who imitated his work. Charles A. Baudouine (active 1845–1900) was one of these; he had a large factory with several hundred employees and got around Belter's patents by running a central dividing seam through the center of a laminated panel (*Plate 246*). Other important Rococo revival cabinetmakers were Gustave Herter, Alexander Roux, and the Meeks Brothers in New York; Daniel Pabst, George Henkels, and Gottlieb Volmer in Philadelphia, François Seignoret in New Orleans, and S. S. Johns in Cincinnati.

By the middle of the century, furniture in the Rococo style was being produced in many parts of the United States. The principal woods were mahogany, rosewood and walnut. Although painted lightwood was used for country pieces, the Rococo furniture was most often produced in sets with seat furniture, tables, and cabinet furniture *en suite*. The new forms which

314

*Plate 245.* SOFA, ROCOCO-RENAISSANCE REVIVAL STYLE, LAMINATED ROSEWOOD. Attributed to John Henry Belter, *circa* 1860. This piece is from the final period of Belter's production and represents a complete transition from the naturalism of his earlier pieces. *Courtesy*, THE METROPOLITAN MUSEUM OF ART, NEW YORK. GIFT OF MR. AND MRS. LOWELL ROSS BURCH AND MISS JEAN MC LEAN MORRON, 1951

*Plate 246.* Card Table, Rococo Revival Style, Laminated Rosewood. Marked by Charles A. Baudouine, New York. Made for the Williams family of Utica, *circa* 1850. The treatment of the legs is an unusual feature in 19th century furniture. This table is one of a pair which were designed to fit together. *Courtesy,* FOUNTAIN ELMS, MUNSON-WILLIAMS-PROCTOR INSTITUTE, UTICA, NEW YORK

were originated at the time were the étagère or "what-not," the balloon-back chair, and the single-end sofa which was derived from an Empire form.

A sub-style of the Rococo was called the "Louis Quatorze" in its day. Cabinet furniture was most often produced in this style and its design elements included broken pediments, geometric detail, heroic figures, and garlands of naturalistic elements. This furniture was massive and clumsy and did not enjoy a great popularity (*Plate 247*).

*Plate 247*. Sideboard, Red Walnut, Louis XIV Revival Style. Attributed to Daniel Pabst, Philadelphia, *circa* 1869. Because of their massive quality, few pieces of this type have survived in the 20th century. The carved medallions represent the full-blown Renaissance revival style. *Courtesy*, philadelphia museum of art

316

*Historical Revivalism, 1865–1900.* From the Civil War period through the end of the century, historical revivalism seemed to increase in popularity and designers and cabinetmakers began to vie with one another for novelty of production. Often the design elements from several styles would be combined into a single piece of furniture and much was produced which was shoddy and grotesque.

The Renaissance revival style was one which was popular throughout the second half of the century. Its exact source of inspiration is not known but design books before 1850 mention the style and Downing mentions it as being popular. In overall design the style was essentially square and massive and examples produced toward the end of the century became more and more heavy. It was characterized by the use of broken pediments, applied medallions, acorn trimmings and the tapering baluster-turned leg.

G. Hunzinger of New York produced some of the best designed furniture in this style. He was of German birth and was working in New York in the 1860's, for in 1866 he patented a folding chair. Often the stationary pieces which he produced contained a similar structural bracing to that found in a folding chair. His work was delicate and he demonstrated a careful knowledge of the design vocabulary with which he worked (*Plate 248*). Other makers of Renaissance revival furniture, some of whom had worked in the rococo revival style, were John Jelliff of Newark, Daniel Pabst of Philadelphia, and Thomas Brooks of Brooklyn. It was the factories at Grand Rapids, however, which made this a universal American style. Quantities of this furniture were made there in the last quarter of the century and they were shipped to all parts of the United States (*Plate 249*).

Another of the important revival styles which continued in popularity through to the end of the century was the Louis XVI. It was apparently in France about the middle of the century that the style was revived. Its source of inspiration was French classicism and the oval back, reeded-tapering leg and classical devices such as bowknots, paterae, classical medallions, and sunbursts were reintroduced. Mahogany was the most popular wood employed although it was often ebonized and inlaid with exotic marquetry and mother of pearl (*Plate 250*). Some of the most elaborate American pieces were fitted with pierced metal gallery edges and were inlaid with imported French porcelain plaques.

Henkels of Philadelphia and Jelliff of Newark also worked in this style as they had in other revival styles, but its center of production was New York where the Sypher firm, Thomas Brooks, Léon Marcotte, and

*Plate 248.*
SIDE CHAIR, RENAISSANCE REVIVAL STYLE, WALNUT. Stamped "Hunzinger N. Y. Pat. March 30, 1869." The bracing of the base resembles that used by the craftsmen in folding chairs although this is a stationary model. Hunzinger was one of the most successful interpreters of the Renaissance revival style. *Courtesy*, NATIONAL TRUST FOR HISTORIC PRESERVATION, WASHINGTON, D. C.

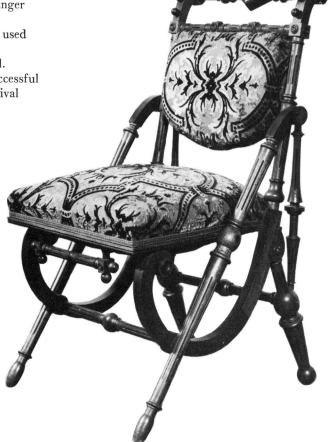

*Plate 249.* BEDROOM SUITE, RENAISSANCE REVIVAL STYLE, WALNUT AND BURL WALNUT. Made by Berkey and Gay Company, Grand Rapids, Michigan, *circa* 1876. Bedroom suites of this kind were one of the most common types of the last forty years of the century. *Courtesy*, GRAND RAPIDS PUBLIC MUSEUM, GRAND RAPIDS, MICHIGAN

319

*Plate 250.*
ARMCHAIR, LOUIS XVI REVIVAL STYLE,
MAHOGANY, EBONIZED AND GILDED,
New York, *circa* 1875. This was one
of the more elaborate productions in
the Louis XVI revival style. *Courtesy*,
MUSEUM OF THE CITY OF NEW YORK

the Herter Brothers were among its best known exponents. Louis XVI
furniture continued to be made into the early 20th century. The later
pieces are often of natural walnut carved in flat relief with caned backs
and seats.

320

*Plate 251.*
SIDE CHAIR AND MATCHING TABLE,
INSPIRED BY LOUIS XVI STYLE, PAINTED
WOOD INLAID WITH NACRE AND GILT
DECORATION. Possibly New York,
*circa* 1880. Such pieces were the height
of fashion in dining rooms of the
1880's. *Courtesy*, MUSEUM OF THE
CITY OF NEW YORK

A style which was not largely adapted into furniture design was the Romanesque. One of America's great architects, Henry Hobson Richardson (1838–1886), who is known for his development of this style, did design some furniture which was to be used *en suite* in architectural settings. The furniture was generally made of oak and had little direct connection with Romanesque detail; rather, in some ways it reflected the principles of the Arts and Crafts Movement (*Plate 252*).

During the last quarter of the century, a new vogue came into being— the quest of the "antique." While collecting had been reserved as the pursuit of the wealthy in earlier times, old furniture was now advised by tastemakers

322

*Plate 252.* SETTEE, OAK. Designed by Henry H. Richardson, *circa* 1875. Richardson's furniture was not conceived in an overall manner and the elements are somewhat distracting; his architecture is more satisfying than his furniture. *Courtesy,* MUSEUM OF FINE ARTS, BOSTON

for people of more modest means. Especially popular were furnishings associated with the Spanish and Italian Renaissance and the Orient. Great public interest was aroused by American furniture of the Colonial period shown at the Philadelphia Centennial Exposition of 1876. Probably this exhibition was largely responsible for the impetus which produced vast quantities of reproduction American colonial furnishings through the end of the century. This furniture, primarily in the Queen Anne and Chippendale styles, is often incorrectly referred to as "centennial."

Another style which was somewhat popular during the entire century, but became increasingly important during the last decade, was the Moorish or Oriental. This style was essentially Near Eastern in its inspiration, but elements from many Oriental design vocabularies were often indiscriminately mixed. The smoking room was most often done in this style, but it began to spread to other rooms of the house through the "Turkish corner." This was an area which contained a Near Eastern divan or a heap of pillows; a tent-like drapery was often put over this, sometimes supported by poles with elaborate Saracenic terminations (*Plate 253*). A Persian or Turkish carpet provided the base for the creation and it was littered with a variety of Koran stands, smoking equipment, teakwood screens, and every other variety of exotic object; large plants were often an integral part of the *ensemble* (*Plate 254*).

The furniture which was incorporated into tnese Moorish rooms was completely under the domination of the upholsterer. The cabinetmaker became less important toward the end of the century and his work was often completely covered by elaborate tufted, fringed, and tasseled surfaces. Often the upholsterer was also an interior decorator and he determined the physical surroundings of the room into which his furniture was to be placed. Moorish upholstered furniture was decorated with a mixture of bizarre embroideries which were borrowed from various design sources. The coil spring provided great comfort to such furniture; this improvement will be discussed under innovative furniture.

An examination of the furniture exhibitions at the Chicago Columbian Exhibition of 1893 gives a good indication of the state of taste by the end

Plate 253.
ARMLESS CHAIR, MOORISH REVIVAL
STYLE. UPHOLSTERY OVER SPRING
CONSTRUCTION. Made for the John D.
Rockefeller house, New York City, *circa*
1880. This piece was designed *en suite*
with other forms for an extraordinary
room; the embroidery attempts to simulate
Saracenic design. *Courtesy*, THE
BROOKLYN MUSEUM, BROOKLYN,
NEW YORK

Plate 254.
SMOKING STAND, MOORISH REVIVAL
STYLE, BRONZE. *Circa* 1870. A perfect
piece for a fashionable Turkish corner.
*Courtesy*, MUSEUM OF THE CITY OF
NEW YORK

324

of the century. Revivalism and eclecticism were reigning supreme. It was now often impossible to determine the revival style in which an individual piece had been conceived because so many extraneous elements were combined into it. Most of the pieces shown were mass produced or special "custom-built" machine creations. The machine dominated furniture making and produced pieces which were poorly constructed and generally tasteless.

*DESIGN REFORM AND INNOVATIVE FURNITURE*

*Design Reformers.* By the middle of the century there was an organized outcry in England against the poor design produced by revivalism and machine production. This movement was spurred on by such leaders as Henry Cole, Owen Jones and John Ruskin. Another Englishman, William Morris, believed that good design could be achieved only through a return to the handcraft and guild method of the Middle Ages. He and his associates turned their attention to many crafts among which was furniture design in the 1860's. His furniture was produced and decorated by hand and proved to be too costly for popular consumption.

Charles J. Eastlake, who was an exponent of good taste in the Morris manner, was especially important in influencing taste in the United States for his *Hints on Household Taste* was first printed in New York in 1872 and continued to be reprinted through the remainder of the century. Eastlake spoke out against revivalism and advocated a straightforward, simple type of furniture which was inspired by Gothic English ornament. His book was widely circulated in the United States and furniture which incorporated his ideas was widely produced although no American piece which is a direct replica of one of his illustrations has yet come to light (*Plate 255*).

One of the English outgrowths of the philosophy and practice of these reformers was the Arts and Crafts Movement which flourished from about 1882 until 1910. Workmen banded together to form guilds, and good hand-workmanship and the proper use of material were emphasized. There was also a return to the simple furniture of English cottages where

*Plate 255.* ORGAN, EASTLAKE INFLUENCE. Made by Jacob Estey Organ Company, Brattleboro, Vermont, *circa* 1880. Most of the top section was cut on a jigsaw and intricacy was the desired effect. Such pieces were middle-class high style in their day. *Courtesy,* THE HENRY FORD MU-SEUM, DEARBORN, MICHIGAN

utility was foremost and decoration secondary. In the United States there was some influence of the Arts and Crafts Movement, but it was not widespread. Some craftsmen did organize communities where a number of different trades were practiced. Notable among these was the

*Plate 256.*
BOOKCASE. By the Roycrofters, East Aurora, New York, *circa* 1900. Elbert Hubbard's design. *Courtesy*, W. HAWKINS FERRY, GROSSE POINTE SHORES, MICHIGAN. PHOTOGRAPH BY JACK O. PETZOLDT

327

community founded at East Aurora, New York, by Elbert G. Hubbard (1856–1915). Although printing and bookmaking were a primary interest of this group, some of the craftsmen fashioned simple furniture which was used in the houses of the community and also sold commercially (*Plate 256*). Another American outgrowth of the Arts and Crafts Movement was the Mission style—a style inspired by the colonial Spanish furniture of the Southwest. Oak was the most common wood for this furniture which was heavy, rectilinear, and largely unornamented.

*Progressive Furniture Forms.* Simultaneous with the interest in design reform and a break with revivalism, other designers and craftsmen were experimenting with technical innovations which could be combined into furniture forms or new materials from which furniture could be made. It was these men who produced some of the most outstanding furniture of the century, for this formed the background for the revolt against tradition in the 20th century.

John Henry Belter has been mentioned for his reintroduction of laminated wood panels into furniture making. This was of extreme importance because it gave furniture greater strength and durability and provided a medium for sensitive shaping and elaborate carved decoration which otherwise could not have been achieved. Another designer who experimented with lamination and bending by steam was the Austrian, Michael Thonet (1796–1871). His earliest attempts were made in Germany and Austria and by 1850 he had perfected a process for bending straight dowels of birch wood into highly elaborate designs. His pieces often show the curved influence of the Rococo revival style but his construction method reduced the elements of a furniture form to its basic structure. Thonet's product was known as bentwood and it enjoyed a wide popularity in Europe and the United States. It was shipped to this country in parts and assembled with screws in the salesroom. Chairs and settees generally had seats and backs which were composed of caned panels. Although Thonet carefully patented his furniture, there were imitators here who produced pieces which can often be distinguished because of their lack of sophistication and inferior quality.

A substance which was not produced in any great quantity in the United States, but is none the less important in 19th-century furniture design, was papier mâché. This material was produced by pressing together under great pressure paper pulp or strips of paper with glue. When the molded piece had hardened, it was removed from the mold and treated with successive coats of heavy paint or lacquer. The decoration was further elaborated through painted scenes and designs and inlaid nacre. Because of technological advances in the steam-driven presses, it was possible to make large pieces of furniture by this method and fanciful curves and swells could be achieved that could not be fashioned from wood. The end product was highly durable unless it was exposed to water or damp surfaces.

The English and French factories exported great quantities of this furniture and other decorative accessories to the United States and papier mâché became one of the popular elegancies of the mid-century parlor. Some attempt was made by the Litchfield Manufacturing Company (Connecticut) from 1850 until 1854 to make papier mâché; small boxes, trays, and a few serving stands were the usual output and the product was inferior to its English counterpart.

Metals also became increasingly popular during the century as a material for furniture production. The most popular of these was cast iron. The Industrial Revolution had brought about great advances in the iron industry and more efficient methods of molding made possible the production of larger single units. The iron works, especially in New York and Philadelphia, produced great numbers of cast iron chairs, settees, and tables which were intended for garden use, as well as umbrella stands and hat trees for interiors. The units of these pieces were shipped unassembled and were fashioned into complete furniture forms by the vendor. Iron furniture could incorporate any of the revival design elements although pieces were often made in a rustic manner which incorporated tree limbs with fruits and flowers (*Plate 257*). The factories which produced iron furniture also generally turned their attention to pieces made from wire. The heavy wire was generally twisted into highly fanciful shapes which were reminiscent of the curves of the Rococo revival (*Plate 258*).

*329*

Furniture constructed from hollow steel tubes was being made in France during the 1840's. It was made in England by the 1850's and brass was added as a material from which the tubing was made. Chairs of this type were generally rockers and a bent section of the metal tubing formed the entire rear member of the piece. It is not known that these chairs were ever produced in the United States, but an example survives of similar design in which the flattened iron elements were substituted for the tubes. This unusual chair is thought to have been made between 1850 and 1860 by Peter Cooper (1791–1883) at his iron foundry in Trenton, New Jersey; the iron frame is painted to imitate tortoise shell (*Plate 259*).

*330*

*Plate 257.* BENCH, CAST IRON, INSPIRED BY ROCOCO REVIVAL STYLE. Marked "E. T. Barnum, Detroit, Michigan." *Circa* 1885. A wonderful example of the combination of naturalistic and rococo elements in cast iron. *Courtesy,* THE HENRY FORD MUSEUM, DEARBORN, MICHIGAN

Another important type of innovative furniture was that which combined a mechanical device with the design and construction of the piece. This was a resurgence of the very old desire for movability and collapsibility in furniture. Comfort became an increasingly important quality of

Plate 258.
GARDEN CHAIR, INSPIRED BY ROCOCO
REVIVAL STYLE, IRON AND WIRE
PAINTED GREEN, *circa* 1870. Such chairs
were made throughout the second half
of the 19th century; they have a strong
appeal today because of their light and
airy construction. *Courtesy*, THE HENRY
FORD MUSEUM, DEARBORN, MICHIGAN

331

seat furniture and designers tried to achieve it in highly imaginative ways. As early as 1840, in his *The Cabinet Maker's Assistant*, Hall showed a chair which could be converted into a day bed. By the middle of the century and until its end, the Patent Office in Washington was flooded by inventions for folding, dual or triple purpose, and convertible furniture forms (*Plate 260*). Closely aligned with this was the concentration on dentists' and barbers' chairs, and built-in furniture for railroads and steamships. Even elaborate pieces of cabinet furniture were patented because of their ingenuity in concealing pigeon-holes and storage com-

332

*Plate 259.* ROCKING CHAIR, IRON PAINTED TO IMITATE TORTOISE SHELL. Believed to have been made by Peter Cooper at Trenton, New Jersey, *circa* 1850. This strongly resembles European prototypes which were made of tubular metal. Such a chair was a great contribution to comfort. *Courtesy,* THE COOPER UNION MUSEUM, NEW YORK, N. Y.

*Plate 260.*
INVALID CHAIR. *Circa* 1880. The iron frame is completely extendible to change the chair into a day bed. The chair can be adjusted to four positions and is the grandfather of the convertible chair of today. *Courtesy*, THE HENRY FORD MUSEUM, DEARBORN, MICHIGAN

333

partments. One of the most elaborate of these was patented by the Wooten Brothers in 1874 (*Plate 261*).

One of the most important innovations of the second half of the century was the widespread use of the metal coil spring. The spiral coil spring was known in the late 18th century, but it was not incorporated in any degree into furniture construction. Just when and why, during the 19th century, the spring achieved such popularity is still not known. One of the American products which was illustrated in the catalog of the

*Plate 261.* DESK, LATE RENAISSANCE REVIVAL STYLE, MAHOGANY AND BURL MAHOGANY. Stamped "The Wooten Brothers Patent 1874." A similar desk was owned by John D. Rockefeller in Cleveland, Ohio. *Courtesy*, THE BROOKLYN MUSEUM, BROOKLYN, NEW YORK

Crystal Palace Exhibition of 1851 was a centripetal spring chair which was patented by the American Chair Company of Troy, New York. This chair had a spring installed in the connection section between base and seat so that the chair would recline when its back was pushed against. The frames of these chairs were generally made of cast iron and they were often upholstered in plush carpet; spring chairs are the ancestors of the reclining desk chair of the 20th century (*Plate 262*).

An even more elaborate use of coil springs was to be seen in the Turkish frame chairs of the 1880's and 1890's. The frames of these chairs were made of iron or steel and all of the parts of the chair were made up of coil springs. The only wood elements to be found were the legs and their connecting members. The entire piece was elaborately upholstered, usually with considerable tufting, and a heavy fringe was placed around the base so that the wood legs were concealed. The concept was one of complete comfort and the art of the upholsterer dominated that of the cabinetmaker. These chairs were often to be found in rooms which were Near Eastern in their inspiration (*Plate 263*).

*Furniture of Natural Organic Substances.* While great strides were being made in the machine production of innovative furniture, another type was being produced completely by hand. This was furniture which was made from organic materials and was intended for country houses and cottages where it would aid in creating a picturesque environment. One of the simplest types of this furniture and the kind which was easiest to fashion was made from the natural branches of trees. The branches were carefully selected so that they essentially followed the contours of the desired furniture form; these were then nailed or screwed together and the product was often very rustic. Two articles of Downing's, posthumously published in his periodical *The Horticulturist* in 1858, described the methods of making furniture from rustic wood.

Closely related to this was the manufacture of furniture from cane (wicker or rattan). The cane was a durable tendril from an Oriental climbing palm. It was imported into the United States and Gervase Wheeler,

writing in his *Rural Homes* (1852), describes the magnitude of the
industry in New York at the time; the chief manufactories were orphan
and insane asylums. The cane was soaked in water until it became pliable
and then it was woven around frames which were fashioned from hickory
or white oak. The cane ornamentation could be as original as the imagination of its creator so that some pieces approached the fantasy world in

*Plate 263.*
ARMCHAIR, TURKISH FRAME
CONSTRUCTION OF COIL SPRINGS,
UPHOLSTERED, CHERRY LEGS UNDER
FRINGE. *Circa* 1880. The art of the
upholsterer reaches its height. Now all
functional members of the chair are
obscured by upholstery. *Courtesy*,
NATIONAL TRUST FOR HISTORIC
PRESERVATION, WASHINGTON, D. C.

their concept. The furniture was light and airy and intended for use on porches or inside summer houses (*Plate 264*). Bamboo was also imported along with cane from the Orient. This was fashioned into seat furniture, tables, and cabinets and pieces of pseudo-Japanese lacquer were set into them to heighten the Oriental feeling.

A final form of highly unusual organic furniture was made from the

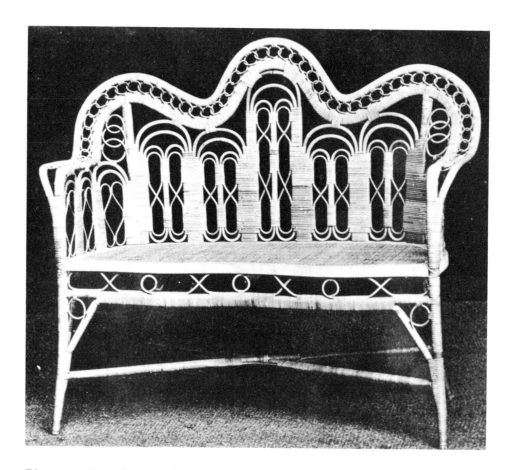

*Plate 264.* CANE SETTEE. Reproduced from catalog of Wakefield Rattan Company, Boston. *Circa* 1885. The fantasy of such furniture is indicative of the laborious hand process which was used to produce it. PHOTOGRAPH BY LOUIS H. FROHMAN

horns of native animals. The great interest in the American West during the second half of the century caused this furniture to be very popular. The horns of deer, antelope, buffalo, steers, etc. were all incorporated into seat furniture and tables. The horns often had to be matched so that a certain amount of symmetry could be achieved in a given piece; chairs and settees were upholstered in the skin of the animal from which the horns had come or in a plush fabric.

## SILVER

BECAUSE of its intrinsic value, silver, next to furniture, generally follows the high style of a period more closely than the other decorative arts. Federal silver was carefully based on imported English models which were in the classical style and characterized by straight structural lines. The urn shape was the most popular for hollow pieces; decoration was achieved through reeded or beaded moldings, bright-cut ornament engraved in delicate parallel bands, and urn-shaped finials.

Silversmithing changed very little in the years following the Revolution. The handcraft method was still perpetuated and a master silversmith evolved through the apprentice system. Famous among silversmiths of the period was Paul Revere (1735–1818) who worked in Boston. Before the Revolution he had worked in the rococo tradition but he now turned his attention to the classical style and produced a pitcher shape about 1800 which was related to the Liverpool jug (*Plate 265*). Benjamin Burt was another important Boston silversmith, while in New York Samuel Johnson, Ephraim Brasher, and Hugh Wishart fashioned pieces which are testimonies to the popularity which they achieved. Philadelphia remained an important center of the silver craft as it had been in colonial times; Joseph Lownes, Abraham Dubois, James Musgrave, and Joseph Anthony, Jr. were all important makers in the classical style. Charles Louis Boehme was probably the leading Baltimore silversmith of the period.

The matching teaset became extremely popular and it served an important decorative function when used on another classical creation—the sideboard (*Plate 266*). The tankard lost popularity and the spoon was still the most common form to be found. During the period 1785–1810 the spoon was characterized by a pointed bowl and down-turned handle.

During the 1820's, French silver forms became a dominant influence on American craftsmen. Pieces became larger in scale and silver stock was of a heavier material. Shapes were round or geometric and antique Greek and Roman vessels such as urns or vases were copied. Die-cast ornament

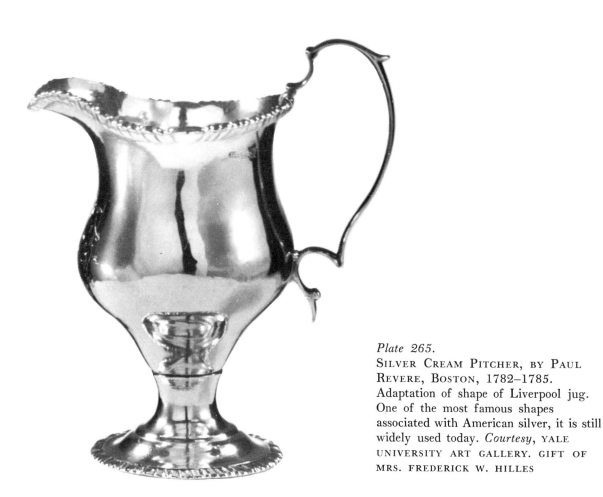

*Plate 265.*
SILVER CREAM PITCHER, BY PAUL
REVERE, BOSTON, 1782–1785.
Adaptation of shape of Liverpool jug.
One of the most famous shapes
associated with American silver, it is still
widely used today. *Courtesy*, YALE
UNIVERSITY ART GALLERY. GIFT OF
MRS. FREDERICK W. HILLES

was often used for decoration, the Greek key, anthemion leaf, oak and
laurel leaves being the most common. Handles varied in shape from
simple scrolls to cast wreaths, sheaves of wheat, or animal forms (*Plate
269*).

These basic characteristics persisted into the 1840's although romantic
elements were often used as decoration on later pieces. Another decorative
device which gained tremendous popularity at this time was *repoussé*.
Although this was in use as early as 1825, *repoussé* became the most
popular decoration by 1840. A Baltimore silversmith, Samuel Kirk
(working 1793–1872), is sometimes given the credit for the introduction

of this decoration; it is known, however, that other craftsmen were using *repoussé* at the same time (*Plate 270*).

Spoons changed in shape from the rounded or coffin-end handle of 1800 to a plain "fiddle back" or spatulate down-curved handle. These were often stamped with a basket of flowers, sheaf of wheat, or shell. "Fiddle back" spoons were popular until the 1830's when the spatulate up-turned handle succeeded them. Knives and forks were not commonly produced in the United States until the 1850's.

Some important silversmiths of the 1830's and 1840's were George Gelston, William Forbes and William Thomson of New York, Anthony Rasch, Thomas Whartenby and Peter Bumm of Philadelphia and Obadiah Rich of Boston.

*Plate 266.* SILVER TEA SET. Made by Abraham Dubois, Philadelphia, 1785–1795. The use of beaded moldings as well as the pierced gallery are characteristics of Philadelphia silver of the day. *Courtesy,* YALE UNIVERSITY ART GALLERY. THE MABEL BRADY GARVAN COLLECTION

Plate 267.
SILVER CANN, by Robert S. Shepard,
Albany, New York, *circa* 1800. Bears an
elaborate engraved script-monogram
"PUC," for Pierre Van Cortlandt II
(1762–1848). *Courtesy,* SLEEPY
HOLLOW RESTORATIONS, TARRYTOWN,
NEW YORK

Plate 268.
PATCH BOX, SILVER AND COWIE SHELL,
by Robert S. Shepard and William B.
Boyd, Albany, New York, *circa*
1810–1813. The elaborate monogram
"A. S." is for its owner, Ann Stephenson
Van Cortlandt (1774–1821). *Courtesy,*
SLEEPY HOLLOW RESTORATIONS,
TARRYTOWN, NEW YORK

342

A revolutionary change of the 1840's was the introduction of electro-plating. This process made it possible to apply a coat of plate to a piece of britannia, pewter, or other metal. Designs were often borrowed directly from the trade catalogs of English competitors. The entire craft, however, was undergoing a great change. By 1840 the effects of mechanization were already to be seen and by 1870 the silver craft had been transformed into a full-scale industry. By 1900, virtually the entire industry had adopted mass production.

*Plate 269.* SILVER TEAPOT, SUGAR BOWL, CREAMER. Made by Shepard and Boyd, Albany, New York, *circa* 1820. The bold Greek key or meander pattern plus the dog finial are characteristics of Empire silver. *Courtesy,* THE ALBANY INSTITUTE OF HISTORY AND ART, ALBANY, NEW YORK

*Plate 270.*
SILVER TEAPOT AND SILVER CONDIMENT SHAKER. Made
by William Forbes, New York City, *circa* 1830. The dawn
of the rococo revival is clearly seen in the cartouche and
naturalistic decoration of this piece. *Courtesy,* NEW-YORK
HISTORICAL SOCIETY, NEW YORK CITY

344

The silver of the 1850's and 1860's is characterized by the use of bulbous forms and rococo ornament, often of a naturalistic type (*Plate 271*). Elaborate tea services often demonstrated the virtuosity of the designer by crowding details of historical ornament into a single piece. During the 1860's, Renaissance ornament became popular; forms were

*Plate 271.*
SILVER PITCHER. Made by Ball and Black, New York City. One of a pair, marked "Elam Williams to Julia A. Vanderpool, 1867." A return to shape and decoration of the mid-18th century is clearly demonstrated in this rococo revival piece. IN THE COLLECTIONS OF THE MUSEUM OF THE CITY OF NEW YORK

decorated with bands of cast architectural ornament and sometimes human figures in relief. The Renaissance style continued to be dominant through the 1870's, although matted or dulled finishes were also used to heighten surface contrasts. Revivalism was at its height during the 1880's and a great variety of Oriental, Louis XVI, Assyrian and other motifs were intermixed although Orientalism was probably the dominant theme (*Plate 272*). By the 1890's, there was a severe reaction to revivalism and forms of the 18th century again were introduced.

346

*Plate 272.* SILVER COMPOTE. Unmarked; possibly New York, *circa* 1880. Eclecticism typifies this high-style piece whose design elements diverge from classical to rococo. IN THE COLLECTIONS OF THE MUSEUM OF THE CITY OF NEW YORK

The second half of the century is especially interesting because it saw the rise of such great jewelry establishments as Tiffany and Company of New York and J. E. Caldwell and Company of Philadelphia. These stores provided a wealthy clientele with a vast number of silver patterns from which to choose. Pieces were made by the store or commissioned from other factories and marked accordingly.

While revivalism dominated silver design during the second half of the century, important innovations were being made through mechanization. This silver can only rarely be thought of as aesthetically pleasing, but it demonstrates the complete absorption which man had with the machine.

GLASS

AMERICA's first sophisticated native glass, comparable to that of Europe, was produced during the last decade of the 18th century. John Frederick Amelung, a native of Bremen, Germany, established two glasshouses near Frederick, Maryland, at a place he called New Bremen—the first in 1784 and the second in 1787. He brought a group of German workmen with him and the factory produced window glass and a variety of blown table wares and commemorative objects. Amelung glass was of the soda-lime type or glass made with no lead added to the sand; this is a light-weight glass and most of the pieces had a greenish or smoky cast. The New Bremen glass is thoroughly German in its concept and execution and the elaborate engraved inscriptions with their floral embellishments are identical with the best German products of the time (*Plate 273*).

In 1808, Benjamin Bakewell and Benjamin Page, both from Derby, England, opened a glasshouse in Pittsburgh—first called Bakewell and Company and later Bakewell and Page. This factory produced flint glass—a heavier type with a lead base which produced a clear bell-like tone when struck. The glass was clear and dense and it lent itself to elaborate cut and engraved decoration. Sets of stemmed tableware were the speciality of the Pittsburgh glass house; indeed, until 1819 Bakewell and Page were the sole producers of these wares in the United States. The cut and engraved

*Plate 273.*
PRESENTATION POKAL, BLOWN GLASS. Made by John F. Amelung, New Bremen, Maryland. Inscriptions read "Old Bremen Success and the New Progress" and "New Bremen Glassmanufactory— 1788." Amelung made the first sophisticated glass in America. Such a piece closely resembles its German contemporaries. *Courtesy,* THE METROPOLITAN MUSEUM OF ART, NEW YORK. ROGERS FUND, 1928

decoration embraced the designs of classicism, and swags, draperies, floral motifs and patriotic emblems dominated these pieces. The Bakewell firm was in operation until 1882; it had the longest life-span of any American 19th-century glasshouse (*Plate 274*).

Inspired by the success of Pittsburgh, a glass factory was established in 1818 in Cambridge, Massachusetts. This was the genesis of the New

*Plate 274.*
WINE GLASS, BLOWN AND CUT. Made by Bakewell and Company, Pittsburgh, *circa* 1860. This type of simple, cut decoration is typical of the period and it greatly appealed to a wide segment of the population. *Courtesy*, THE BROOKLYN MUSEUM, BROOKLYN, NEW YORK

England Glass Company and Deming Jarves (1790–1869), father of the critic, James Jackson Jarves, was its first manager. The output of this factory was primarily stemmed table glass and the cutting technique of decoration was emphasized. While the workmen at the New Bremen and Pittsburgh factories had been German, the Cambridge factory employed glassmakers from England and Ireland who were trained in the best British tradition. One of the innovative developments of this company which can surely be called distinctively American was three-mold glass. In order to achieve a uniformity in table wares, glass was blown into a full mold which generally had three parts. The mold was hinged and the seams where the sections fit together were usually devised so that they would become a part of the design. A great variety of different articles was made by this method and often a single mold could be utilized in making more than one object. Generally pieces of this type were clear but such colors as purple, amethyst, blue, green, and yellow were sometimes artificially produced (*Plate 275*).

Deming Jarves left Cambridge in 1825 and founded his own Boston and Sandwich Glass Company at Sandwich on Cape Cod. The earliest products of this factory were of the blown and three-mold type. In 1827, Jarves, aided by a practical workman, produced an object which was to revolutionize the glassmaking industry—a mold and a hand-operated machine by which a pressed glass tumbler could be made. This invention was so revolutionary that Jarves' own workmen threatened his life for they feared that this machine process would turn all of them out of work.

Molds had been developed in the 1820's from which pieces of flat or shallow glass, such as salts or cup plates, could be made. However, it was not until Jarves' invention that a complete piece of hollow ware could be fashioned; this opened the way for the great wave of mass production which followed and put glass within the economic reach of everyone. The Sandwich pressed pieces were made in elaborately designed molds. Often the background was covered with a fine stippling which suggested lace and gave the name "lacy glass" to the type. The designs of most pieces of lacy glass are so contrived that the background covers the entire piece. The design motifs were borrowed directly from the Empire idiom and cornucopias, lyres, acanthus leaves, and patriotic symbols all began to appear; in the 1840's and 1850's, Gothic pointed arches became the most popular design. Soon lacy pressed glass was being made at other factories but none surpassed Sandwich in its output. Between 1820 and 1840 it is known that there were slightly over one hundred independent glasshouses operating in various parts of the United States (*Plate 276*).

*Plate 275.* PITCHER, BLOWN THREE-MOLD CLEAR GLASS. Midwestern or Massachusetts, *circa* 1825–1835. The Roman rosette motif was very popular in this type of glass. *Courtesy,* THE CORNING MUSEUM OF GLASS, CORNING, NEW YORK

Other types of glass were being made in the 1830's, however. A pressed glass, much simpler than the lacy variety, imitated the direct fluted patterns of cut glass; the first pressed goblets were of this type. This was the beginning of the production of pattern glass or pressed glass in complete matching table sets. The vogue for this was to last throughout the century and the popular market was flooded with it in clear glass and various colors. The earlier pieces were generally made of flint glass and the patterns were largely geometric. In the 1860's William Leighton in Wheeling, West Virginia, originated a formula for soda-lime glass which made it especially appropriate for pressing. More ornate patterns of a naturalistic or com-

352

*Plate 276.* DISH, PRESSED LACY GLASS, SANDWICH, MASSACHUSETTS. *Circa* 1840. American pressed glass often found design inspiration, as in this piece, in the products of the French Baccarat factory. *Courtesy*, THE METROPOLITAN MUSEUM OF ART, NEW YORK. GIFT OF MRS. F. N. CROSBY, 1948

memorative nature were incorporated into the pressed glass of the 1870's and 1880's; often the designs were ill-composed and not suited to the shape of the vessel (*Plate 277*).

353

*Plate 277.* COVERED COMPOTE, PRESSED PATTERN GLASS ("Westward Ho" pattern), by James Gillinder and Sons, Philadelphia, *circa* 1875. Pattern glass had great popularity with the average American. Sets were sold as well as individual pieces; the patterns numbered in the thousands. *Courtesy*, THE BROOKLYN MUSEUM, BROOKLYN, NEW YORK

One of the important branches of glassmaking was the manufacture of lighting devices. Before 1830, lamps were being made in great quantity; often they were nothing more than a stepped base with a globular reservoir which held a whale oil wick. By the middle of the century the lamp industry at Sandwich was highly developed; these were often made in one of the popular lacy patterns. The advent of kerosene as a burning fluid in the third quarter of the century, created a market for glass lamps—often designed in a pattern so that the lamp was *en suite* with a table setting. About the middle of the century, pressed glass candlesticks began to be made; these were a standard product of all factories.

The vogue for blown glass never died out during the 19th century; there was a growing market after 1850 for more expensive handmade products. An American version of Bohemian glass was being produced by Louis Vaupel at the New England Glass Company in the 1850's. A casing of colored glass was put over a clear base and the pieces were cut or engraved through so that the end product was of two colors. This process was also practiced at Sandwich where the large and elaborate overlay kerosene lamps became one of the major products of the factory. Designs on the Bohemian and overlay pieces were realistic; they showed foliage, animals, and hunting scenes. While the earlier 19th-century blown pieces used a discreet cutting for decoration, after 1875 table glass was introduced which was covered with cutting. This decoration was often so elaborate that the body of the piece had to be thick and heavy to accommodate it.

Paperweights were important novelties of 19th-century blown glass. They were first introduced here by craftsmen who had been trained at French glasshouses. Paperweights were highly individual creations and depended on the ingenuity of the craftsman; they were of the *millefiori* type, contained sulphide busts of celebrities, or were made in the shapes of fruits. Silvered glass was another American novelty; it was patented as early as 1855 by the New England Glass Company and later produced by other factories. It attempted to be an imitation of silver and was blown double, the interior painted with a solution of silver nitrate. Sometimes there was an engraved or painted decoration to further enrich the piece.

A minor revolution took place in glass blowing during the 1880's. The exhibitions at the Philadelphia Centennial of 1876 had exposed Americans to the ceramics of the Orient and craftsmen tried to imitate their shapes and colors in glass. These pieces were referred to as "art glass"; color and surface treatment were the keynotes to this type of glass. Colored glass was given shadings through reheating; amberina and peachblow were the two basic types produced by this method. Peachblow is a term which was derived from the Chinese peachbloom porcelain vase which created a sensation through the high price paid by J. P. Morgan at auction in the 1880's. The peachblow produced by the Hobbs, Brockunier Company of Wheeling, West Virginia, shades from a light yellow to red white; that made at Cambridge ranges from opaque white to deep rose; both often had an acid finish (*Plate 278*). Amberina was a transparent flint glass which

*Plate 278.*
MATCH HOLDER, BLOWN PEACHBLOW
GLASS. Made by New England Glass
Company, Cambridge, Massachusetts,
*circa* 1885. The shapes achieved in
peachblow glass were among the most
advanced of the 19th century. *Courtesy*,
THE BROOKLYN MUSEUM, BROOKLYN,
NEW YORK

355

*Plate 279.* BOWL, BLOWN AMBERINA GLASS. Provenance unknown, *circa* 1885. Dessert sets as well as stemmed glassware were produced in this popular coloring. *Courtesy,* THE BROOKLYN MUSEUM, BROOKLYN, NEW YORK

shaded from amber to deep red; it was made at Cambridge and at the Mount Washington Glass Company at New Bedford, Massachusetts (*Plate 279*). Closely related was Burmese glass which was also produced at New Bedford; it had a dull finish, shaded from yellow to pink, and often had enameled decoration.

By the 1890's all varieties of novelties were being produced; often naturalistic flowers in different colors were applied, or mineral flakes were put in the glass to achieve a spangled metallic appearance. One of the great innovators of this period was Louis Comfort Tiffany (1848–1933) who first turned his attention to glassmaking in the 1870's. Tiffany was interested in excavated ancient glass which was iridescent and at-

*Plate 280.* VASES, BLOWN FAVRILE GLASS, by Louis Comfort Tiffany, New York, 1890–1910.
The organic shapes achieved by Tiffany were the best interpretation of Art Nouveau in America.
*Courtesy,* THE METROPOLITAN MUSEUM OF ART, NEW YORK

tempted to recreate this appearance in some of his pieces. By 1880 he had applied for patents on his iridescent finishes and in 1893 he founded his own glass furnaces at Corona, Long Island. Tiffany was especially important because he was one of the few Americans who became an exponent of Art Nouveau—an organized European movement (*circa* 1890–*circa* 1919) which rejected the design of the past and turned to nature for its inspiration. This movement enjoyed great popularity in Europe at the time (*Plate 280*).

## CERAMICS

AT the close of the 18th century there were few innovations in the potter's craft beyond those which were known at its beginning. Pottery, which was chiefly made in New England, New York and Pennsyl-

*Plate 281.* FIVE VASES AND BOWLS, BLOWN FAVRILE GLASS, by Louis Comfort Tiffany, New York, 1890–1910. More naturalistic forms and decorations can be seen here. *Courtesy*, THE MUSEUM OF MODERN ART, NEW YORK CITY. THE JOSEPH H. HEIL TIFFANY COLLECTION

Plate 282.
TWO PITCHERS, DECORATED
EARTHENWARE, CONNECTICUT, early
19th century. The shapes of these pieces
are of the simplest type and could be
produced by a village potter; such forms
have persisted for hundreds of years.
*Courtesy*, THE BROOKLYN MUSEUM,
BROOKLYN, NEW YORK

359

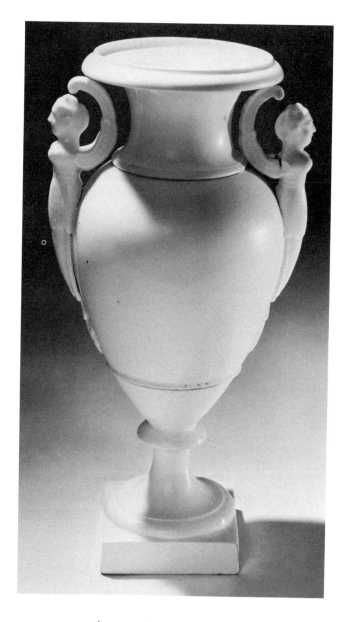

Plate 283.
PORCELAIN URN, UNDECORATED, by
Dr. Henry Mead, New York, 1816. The
direct inspiration of this porcelain urn lies
in French porcelain of the period.
*Courtesy*, PHILADELPHIA MUSEUM
OF ART

vania, was fashioned by the time-honored method of hand-throwing; most
of the products were utilitarian and under the design influence of the
peasant or popular crafts of the country from which the potters had
migrated (*Plate 282*). There had been some attempts to manufacture
pottery commercially, but none of these succeeded and the handcraft
method persisted. Although contemporary accounts refer to the manufacture of "porcelain," it would seem that a kind of tin-glazed earthenware is what was probably meant.

*Plate 284.*
VASES, POLYCHROME DECORATED
PORCELAIN, by Tucker and Hemphill,
Philadelphia, *circa* 1830. Tucker was the
first American to produce porcelain in
any quantity or in a successful manner;
his work is imitative of French sources.
*Courtesy*, PHILADELPHIA MUSEUM
OF ART

361

Actual porcelain was not made successfully in the United States until 1816. Dr. Henry Mead of New York was the manufacturer and only a few pieces in the Empire style survive today with a documented history of origin in this factory (*Plate 283*). Other brief attempts were made in Philadelphia and Jersey City, but it was not until 1827 that a factory was established which was to have a continuous existence of eleven years. This was founded in Philadelphia by William Ellis Tucker whose object was to emulate the popular porcelain which was imported in considerable quantity from France. Vases and urns were important products of this factory, but the most ordinary productions were useful tableware. The earliest pieces were plain white; later, gold or sepia

*Plate 285.*
PITCHER, GILT DECORATED PORCELAIN, Union Porcelain Company, Greenpoint, Long Island, New York, *circa* 1864. The influence of the rococo revival is seen in the molded design and gilt tracery. *Courtesy*, THE HENRY FORD MUSEUM, DEARBORN, MICHIGAN

decoration was added, and finally elaborate polychrome decorations were used (*Plate 284*).

Another factory which was successful in producing a soft paste porcelain was established in 1847 by Charles Cartlidge at Greenpoint, Long Island. Its products were generally table wares, buttons and door knobs; these were generally decorated only in black and gold. This enterprise lasted until 1856, only to be followed a year later by William Bock and Brothers which existed until 1861. The factory then became known as the Union Porcelain Works; it had a long history (*Plate 285*).

Just as molds were being developed during the second quarter of the century for pressing glass, so the pottery industry turned to more mechanized methods. The earliest pottery molds were for shallow forms with a simple decoration. Most of these pieces were of earthenware and the factories which produced them were large. One of these was the Ameri-

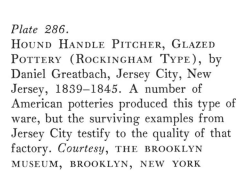

*Plate 286.*
HOUND HANDLE PITCHER, GLAZED POTTERY (ROCKINGHAM TYPE), by Daniel Greatbach, Jersey City, New Jersey, 1839–1845. A number of American potteries produced this type of ware, but the surviving examples from Jersey City testify to the quality of that factory. *Courtesy*, THE BROOKLYN MUSEUM, BROOKLYN, NEW YORK

can Pottery Manufacturing Company which was established in Jersey City by David Henderson. The factory was greatly influenced by English pottery of the time and many of the pieces were under the influence of so-called Rockingham wares (*Plate 286*). The United States Pottery Company at Bennington, Vermont, began to make wares of this type by the middle of the century. This factory was highly successful and became famous for its unglazed porcelains which sometimes incorporated contrasting white and colored areas (*Plate 287*).

By the Civil War, virtually all ceramic wares were mass-produced. Since the design or decoration was determined by the maker of the

*Plate 287.*
VASE, UNGLAZED PORCELAIN, BENNINGTON, VERMONT, *circa* 1850. While Bennington was noted as a great pottery center, the most successful of its productions were of parian or unglazed porcelain. *Courtesy*, THE HENRY FORD MUSEUM, DEARBORN, MICHIGAN

*Plate 288.* ROCKINGHAM AND FLINT ENAMEL CANDLESTICKS, Bennington, Vermont, 1849–1858. The two on the top row are Rockingham and the remaining three are flint enamel. *Courtesy,* THE BENNINGTON MUSEUM, BENNINGTON, VERMONT. PHOTOGRAPH BY LLOYD STUDIO

*Plate 289.*
VASE, POLYCHROME DECORATED
PORCELAIN. Painted by Antoine Heidrick
for Lenox, Incorporated, 1896. Marked
"Lenox." Lenox Incorporated, which is
still a thriving ceramics company, has
always been known for quality work.
*Courtesy,* LENOX INCORPORATED
COLLECTION, TRENTON, NEW JERSEY.
DONATED BY MR. WILLIAM CLAYTON,
FEBRUARY 1950

molds, the individual craftsman lost most of his influence on the finished product. Many pieces were conceived in the vocabulary of revivalism which became as mixed and confused as in other decorative art categories. One of the important areas in which great strides were made was the production of porcelain. After the attempts and successes of the first half of the century, a number of highly enterprising firms evolved—Knowles, Taylor and Knowles Company of East Liverpool, Ohio; in 1872, the Onondaga Pottery Company (founded in 1870 by James Pass); and in 1889, Walter Scott Lenox's pottery at Trenton, New Jersey (*Plate 289*).

The character of American Victorian ceramics could be observed in the wares displayed at the Philadelphia Centennial Exhibition of 1876. Naturalism was the dominant force in all of the creations; indeed, the ability to reproduce minutiae from nature received the highest praise. One of the pieces most noted was "The Century Vase" which was designed and decorated by Karl Müller for the Union Porcelain Works. This vase had handles at either side which were the shape of bison heads and the piece was decorated with historical scenes and portraits. The conception of the piece displays the virtuosity of the designer-decorator but completely negates the properties of the porcelain from which it was made (*Plate 290*). This might be stated as the nature of ceramics by the late 1870's—a concept of the proper use of basic materials had been lost. This was to be changed, however, within the next decade.

A group of lady amateurs in Cincinnati, Ohio were inspired by the English Arts and Crafts Movement and decided to design pottery so that the shape and decoration would have continuity. They were also greatly interested in the arts of the Orient and attempted to simulate decoration drawn from this source. From this group the Rookwood Pottery—still in existence—was organized in 1880 by Maria Longworth Storer, wife of the diplomat Bellamy Storer. This was America's first art pottery and each piece was individually thrown on the wheel and decorated. Great individuality was encouraged and pieces were signed by their creator, dated, and numbered for shape. Some of America's best potters, such as A. Van Briggle, M. A. Daly, W. McDonald, and A. R. Valentien, worked at

*Plate 290.* VASE, POLYCHROME DECORATED PORCELAIN. By Karl Müller at Union Porcelain Works, Greenpoint, Long Island, New York, *circa* 1876. This famous vase, whose decoration is completely American in inspiration, was exhibited at the Philadelphia Centennial Exhibition. *Courtesy,* THE BROOKLYN MUSEUM, BROOKLYN, NEW YORK

*Plate 291.* VASE, UNDERGLAZE DECORATED POTTERY. By A. Van Briggle at Rookwood Pottery, Cincinnati, Ohio, *circa* 1900. The Rookwood Pottery, which is still in existence, produced many pieces which were Art Nouveau in their inspiration. *Courtesy*, DR. AND MRS. ROBERT KOCH. PHOTOGRAPH BY FERDINAND BOESCH

this pottery (*Plate 291*). Other potteries founded in the late 1880's and based on the example of Rookwood were the Weller Pottery at Zanesville, Ohio and J. S. Tafts' Hampshire Pottery at Keene, New Hampshire.

Another field which offered a possibility for creative ceramics was the design of terra-cotta ornaments. These were intended to be incorporated into buildings and were made from molds designed by some of the leading architects of the day—for instance, James Renwick, Jr., Louis Sullivan and Bernard R. Maybeck. Probably the most successful were Sullivan's in which motifs drawn from nature were treated in a highly organic and complex manner (*Plate 292*). The molds for the tiles were supplied to construction firms all over the country. The terra-cotta factories in Boston, New York and Chicago were probably the most important.

Tiles for use in interior architecture were also produced in large quantities and many of them were important because of the quality of

*Plate 292.* TERRACOTTA TILE DESIGNED BY LOUIS SULLIVAN FOR THE REUBEN RUBEL HOUSE, Chicago, 1884. Demolished 1958. This tile was part of a stringcourse at shoulder height adjoining the front door of the house. PHOTOGRAPH BY RICHARD NICKEL, PARK RIDGE, ILLINOIS

the painted decoration which adorned them. Chelsea, Massachusetts, became the center of the tile industry about 1880 and the best tiles done there were produced by John G. Low.

By the end of the century, Art Nouveau had a widespread influence on the pottery industry. A. Van Briggle had left the Rookwood Pottery and gone to Colorado Springs for his health and some of the best Art Nouveau pottery came from his establishment there. In 1897, William H. Grueby, who had made great advances in the tile industry, began to make vases and glaze them with a matte finish. Louis C. Tiffany greatly admired this pottery and ordered some lamp bases made of it. Grueby's firm went out of business in 1907 and Tiffany carried on the pottery tradition in his own establishment, incorporating many of his naturalistic designs, which were famous in his glass, into pottery.

CHANGING DOMESTIC INTERIORS, 1789–1900

In conclusion, it might be well to discuss briefly some key domestic interiors which span our time period and analyze the changing taste which dominates them. Unhappily, there is room for little more than the most surface of treatments.

In the 1790's, Oliver Phelps remodeled a house in Suffield, Connecticut in the then fashionable classical style. The parlor from this house, now installed in the Henry F. du Pont Winterthur Museum, has a paneled fireplace wall which displays the vocabulary of classical design. It is carved with urns, paterae, swags, etc. and is supported by simple classical orders. The dentilled cornice pattern which runs around the ceiling is also borrowed from classical architecture. The paneling is painted a soft gray and the walls are papered in a colorful wallpaper. All of the furniture is in the Hepplewhite or Sheraton styles and the accessories, many of which are imported, are in the classical taste. In general, the arrangement of the room is highly rigid and formal but an airy quality is given to the whole because of the delicacy of the objects (*Plate 293*).

The heavy influence of archaeological classicism of the Empire style is to be seen in a drawing which Alexander J. Davis did in 1845 of a New York double parlor. The room now resembles the interior of a classical temple—full Doric orders are used to separate the two sections of the parlor and the trim around the ceiling and doorways is directly copied from antique ornamentation. The woodwork is painted white to simulate marble and the walls are a light gray. There is little furniture and it is in the Empire taste; the chairs are *klismos* in shape. The few decorative items such as torchiéres, an urn, and a pole screen are copies of Roman

*Plate 293.* CLASSICAL PARLOR, FROM OLIVER PHELPS HOUSE AT SUFFIELD, CONNECTICUT, *circa* 1790. The symmetry, use of classically inspired motifs, and general lightness of this room are all typical of classicism in America. *Courtesy,* HENRY FRANCIS DU PONT WINTERTHUR MUSEUM, WINTERTHUR, DELAWARE

prototypes. Although the room is sparsely furnished, the massive character
of the woodwork and furniture give it a heavy feeling (*Plate 294*).

The parlor of the Robert Milligan house from Saratoga, New York,
which is now installed in the Brooklyn Museum, well represents the revival
taste of 1853. Here is an eclectic spirit for there are full-length classical
pilasters, moldings in a heavy classical style, and embellishments in the
rococo taste. The elaborate white marble mantelpiece is a splendid mixture
of classical and rococo details. The overmantel looking glass and furniture

*Plate 294.* EMPIRE DOUBLE PARLOR FOR A NEW YORK HOUSE, DRAWN BY ALEXANDER J.
DAVIS, 1845. The archaeological exactness and massive quality of the Empire style are to be
observed in this remarkably clear drawing. *Courtesy*, THE NEW-YORK HISTORICAL SOCIETY,
NEW YORK CITY

*Plate 295.* PARLOR FROM ROBERT MILLIGAN HOUSE AT SARATOGA, NEW YORK, 1853. Although some classical elements still persist in the architecture, the furnishings of this room typify the height of lushness of the Rococo revival. *Courtesy*, THE BROOKLYN MUSEUM, BROOKLYN, NEW YORK

are fully developed rococo pieces. The draperies are of floral patterned silk damask and the broadloom carpet is a swirl of floral and rococo detail. While there is a formality to the arrangement of furniture around the table in the center of the room, it has a cozy, comfortable appearance. Instead of letting in daylight, the oppressive draperies and inside shutters seem to shut it out. The profusion of decorative objects and color give a cluttered and confused appearance (*Plate 295*).

In 1879 the extraordinary millionaire William Henry Vanderbilt began to build a brownstone house in New York which stretched for one block (51st Street to 52nd Street) on the west side of Fifth Avenue. The interiors of this house represented the height of eclecticism which was considered the best taste of the time. A sumptuous picture album (*Mr. Vanderbilt's House and Collection*) was produced which showed the glories of the house. The commentary, signed by Edward Strahan, noted two solid ivory statues by Moreau-Vauthier in the drawing room. "Both are completely adapted for parlor meditation. They are completely elegant, refined, artistic, without deep mythological meanings to disturb the equipoise of the evening parlor." It is apparently these statues which are visible in the right and left corners of the room in the photograph from the album (*Plate 296*).

The ceiling of the drawing room was decorated very much in the taste of the time with an elaborate painted mural. The artist remains anonymous. Another American, James McNeill Whistler (1834–1903), was probably the most advanced practitioner of this art. His murals were conceived in small panels which were surrounded by architectural woodwork. Among his most famous English commissions were the dining room at Aubrey House (1873) and the Peacock Room (1876–77) which is now installed at the Freer Gallery of Art in Washington, D. C.

But in the Vanderbilt house, the photograph of the Japanese room (*Plate 297*) shows a treatment diametrically opposed to Whistler's ideas. This room well illustrates another of Strahan's extravagant statements, although, in retrospect we might well be suspicious of the word "typical": "In these volumes, we are permitted to make a revelation of a private home which better than any other possible selection may stand as a repre-

sentative of the new impulse now felt in the national life. Like a more
perfect Pompeii, the work will be the vision and image of a typical American
residence, seized at the moment when the nation begins to have a taste of
its own . . . the country, at this moment, is just beginning to be astonishing."

In 1892, Richard Morris Hunt designed "The Breakers" in Newport,
Rhode Island, for Cornelius Vanderbilt. Architecturally, the house was in the
16th-century Italian manner and the interiors were conceived as back-

*Plate 296.* DRAWING ROOM FROM WILLIAM H. VANDERBILT HOUSE, NEW YORK CITY, 1879.
Grandeur and the taste for princely surroundings and possessions is reflected in such a room.
Eclecticism has reached a height and borrowings from every design source are included. PHOTO-
GRAPH BY BROWN BROTHERS, NEW YORK

ground for the courtly life of a wealthy American financier. Many architectural details in the dining room were borrowed from 16th-century design, but there is a liberal mixing of elements from other sources. Some of the pieces of furniture are European antiques; the majority, however, are 19th-century reproductions in the antique spirit. The age of the architect-decorator had arrived and the elaboration and stateliness of the room match its rigidity. The taste for such splendors as these were confined to the wealthy

*Plate 297.* Japanese Room from William H. Vanderbilt House, New York City, 1879. The taste for the exotic and fascination for the Orient are represented in a room which would be considered garish by 20th century standards; this was the taste of the *very* rich. Photograph by Brown Brothers, New York

*Plate 298.* STUDIO FROM NEW YORK CITY HOUSE OF LOUIS C. TIFFANY. *Circa* 1890. As Tiffany excelled in the products which he produced, so his interiors exhibit a remarkable freedom from the eclecticism which was so prevalent. This photograph is reproduced from Desmond and Croly, *Stately Homes in America*, NEW YORK, N. Y., 1903.

few and did not filter to the great masses other than in the taste for the "antique" and reproductions which developed at the end of the century.

One of the most extraordinary domestic interiors was the studio which Louis C. Tiffany created (*circa* 1890) for his New York City house. The fireplace stood in the center of the room and had a highly organic shape. All manner of Moorish lamps, ostrich eggs and innumerable decorative objects were suspended at varying heights from the ceiling around the fireplace. The furniture was reduced to a minimum and was simple and functional, in a relaxed and comfortable arrangement. Against a wall a collection of pictures and other memorabilia was displayed. The room was lighted by sky lights and the *ensemble* had a pleasantly bizarre appearance. Surely, such an interior was the direct antecedent of the informal interiors of the 20th century (*Plate 298*).

The architectural firm of McKim, Mead, and White eventually dominated the New York architectural scene of the 1890's. Indeed, John Jay Chapman said of Stanford White:

*If you were walking down Fifth Avenue and caught sight of a turkey red curtain at the upper window of a new Renaissance apartment, you knew who it was who hung his flag there. If you went to a charity ball, and saw on the stage a set of gilt twisted wooden columns eighteen feet high and festooned with laurel, you looked about till you found Stanford on top of a ladder draping a tapestry.*

About 1895, White redecorated the New York brownstone house of William C. Whitney which stood on the northeast corner of Fifth Avenue and 69th Street. Photographs of the rooms reveal that they were conceived in various period styles and their interpretation was intended to be careful. The drawing room (*Plate 299*) was in the Louis XV style in its overall inspiration although there is some mixing of Regence furniture. The library (*Plate 300*) was in the Renaissance style with what appears to be a mixture of architectural elements and objects from Italian, French and Spanish sources. While it is known that White was a furniture designer, it is difficult, because of the lack of exact knowledge, to distinguish which pieces were his own designs, which were designed by members of his firm, or which were actual antiques.

Fashionable Newport was naturally another center of work for the McKim, Mead, and White firm. During the 1890's, the dining room of an earlier Newport house was redecorated and expanded by White for the Armstrong family (*Plate 301*). One of the most interesting features of this room was the mosaic glass screen which was designed by Louis C. Tiffany and thus united the work of a great designer and a great architect.

*Plate 299.* DRAWING ROOM FROM WILLIAM C. WHITNEY HOUSE, NEW YORK CITY. *Circa* 1895. Stanford White created a Europe in America and this room shows his careful attempt to simulate a salon of the reign of Louis XV. *Courtesy,* MUSEUM OF THE CITY OF NEW YORK

At the end of the century, the novelist Edith Wharton was one of America's greatest advocates of a return to a careful study of the monuments of Europe. With Ogden Codman, Jr. she published *The Decoration of Houses* (1897), a history of the decorative arts plus a guide for wealthy Americans for the creation of houses which would rival in taste the great palaces of Europe. To her, good taste was established in Europe

*Plate 300.* LIBRARY FROM WILLIAM C. WHITNEY HOUSE, NEW YORK CITY. *Circa* 1895. If a European palace could be added to in various periods, so a princely American house could have rooms inspired by different epochs and lands. *Courtesy,* MUSEUM OF THE CITY OF NEW YORK

and the best that Americans could do was to imitate it. In the *Age of Innocence* (1920) she wrote with disgust of a 19th-century room which was "the purest 1830, with a grim harmony of cabbage-rose-garlanded carpets, rosewood consoles, round-arched fireplace with black marble mantels, and immense glazed bookcases of mahogany."

This, then, was the taste of wealthy Americans at the beginning of the 20th century—a desire for things European and a distaste for American products of the earlier 19th century. This impression unfortunately exists to some extent today. It is hoped that this essay will at least point out a few accomplishments of the period.

*Plate 301.* DINING ROOM FROM ARMSTRONG HOUSE, NEWPORT, RHODE ISLAND, 1880. The collaboration of White and Tiffany created a room which was remarkably progressive for the end of the century. PHOTOGRAPH BY WAYNE ANDREWS

# BIBLIOGRAPHY

## A Century of Aspiration

ADAMS, BROOKS, *The Degradation of the Democratic Dogma*. New York, 1919.

ADAMS, CHARLES FRANCIS, *An Autobiography*. Boston, 1916.

ADAMS, HENRY, *The Education of Henry Adams: An Autobiography*. Boston, 1918.

———, *History of the United States During the Administrations of Jefferson and Madison*. 9 vols. New York, 1888–1891.

BEARD, CHARLES A., *Economic Origins of Jeffersonian Democracy*. New York, 1915.

BEER, THOMAS, *The Mauve Decade: American Life at the End of the Nineteenth Century*. New York, 1926.

BERMAN, ELEANOR D., *Jefferson Among the Arts*. New York, 1947.

BILLINGTON, RAY A., *Westward Expansion*. New York, 1949.

BIRKBECK, MORRIS, *Notes on a Journey in America, from Virginia to Illinois*. Philadelphia, 1817.

BLAU, JOSEPH N., *Men and Movements in American Philosophy*. New York, 1952.

———, *Social Theories of Jacksonian Democracy*. New York, 1954.

BODE, CARL, *The Anatomy of American Popular Culture, 1840–1861*. Berkeley, 1959.

BOND, B. W., *Civilization of the Old Northwest*. New York, 1934.

BOORSTIN, DANIEL J., *America and the Image of Europe*. New York, 1960.

———, *The Americans: The National Experience*. New York, 1965.

———, *The Lost World of Thomas Jefferson*. New York, 1948.

BRANCH, E. DOUGLAS, *The Sentimental Years*. New York, 1934.

BRISSOT DE WARVILLE, J. P., *New Travels in the United States of America*. 2 vols. London, 1794.

BROOKS, VAN WYCK, *The Dream of Arcadia*. New York, 1958.

———, *The Flowering of New England*. Boston, 1936.

———, *The World of Washington Irving*. Boston, 1944.

BRYCE, JAMES, *The American Commonwealth*. 2 vols. New York, 1893.

BURNS, EDWARD M., *The American Sense of Mission*. New Brunswick, N.J., 1957.

CASH, W. J., *The Mind of the South*. New York, 1941.

COCHRAN, THOMAS C., *Railroad Leaders, 1845–1890: The Business Mind in Action*. Cambridge, 1953.

———, AND WILLIAM MILLER, *The Age of Enterprise: A Social History of Industrial America*. New York, 1956.

CONSTABLE, W. G., *Art Collecting in the United States of America: An Outline of a History*. New York, 1964.

COOPER, JAMES FENIMORE, *The American Democrat*. Cooperstown, N.Y., 1838.

CRAVEN, WAYNE, *Sculpture in America*. New York, 1968.

CREMIN, LAWRENCE C., *The Transformation of the School: Progressivism in American Education, 1876–1957*. New York, 1961.

CRÈVECOEUR, MICHEL GUILLAUME ST. JOHN DE, *Letters from an American Farmer*. London, 1782 (many later editions).

CROSS, WHITNEY R., *The Burned-Over District*. Ithaca, 1950.

CURTI, MERLE, *The Growth of American Thought*. New York, 1943.

———, *The Roots of American Loyalty*. New York, 1946.

DANGERFIELD, GEORGE, *The Awakening of American Nationalism, 1815–1828*. New York, 1965.

# Bibliography

———, *The Era of Good Feelings*. New York, 1952.

DAVIDSON, MARSHALL, *The American Heritage of American Antiques from the Revolution to the Civil War, 1783–1860*. New York, 1968.

———, *Life in America*. 2 vols. Boston, 1951.

DICKENS, CHARLES, *American Notes for General Circulation*. 2 vols. New York, 1842.

DORFMAN, JOSEPH, *The Economic Mind in American Civilization, 1606–1865*. 3 vols. New York, 1946–1949.

DUNLAP, WILLIAM, *Diary*, ed. by Dorothy C. Barck. 3 vols. New York, 1930.

———, *History of the Rise and Progress of the Arts of Design in the United States*, ed. by Frank W. Bayley and Charles Goodspeed. 3 vols. Boston, 1918.

DURAND, JOHN B., *The Life and Times of A. B. Durand*. New York, 1894.

DWIGHT, TIMOTHY, *Travels in New England and New York*. 4 vols. New Haven, 1821–1822.

EKIRCH, ARTHUR, *The Idea of Progress in America, 1815–1860*. New York, 1944.

FLAGG, JARED B., *Life and Letters of Washington Allston*. New York, 1892.

FLEXNER, JAMES THOMAS, *That Wilder Image: The Painting of America's Native School from Thomas Cole to Winslow Homer*. Boston, 1962.

GINGER, RAY, *Age of Excess: The United States from 1877 to 1914*. New York, 1965.

———, *Altgeld's America: The Lincoln Ideal versus Changing Realities*. New York, 1958.

GREENOUGH, HORATIO, *Form and Function: Remarks on Art*, ed. by Harold A. Small. Berkeley, 1947.

———, *The Travels, Observations, and Experiences of a Yankee Stonecutter*. New York, 1852.

GRUND, FRANCIS J., *The Americans in Their Moral, Social, and Political Relations*. 2 vols. London, 1839.

HAGEN, OSCAR, *The Birth of the American Tradition in Art*. New York, 1940.

HALL, FRANCIS, *Travels in Canada and the United States in 1816 and 1817*. Boston, 1818.

HAMILTON, THOMAS, *Men and Manners in America*. 2 vols. Philadelphia, 1833.

HANDLIN, OSCAR, *This Was America*. Cambridge, 1949.

———, AND MARY HANDLIN, *Commonwealth, A Study of the Role of Government in the American Economy: Massachusetts, 1774–1861*. New York, 1947.

HARDING, CHESTER, *My Egotistigraphy*. Cambridge, 1866.

HARRIS, NEIL, *The Artist in American Society: The Formative Years, 1790–1860*. New York, 1966.

HEALY, G. P. A., *Reminiscences of a Portrait Painter*. Chicago, 1894.

HIGHAM, JOHN, *Strangers in the Land: Patterns of American Nativism, 1860–1925*. New Brunswick, N.J., 1955.

HOFSTADTER, RICHARD, *The American Political Tradition*. New York, 1951.

———, *Social Darwinism in American Thought, 1860–1915*. Philadelphia, 1944.

HONE, PHILIP, *The Diary of Philip Hone, 1828–1851*, ed. by Allan Nevins. 2 vols. New York, 1927.

HOUGHTON, WALTER E., *The Victorian Frame of Mind, 1830–1870*. New Haven, 1957.

ISHAM, SAMUEL, *The History of American Painting*. New York, 1936.

JARVES, JAMES JACKSON, *The Art-Idea: Sculpture, Painting, and Architecture in America*, ed. by Benjamin Rowland, Jr. Cambridge, 1960.

KEMBLE, FANNY A., *Journal*. 2 vols. London, 1835.

KIRKLAND, EDWARD C., *Dream and Thought in the Business Community, 1860–1900*. Ithaca, 1956.

———, *A History of American Economic Life*. 3rd edn. New York, 1951.

———, *Industry Comes of Age: Business, Labor, and Public Policy, 1860–1897*. New York, 1961.

KOUWENHOVEN, JOHN A., *Made in America, The Arts in Modern Civilization*. Garden City, 1962.

LARKIN, OLIVER W., *Art and Life in America*. New York, 1949.

LERNER, MAX, *America as a Civilization.* New York, 1957.

LIEBER, FRANCIS, *The Stranger in America.* Philadelphia, 1835.

McKITRICK, ERIC L., *Andrew Johnson and Reconstruction.* Chicago, 1960.

MANN, ARTHUR, *Yankee Reformers in the Urban Age.* Cambridge, 1954.

MARRYAT, FREDERICK, *Diary in America, with Remarks on its Institutions.* 2 vols. Philadelphia, 1839.

MARTINEAU, HARRIET, *Society in America.* 3 vols. London, 1837.

———, *Retrospect of Western Travel.* 3 vols. London, 1838.

MARX, LEO, *The Machine in the Garden: Technology and the Pastoral Ideal in America.* New York, 1964.

MESICK, JANE, *The English Traveller in America, 1785–1835.* New York, 1922.

MILLER, JOHN C., *The Federalist Era, 1789–1801.* New York, 1960.

MILLER, LILLIAN B., *Patrons and Patriotism: The Encouragement of the Fine Arts in the United States, 1790–1860.* Chicago, 1966.

MILLER, PERRY, *The Transcendentalists.* Boston, 1953.

MENNINGERODE, MEADE, *The Fabulous Forties.* New York, 1924.

MONROE, PAUL, *Founding of the American Public School System.* New York, 1940.

MORGAN, H. WAYNE, ed., *The Gilded Age: A Reappraisal.* Syracuse, 1963.

NEVINS, ALLAN, *American Social History as Recorded by British Travellers.* New York, 1923.

NOBLE, LOUIS LEGRAND, *The Life and Works of Thomas Cole,* ed. by Elliot S. Vessell. Cambridge, 1964.

NYE, RUSSEL B., *The Cultural Life of the New Nation, 1776–1830.* New York, 1960.

RICHARDSON, EDGAR, *American Romantic Painting.* New York, 1944.

———, *Painting in America; The Story of 450 Years.* New York, 1956.

ROBERTS, KENNETH, AND ANNA ROBERTS, *Moreau de St. Méry's American Journey.* Garden City, N.Y., 1947.

PATTEE, FRED LEWIS, *The Feminine Fifties.* Port Washington, 1940.

PIERSON, GEORGE W., *Tocqueville and Beaumont in America.* New York, 1938.

POLLACK, NORMAN, *The Populist Response to Industrial America: Midwestern Populist Thought.* Cambridge, 1962.

POTTER, DAVID M., *People of Plenty: Economic Abundance and the American Character.* Chicago, 1954.

SCHLESINGER, ARTHUR M., JR., *The Age of Jackson.* Boston, 1945.

SHANNON, FRED A., *The Farmer's Last Frontier: Agriculture, 1860–1897.* New York and Toronto, 1945.

SMITH, HENRY NASH, *Virgin Land: The American West as Symbol and Myth.* Cambridge, 1950.

SPENCER, BENJAMIN, *The Quest for Nationality.* Syracuse, 1957.

STAMPP, KENNETH, *And The War Came.* Baton Rouge, 1957.

STEIN, ROGER B., *John Ruskin and Aesthetic Thought in America, 1840–1900.* Cambridge, 1967.

STRONG, GEORGE TEMPLETON, *The Diary of George Templeton Strong,* ed. by Allan Nevins and Milton Halsey Thomas. 4 vols. New York, 1952.

SUSSMAN, HERBERT L., *Victorians and the Machine: The Literary Response to Technology.* Cambridge, 1968.

SYDNOR, C. S., *The Development of Southern Sectionalism.* Durham, 1948.

TAYLOR, GEORGE ROGERS, *Transportation Revolution, 1815–1860.* New York, 1951.

TOCQUEVILLE, ALEXIS DE, *Democracy in America,* ed. by Phillips Bradley. 2 vols. New York, 1945.

TROLLOPE, ANTHONY, *North America,* ed. by Donald Smalley and B. A. Booth. New York, 1951.

TROLLOPE, MRS. FRANCES, *Domestic Manners of the Americans,* ed. by Donald Smalley. New York, 1949.

TRUMBULL, JOHN, *The Autobiography of Colonel John Trumbull, Patriot-Artist, 1756–1843,* ed. by Theodore Sizer. New Haven, 1953.

TUCKERMAN, HENRY T., *Book of the Artists: American Artist Life.* New York, 1867.

# Bibliography

TURNER, FREDERICK JACKSON, *The Frontier in American History*. New York, 1921.

WADE, RICHARD C., *The Urban Frontier; the Rise of Western Cities, 1790–1830*. Cambridge, 1959.

WARD, JOHN, *Andrew Jackson, Symbol for an Age*. New York, 1955.

WARE, NORMAN, *Industrial Workers, 1840–1860*. New York, 1924.

WEBB, WALTER PRESCOTT, *The Great Plains*. Boston, 1931.

WECTER, DIXON, *The Saga of American Society*. New York, 1937.

WHITE, MORTON, *Social Thought in America: The Revolt Against Formalism*. New York, 1949.

WILLIAMS, WILLIAM APPLEMAN, *The Contours of American History*. Cleveland, 1961.

WOODWARD, C. VANN, *Origins of the New South, 1877–1913*. Baton Rouge, 1951.

WRIGHT, FRANCES, *Views of Society and Manners in America*. New York, 1821.

WYLLIE, IRVIN G., *The Self-Made Man in America: The Myth of Rags to Riches*. New Brunswick, N.J., 1954.

## Architecture

### GENERAL

ALEXANDER, DRURY B., *Texas Homes of the Nineteenth Century*. Austin, 1966.

ANDREWS, WAYNE, *Architecture, Ambition and Americans*. New York, 1955 (paper, New York, 1964).

BURCHARD, JOHN E. AND BUSH-BROWN, ALBERT, *The Architecture of America*. Boston, 1961.

BURNHAM, ALAN, *New York Landmarks*. Middletown, Conn., 1964.

CONDIT, CARL W., *The Chicago School of Architecture*. Chicago, 1964.

DOWNING, ANTOINETTE F. AND SCULLY, VINCENT J., *The Architectural Heritage of Newport, Rhode Island, 1640–1915*. Cambridge, 1952.

FITCH, JAMES M., *American Building; the Forces that Shape It*. Boston, 1948.

GIEDION, SIEGFRIED, *Space, Time and Architecture*. Cambridge, 1941 (and later editions).

GOWANS, ALAN, *Images of American Living*. Philadelphia, 1964.

HAMLIN, TALBOT F., *Greek Revival Architecture in America*. New York, 1944.

HITCHCOCK, HENRY-RUSSELL, *Rhode Island Architecture*. Providence, 1939 (reprinted, New York, 1968).

———, *Architecture: Nineteenth and Twentieth Centuries*. Harmondsworth, Baltimore, Victoria, 1958.

HOWLAND, RICHARD AND SPENCER, ELEANOR, *The Architecture of Baltimore*. Baltimore, 1953.

JACKSON, HUSON, *New York Architecture, 1650–1952*. New York, 1952.

MAASS, JOHN, *The Gingerbread Age*. New York and Toronto, 1957.

MEEKS, C. L. V., *The Railroad Station*. New Haven, 1956.

MUMFORD, LEWIS, *The Brown Decades*. New York, 1931 (paper, 1955).

RANDALL, FRANK A., *History of the Development of Building Construction in Chicago*. Urbana, 1949.

SCHUYLER, MONTGOMERY, *Architecture and other Writings*, 2 vols., edited by William H. Jordy and Ralph Coe. Cambridge, 1961.

SCULLY, VINCENT J., *The Shingle Style*. New Haven, 1955.

STANTON, PHOEBE B., *The Gothic Revival and American Church Architecture*. Baltimore, 1968.

TATUM, GEORGE B., *Penn's Great Town*. Philadelphia, 1961.

### MONOGRAPHS

#### BULFINCH

Place, Charles A., *Charles Bulfinch, Architect and Citizen*. Boston, 1925.

BURGES

Pullan, R. P., *Architectural Designs of William Burges*, 2 vols. London, 1883–87.

BURNHAM

Moore, Charles, *Daniel H. Burnham*, 2 vols. Boston and New York, 1921.

JEFFERSON

Kimball, S. Fiske, *Thomas Jefferson, Architect*. Boston, 1916 (reprinted, New York, 1968).

LATROBE

Hamlin, Talbot F., *Benjamin Henry Latrobe*. New York, 1955.

L'ENFANT

Caemmerer, H. Paul, *The Life of Charles L'Enfant*. Washington, 1950.

Kite, Elizabeth S., *L'Enfant and Washington*. Baltimore, 1929.

McINTIRE

Kimball, S. Fiske, *Mr. Samuel McIntire, Carver, The Architect of Salem*. Portland, 1940.

McKIM, MEAD AND WHITE

*A Monograph of the Work of McKim, Mead and White, 1879–1915*, 4 vols. New York, 1915–25.

Baldwin, Charles C., *Stanford White*. New York, 1931.

Moore, Charles, *Charles Follen McKim*. Boston, 1929.

MILLS

Gallagher, H. M. Pierce, *Robert Mills*. New York, 1935.

OLMSTED

Fabos, Julius; Milde, Gordon; and Weinmayr, V. Michael, *Frederick Law Olmsted, Jr.* Amherst, Mass., 1968.

RICHARDSON

Hitchcock, Henry-Russell, *The Architecture of H. H. Richardson and his Times*. New York, 1936 (2nd revised edition, Hamden, Conn., 1961; paper, Cambridge, 1966).

Van Rensselaer, Marianna G., *Henry Hobson Richardson and His Works*. Boston and New York, 1888 (reprinted, 1968).

ROOT

Hoffma, Donald (ed.), *The Meanings of Architecture*. New York, 1967.

Monroe, Harriet, *John Wellborn Root*. Boston, 1896 (reprinted 1966).

STRICKLAND

Gilchrist, Agnes Addison, *William Strickland: Architect and Engineer*. Philadelphia, 1950.

SULLIVAN

Morrison, Hugh, *Louis Sullivan*. New York, 1935 (paper, 1962).

Paul, Sherman, *Louis Sullivan, An Architect in American Thought*. Englewood Cliffs, N.J., 1962.

TOWN AND DAVIS

Newton, R. H., *Town and Davis: Architects*. New York, 1942.

UPJOHN

Upjohn, Everard M., *Richard Upjohn, Architect and Churchman*. New York, 1939.

WRIGHT

Hitchcock, Henry-Russell, *In the Nature of Materials*. New York, 1942.

Manson, Grant, C., *Frank Lloyd Wright to 1910*. New York, 1958.

Smith, Norris Kelly, *Frank Lloyd Wright*. Englewood Cliffs, N.J., 1966.

PERIODICALS AND SERIALS

American Architect and Building News (1876—).

American Guide Series. Boston in 1930's and 40's. Written for the Federal Writers' Project of the W.P.A.

Architectural Forum (1892—).

Architectural Record (1891—).

Inland Architect and News Record (1883–1908).

Journal of the Society of Architectural Historians (1941—).

*Painting and Sculpture*

The Bibliographical note to this section appears at the end of the text, page 284.

# Bibliography

## The Decorative Arts

BUHLER, KATHRYN C., *American Silver.* Cleveland, 1950.

BUTLER, JOSEPH T., *American Antiques 1800–1900: A Collector's History and Guide.* New York, 1965.

COMSTOCK, HELEN, *American Furniture.* New York, 1962.

DESMOND, HARRY W., AND HERBERT CROLY, *Stately Homes in America.* New York, 1903.

ENSKO, STEPHEN G. C., *American Silversmiths and Their Marks.* New York, 1927–1948.

GIEDION, SIEGFRIED, *Mechanization Takes Command.* New York, 1948.

LICHTEN, FRANCES, *Decorative Art of Victoria's Era.* New York, 1950.

McKEARIN, GEORGE S. AND HELEN, *American Glass.* New York, 1941.

———, *Two Hundred Years of American Blown Glass.* New York, 1950.

MONTGOMERY, CHARLES F., *American Furniture: The Federal Period.* New York, 1966.

Museum of Contemporary Crafts, *Forms from the Earth—1000 Years of Pottery in America.* Loan exhibition Catalogue. n.d.

———, *Louis Comfort Tiffany.* Loan exhibition Catalogue. New York, 1958.

Newark Museum, *Classical America, 1815–1845.* Loan exhibition Catalogue. Newark (N.J.), 1963.

Philadelphia Museum of Art, *Tucker China: 1825–1838.* Loan exhibition Catalogue. 1957.

WHARTON, EDITH, AND OGDEN CODMAN, JR., *The Decoration of Houses.* New York, 1902.

# INDEX

395

## Index

# Index

410